The Modern Afterlives of Old Irish Travel Narratives

Literary Reception & Art Reception

VOLUME 1

The titles published in this series are listed at *brill.com/lrar*

The Modern Afterlives of Old Irish Travel Narratives

From Gulliver to Star Trek

By

Natalia I. Petrovskaia

BRILL

LEIDEN | BOSTON

Cover illustration: Gallica Public Domain. Bibliothèque nationale de France, département Réserve des livres rares, RES P-Y2-2320 (1), p. III. ark:/12148/BTV1B8600288K

The Library of Congress Cataloging-in-Publication Data is available online at https://catalog.loc.gov
LC record available at https://lccn.loc.gov/2025013316

Typeface for the Latin, Greek, and Cyrillic scripts: "Brill". See and download: brill.com/brill-typeface.

ISSN 2949-8597
ISBN 978-90-04-73450-0 (hardback)
ISBN 978-90-04-73454-8 (e-book)
DOI 10.1163/9789004734548

This book is printed on acid-free paper and produced in a sustainable manner.

Contents

Acknowledgements

Several important intellectual debts were incurred in the preparation of this book. I would like to thank the editorial board of the Literary Reception and Art Reception series and the anonymous reviewers whose comments were conveyed to me through the editors of Brill, for their suggestions and advice. Series editor and Utrecht colleague Gandolfo Cascio I would like to thank for his enthusiastic reception of an informally pitched experimental book idea. I would also like to thank Iulia Ivana, Masja Horn, Thalien Colenbrander and Pieter Boeschoten at Brill for their expertise, professionalism and patience. At Utrecht University thanks are due in particular to Nike Stam and Peter Schrijver for reading drafts of the book. Nike I would like to thank for not only carefully and enthusiastically reading the introduction and the Star Trek chapter but for encouraging me to put in more Old Irish quotations. Any errors and inaccuracies that might remain are my responsibility.

Celtic Studies at Utrecht University celebrated its centenary in 2023. To the many colleagues and friends from across the world who have written in 2024 to say how important the continued existence of Celtic Studies as a discipline is to the academic landscape of today, just as I was in the process of copy-editing this book, thank you.

Figures and Tables

Figures

Tables

CHAPTER 1

Introduction: These are the Voyages…

This book explores the reception of the medieval Irish tradition of fantastic journey tales in a selection of major post-medieval fantastic travel narratives, textual and visual. To quote John Carey's definition, the '"voyage tale", in the context of medieval Irish literature, may be defined as a story which describes a visit to an Otherworld region or regions, reached after a sea journey'.[1] The medieval Irish tradition of voyage narratives is composed of two categories, recognised as such already in the medieval period: *immrama* 'rowings-about' (singular form *immram*) and *echtrai* 'adventure-tales' (singular form *echtra*).[2] Most, though not all, of the medieval Irish texts discussed in this book date approximately to the period between the late eighth and the early tenth centuries, which roughly corresponds to the period which in history of the Irish language is defined as 'Classical Old Irish' (though most were transmitted in later manuscripts).[3] The term 'medieval Irish literature' is thus used in this book to refer to Irish literature of the medieval period in broad terms, while 'Old Irish literature' is used more specifically for texts the composition of which is generally considered to date to around the ninth century.

Reception studies of medieval material usually fall under the broad umbrella of the flourishing and ever-expanding academic field of

1 John Carey, 'Voyage Literature', in *Celtic Culture: A Historical Encyclopedia*, ed. by John T. Koch (Santa Barbara: ABC-CLIO, 2006), pp. 1743–46 (p. 1743).

2 For a brief explanation of the genres, see Wooding, 'Introduction', in *The Otherworld Voyage in Early Irish Literature. An Anthology of Criticism*, ed. by Jonathan Wooding (Dublin: Four Courts Press, 2000), pp. xi–xxviii (pp. xi–xii). The spelling *echtrae* for the singular form of the second term is used in some scholarship and is maintained in quotations and references. For spellings of titles of medieval Irish tales I in each case follow the spelling of the edition and translation used. This may yield some inconsistencies between texts but hopefully will make the use of the index and bibliography easier for the non-specialist reader. The categories are discussed in detail in section 1.1 below, pp. 23–29.

3 For the periodization and literary context, see Máire Ní Mhaonaigh, 'The Literature of Medieval Ireland, 800–1200: from the Vikings to the Normans', in *The Cambridge History of Irish Literature*, ed. by Margaret Kelleher and Philip O'Leary (Cambridge: Cambridge University Press, 2006), pp. 32–73 (p. 32).

 | DOI:10.1163/9789004734548_002

'medievalism'.[4] The relation between the two fields – or 'turns' – both historic and theoretical, is only beginning to garner the attention it deserves.[5] As Ika Willis and Ellie Crookes observe, the term 'reception' in medievalist discussions 'appears most often in passing references in footnotes'.[6] Yet, to quote Willis and Crookes again, 'Reception can help medievalism reflect more explicitly on its theoretical underpinnings, while medievalism can help overcome reception's overreliance on a textual paradigm'.[7] The place of this book in this broader field is on the intersection between medievalism and reception – indeed some of the reception examined here is by medievalists who theorised medievalism. Its objective is triple. The book aims to demonstrate that established paradigms for thinking about the afterlives of texts and literary history can be given a good nudge by approaching the modern material through the lens of the medieval. It provides a case-study for using reception studies to give a more theorised articulation to medievalism. Through this it fulfils its second objective: to query whether taking a different approach to narratives as vehicles of reception might not alter what these narratives tell us. Finally, and not least, it seeks to show the continued relevance of medieval Irish literature for the analysis of modern cultural phenomena.[8]

The act of travel or journeying, whether to real or to imaginary places, has occupied a central place in the cultural imagination for centuries. Echoes of themes borrowed by direct or indirect routes from *immrama*, from *echtrai*, and from related Latin tales such as the immensely popular Hiberno-Latin (meaning Latin written in Ireland) *Navigatio sancti Brendani* (Voyage of Saint Brendan) become visible once we open our minds to the possibility that texts such as Jonathan Swift's *Gulliver's Travels*, Umberto

4 David Matthews, *Medievalism: A Critical History* (Cambridge: D. S. Brewer, 2015), pp. 6, 36–37, 119; <https://doi.org/10.1515/9781782043973>. See also further discussion at p. 71 below.

5 Notably with the publication of Ika Willis and Ellie Crookes, ed., *Medievalism and Reception* (Cambridge: D. S. Brewer, 2024).

6 Ika Willis and Ellie Crookes, 'Introduction', in *Medievalism and Reception*, ed. by Ika Willis and Ellie Crookes (Cambridge: D. S. Brewer, 2024), pp. 1–10 (p. 3).

7 Willis and Crookes, 'Introduction', p. 5.

8 Celtic materials, partly perhaps because of a language barrier, remain on the margins of medievalism and reception studies and the many examples of 'complex, original and nuanced entanglements with the Celtic past' in modern fantasy writing, for instance, 'have not attracted the attention they warrant', as Dmitra Fimi observes in her introduction to the recent volume that goes some way to redressing that imbalance; Fimi, 'Introduction', in *Imagining the Celtic Past in Modern Fantasy*, ed. by Dmitra Fimi and Alistair J. P. Sims (London: Bloomsbury Academic, 2023), pp. 1–8 (p. 4).

Eco's *Baudolino*, and C. S. Lewis's *Voyage of the Dawn Treader* and television series such as *Star Trek* and *Stargate* can be placed not on the generic scale fantasy-science fiction but on that of *immram-echtra*.[9]

The use of medieval genre classifications here builds on previous suggestions. Lewis, whose own work is examined in Chapter 2 as an example of the *immram* tradition, hints at such cross-generational genre families in his description of Orwell's *Animal Farm*. He describes Orwell's text as a descendent of 'Rabelais, Cervantes, the *Apocolocyntosis*, Lucian, and the *Frogs and Mice*' (the latter by Aristophanes).[10] Indeed, for Lewis's own *Voyage of the Dawn Treader*, the genre assignation proposed in this book is hardly controversial. In its reliance on the Brendan legend as model, combined with the religious and educational overtone of the narrative, the *Voyage of the Dawn Treader* seems to fit quite snugly into not a modern genre, but a medieval one: the Irish *immram*.[11]

---

9 The *Navigatio* is a Hiberno-Latin text, probably of late eighth- or ninth-century origin (in its current form), and concerns the sea-travels of a sixth-century Irish saint. For a very brief introduction to Saint Brendan, see Thomas O'Loughlin, 'Brendan, St', in *Celtic Culture: A Historical Encyclopedia*, ed. by John T. Koch (Santa Barbara: ABC-CLIO, 2006), pp. 244–45 (p. 244), and Tom Moylan, 'Irish Voyages and Visions: Pre-figuring, Re-configuring Utopia', *Utopian Studies*, 18, Special issue 'Irish Utopian' (2007), 299–323 (p. 304). For further discussion of the *Navigatio*, and further references, see below, pp. 4–5, 29. For an argument that *immrama* can be taken as 'proto-science-fiction', as part of a teleological reconstruction of the history of the modern genre, see Chris Loughlin, 'When was Celtic Futurism? The Irish *Immrama* as Proto-Science-Fiction', *SFRA Review*, 52.1 *Selected LSFRC 2021 Papers* (2022), 214–22 <https://sfrareview.files.wordpress.com/2022/02/5201-ls-immarama.pdf> [accessed 7 April 2024]. By contrast, I do not see the Old Irish voyage narratives as the precursors to modern science-fiction, but rather see in modern works (not all of them generically identifiable as science fiction) traces of the reception of the *immram* and *echtra* genres.

10 C. S. Lewis, *English Literature in the Sixteenth Century, Excluding Drama* (Oxford: Clarendon Press, 1954), p. 468; quoted and discussed in Joe R. Christopher, 'Modern Literature', in *Reading the Classics with C. S. Lewis*, ed. by Thomas L. Martin (Grand Rapids, MI: Baker Academic, and Carlisle: Paternoster Press, 2000), pp. 145–264, who points out the importance of the 'generic classification': 'fantastic or mock heroic narratives' (p. 256). Lucian's *True History* features in the discussion below, p. 123.

11 John E. Lawyer, 'Three Celtic Voyages: Brendan, Lewis and Buechner', *Anglican Theological Review*, 84 (2002), 319–43 (p. 230), crediting Jonathan Wooding for the idea in n. 38 (referring to personal communication); see also Kris Swank, 'The Child's Voyage and the *Immram* Tradition in Lewis, Tolkien, and Pullman', *Mythlore*, 38 (2019), 73–96. For a discussion of some of the potential problems of using 'genre' in relation to Old Irish taxonomic systems, see, for example, Kevin Murray, 'Genre Construction: the Creation of the *Dinnshenchas*', *Journal of Literary Onomastics*, 6 (2017), 11–21 and references therein.

Umberto Eco, meanwhile, is famous for drawing on medieval material both for content and for form, and it will be shown in Chapter 3 that this includes the Old Irish voyage tales. As Eco confessed – rather rhetorically, one suspects – in one of his essays, he sometimes wondered whether his fiction was written 'purely in order to put in hermeneutic references' intelligible only to him.[12] This self-proclaimed goal may render any attempt at a full decoding of the novel a futile effort, but a scholarly annotated edition of *Baudolino* is certainly a desideratum. The discussion in this book, therefore, does not aim to provide a play-by-play comparison of Eco's text and his medieval sources, but rather to explore some of the techniques in the novel which put it in the Old Irish category of voyage literature, as partly *echtra* and partly *immram*.

Star Trek and more explicitly *Stargate* draw heavily on literature, legend and mythology, sometimes mapping individual storylines onto well-known patterns. Here, too, the Irish model is present, as Chapters 5 and 6 show. The most controversial choice, perhaps, within the present corpus, is Swift's *Gulliver's Travels*, but the influence of this text permeates the others examined here. Vivian Mercier, in 1962, suggested that *Gulliver's Travels* owed something to the *immram* tradition: 'as a medievalist recently pointed out to me, no other work in English exemplifies so well the Early Irish *immram* (voyage) tradition and its marvels'.[13] This suggestion was subsequently dismissed as 'far-fetched' by Denis Donoghue, writing that 'Elizabethan travel-literature is a much closer model, if Swift required one, at least as monstrous and fantastic as the *immram* and far more readily available to one whose knowledge of Irish was doubtful and, at best, small'.[14] However, the *immram* does offer a better model for the allegorical reading mode enabled by Swift's text, and is represented by later Continental tradition (because it influenced the latter heavily), so does not require a knowledge of Irish.[15] One thinks specifically of the wider tradition based on the Latin *Navigatio sancti Brendani* (henceforth *Navigatio*).[16] This text, which will

12 Eco, 'To See Things and Texts', in Eco, *Mouse or Rat? Translation as Negotiation* (London: Phoenix, 2004), pp. 104–22 (p. 118).

13 Vivien Mercier, *The Irish Comic Tradition* (Oxford: Oxford University Press, 1962), p. 188, with reference (n. 2) to a conversation with William Matthews of the English Department at UCLA.

14 Denis Donoghue, 'Hibernus Ludens', *The Hudson Review*, 16 (1963), 450–54 (p. 451).

15 See the discussion in Chapter 4, pp. 114–17, 123–24.

16 Editions of the text include Carl Selmer, ed., *Navigatio sancti Brendani abbatis: From Early Latin Manuscripts* (Notre Dame, Indiana: University of Notre Dame Press, 1959)

feature heavily in this book, is a narrative concerning the sea-voyage of Saint Brendan and his companions in search of a 'Promised Land of Saints', composed in Ireland in Latin in the eighth or ninth centuries.[17] In the course of the journey, the monks visit many strange islands and witness a wide variety of marvels. The story enjoyed great popularity in the medieval period, circulating widely throughout Europe in Latin, and was also adapted and translated into multiple European vernacular languages.[18] The suggestion that Swift's text draws on the *immram* tradition, therefore, merits a revisit.

These are the 'texts' (in the broad sense of the term) explored in the following chapters.[19] Starting with the Irish material, this book is therefore

---

and more recently Giovanni Orlandi, and Rossana E. Guglielmetti, ed. and trans., *Navigatio sancti Brendani: alla scoperta dei segreti meravigliosi del mondo*, Per Verba, 30 (Florence: Galluzzo and Fondazione Ezio Franceschini, 2014). For more on the *Navigatio sancti Brendani* and references to earlier discussions, see below, p. 8 n. 26 and p. 29.

17 For a brief introduction, see Jonathan M. Wooding, 'Navigatio Sancti Brendani' in *Celtic Culture: A Historical Encyclopedia*, ed. by John T. Koch (Santa Barbara: ABC-CLIO, 2006), p. 1348; and Carey, 'Voyage Literature', p. 1744. See also John D. Anderson, 'The *Navigatio Brendani*: A Medieval Best Seller', *The Classical Journal*, 83 (1988), 315–22.

18 The literature on this tradition is vast; see, for instance, Renata Anna Bartoli, *La Navigatio sancti Brendani e la sua fortuna nella cultura romanza dell'età di mezzo* (Fasano, Brindisi: Schena, 1993); Clara Strijbosch, *The Seafaring Saint: Sources and Analogues of the Twelfth-Century Voyage of Saint Brendan* (Dublin: Four Courts Press, 2000); W. R. J. Barron and Glyn S. Burgess, ed., *The Voyage of Saint Brendan. Representative Versions of the Legend in English Translation* (Exeter: University of Exeter Press, 2002); Glyn S. Burgess and Clara Strijbosch, ed., *The Brendan Legend. A Critical Bibliography* (Dublin: Royal Irish Academy, 2000); Glynn S. Burgess and Clara Strijbosch, ed., *The Brendan Legend: Texts and Versions* (Leiden and Boston: Brill, 2006); J. S. Mackley, *The Legend of St Brendan. A Comparative Study of the Latin and Anglo-Norman Versions* (Leiden: Brill, 2008), Mattia Cavagna and Silvère Menegaldo, 'Entre la terre et la mer, entre le Paradis et l'Enfer: l'île dans la *Navigatio sancti Brendani* et ses versions en langues romanes', *Les lettres romanes*, 66 (2012), 7–35.

19 Fantasy and science fiction are usually seen as independent genres, albeit closely related ones. See, for instance, Elena Gomel and Danielle Gurevitch, 'What is Fantasy and Who Decides?', in *The Palgrave Handbook of Global Fantasy*, ed. by Elena Gomel and Danielle Gurevitch (Cham: Springer and Palgrave Macmillan, 2023), pp. 3–13 (p. 3). The essays in the first part of Gomel and Gurevitch's volume represent various takes on the definition of fantasy. For comments on the proximity of the two genres see, for instance, Kingsley Amis, *New Maps of Hell. A Survey of Science Fiction* (London: Victor Gollancz, 1961), pp. 21–23. Amis distinguishes the two by postulating that science fiction 'maintains a respect for fact or presumptive fact', while fantasy does not (p. 22). For further discussion of categories of fantasy and science fiction in relation to the material covered in *The Modern Afterlives of Old Irish Travel Narratives*, see below, pp. 20–21.

about travel narratives. We begin with earth-bound narratives, both land-bound and directed eastwards, and sea-bound and directed towards the far west, starting out from what we now conventionally call 'Western Europe'. We then move to the twentieth- and twenty-first-century equivalents of exploration fantasies, which transfer this dimensionality into outer space, with Earth as the starting point and deep space as the new equivalent of the far east and far west of the earlier tradition.[20]

My objective in the following chapters is to explore the tradition of fascination with travel and with distant lands that guides these various expressions of storytelling. I do this by charting a trajectory through what may seem at first blush to be a rather eclectic selection of texts ('texts' broadly defined, including television series), that ranges from Old Irish sea-voyage and otherworld voyage narratives, Eco's experimental postmodernist medievalist novel *Baudolino*, Lewis's children's book *The Voyage of the Dawn Treader*, Swift's *Gulliver' Travels*, as well as a selection of texts belonging to the two major franchises starting with the 1960s television series *Star Trek* and the 1990s movie *Stargate*.[21] In using the term 'text' for the visual media

20 This is not to negate the importance of classical and medieval narratives concerning space travel (such as Lucian's *True History* or Cicero's *Somnium Scipionis*), but rather to place the accent on another aspect of the tradition, highlighting a different set of connections that are less immediately apparent in traditional histories of science fiction. In this book, I focus on two major twentieth-century science fiction series which are not normally discussed as part of *Nachleben* of Celtic literatures: *Star Trek* and *Stargate*, as my primary goal is to show that the Old Irish taxonomies have a wider use and application, which can be extended beyond purely 'Celtic' adaptations. For recent discussions of science-fiction inspired directly by medieval Irish and Welsh traditions, see for example, Cheryl Morgan, 'Celts in Spaaaaace!', in *Imagining the Celtic Past in Modern Fantasy*, ed. by Dimitra Fimi and Alistair J. P. Sims (London: Bloomsbury Academic, 2023), pp. 117–34. Lucian's *True History* features below in the context of discussion of Swift's *Gulliver's Travels*, pp. 15, 123. For a discussion of the *Somnium Scipionis* in the context of the history of science fiction, see Ryan Vu, 'Science Fiction before Science Fiction: Ancient, Medieval, and Early Modern SF' in *The Cambridge History of Science Fiction*, ed. by Gerry Canavan and Eric Carl Link (Cambridge: Cambridge University Press, 2018), pp. 13–34 (pp. 18–19). I am grateful to the anonymous reviewer for the reminder of the importance of these pre-modern space-travel narratives to the history of science fiction.

21 The literature on Old Irish otherworld voyages is extensive. An accessible, though somewhat dated, starting point is Chapter VI 'Voyages' in Miles Dillon, *Early Irish Literature. An Introduction to the Sagas and Legends of Ancient Ireland* (Chicago: Chicago University Press, 1948), pp. 124–31. For a brief and accessible summary of the premise of *Stargate*, see Sarah R. MacKinnon, '*Stargate Atlantis:* Islandness of the Pegasus Galaxy', *Shima*, 10 (2016), 36–49 (p. 36) <https://doi.org/10.21463/shima.10.2.06>. Since both the *Star Trek* and *Stargate* franchises are extensive mega-texts (*Star Trek* particularly) it is impossible to address all their constituent texts within the scope of this

of film and television series, I follow convention, taking works of film and television 'as a signifying discourse (text), or as a *linguistic object*', as formulated in Christian Metz's foundational definition.[22] I return to my selection from the two franchises further below.

It will be noticed that the texts are listed here not in chronological order. The order of the list is the order in which they feature in this book. The reason for this arrangement of the material is that my objective is not to present a teleological narrative of the development of fantasy and science fiction, or of what is known as the 'island narrative' genre.[23] Rather, the goal here is to bring into focus a phenomenon that I describe as an 'intertextual matrix', as these narratives show a complicated network of connections on multiple levels.[24] The grouping of texts is also based not only on the loose notion of the 'travel narrative' but on a taxonomy of narrative types which does not quite correspond to modern genre divisions and belongs to an established medieval system: the Old Irish taxonomic system of text types, often referred to as the 'Old Irish genre system'.[25] The Old Irish genre

book. The selection is guided by considerations of thematic suitability to the analysis, and by considerations of size, see below, pp. 11–14.

22 Christian Metz, *Language and Cinema* (The Hague: Mouton, 1974), p. 13, the brackets and emphasis Metz's. See, e.g. Sean Guynes and Dan Hassler-Forest, ed., *Star Wars and the History of Transmedia Storytelling* (Amstedam: Amsterdam University Press, 2017), discussion of terminology relating to Star Wars on p. 9; Leimar Garcia-Siino, Sabrina Mittermeier and Stefan Rabitsch, 'Introduction: Open Hailing Frequencies', in *The Routledge Handbook of Star Trek*, ed. by Leimar Garcia-Siino, Sabrina Mittermeier, and Stefan Rabitsch (New York and London: Routledge, 2022), pp. 1–5, describe *Star Trek* as 'a massive mega-text' (p. 1).

23 Various accounts are given for the timeline of the development of fantasy and science fiction as genres. Pre-modern precursors are postulated in such narratives more often for fantasy than for science fiction; see Amis, *New Maps*, pp. 22, 26–27. For references to discussions, see note 62 below.

24 This study thus presents a formalised analysis of a phenomenon of the 'deeply embedded and further reaching' interconnections between texts in such thematically linked corpora that was noted in Christoph Singer, *Sea Change: The Shore from Shakespeare to Banville*, Spatial Practices. An Interdisciplinary Series in Cultural History, Geography and Literature, 20 (Amsterdam and New York: Rodopi, 2014), pp. 16–17. The related term 'cultural matrix' is used by Maryna Romanets in her discussion of the spatial aspects of contemporary Irish poetry which includes *immram* influences; Romanets, 'Travellers, Cartographers, Lovers: Ideologies of Exploratory Desire in Contemporary Irish Poetry', *Nordic Irish Studies*, 3 (2004), 35–49.

25 For a brief introduction to the Old Irish travel narratives, see Carey, 'Voyage Literature', and further references in n. 91 below. Medieval Irish genre types also include the categories *comperta* 'births', *tána* 'cattle-raids', and *tochmarca* 'wooings', among others. For an introduction to these, see Proinsias Mac Cana, *The Learned Tales of Medieval Ireland* (Dublin: DIAS, 1980).

system is not widely known today (beyond the narrow circles of Celtic Studies) but it must be remembered that to it belonged some of the international medieval best-sellers which still capture our imagination (such as the *Navigatio*), and that this particular literary tradition is already well-known for punching above its weight.[26] This book will simply argue that this is slightly more so than has hitherto been acknowledged.

The typology proposed in this book seeks to provide a new way of reading the narratives concerned that is intended to supplement rather than replace existing alternative readings. Most of the primary sources selected for analysis here are also intentionally and overtly polyphonic. The choice to begin the story with Lewis's *The Voyage of the Dawn Treader* and Umberto Eco's *Baudolino* is dictated partly by the desire to emphasise this fact. Throughout the book, I will also highlight points of contact between the intertextual matrix examined here and other texts, as well as the various matrices to which these other texts belong. In particular, this book reads C. S. Lewis and Umberto Eco as medievalists, paying attention principally to the Irish elements in their interests. The aim here is not to trace the influence of their professional occupation as scholars of the Middle Ages on their creative output as a whole, but to focus on a specific aspect thereof, in light of a study of the reception of the Old Irish voyage tales.

While medieval elements in the two authors' work, and their sources, have been discussed before, Lewis is usually read primarily as a Christian thinker. Although born in Belfast, in Northern Ireland, he is generally not associated with the Irish literary tradition, mostly because his publications have dealt primarily with medieval and Renaissance English literature.[27] Similarly, Eco is primarily read as a semiotician, though the medieval focus of *Il nome della Rosa* (*The Name of the Rose*) and *Baudolino* has meant that

26 For the *Navigatio* as *immram*, see, for instance, David N. Dumville, '*Echtrae* and *Immram*: Some Problems of Definition', *Ériu*, 27 (1976), 73–94 (p. 75). That the *Navigatio sancti Brendani* is intricately connected to the vernacular *immrama* is also highlighted in Jonathan M. Wooding, 'The Date of *Navigatio S. Brendani abbatis*', *Studia Hibernica*, 37 (2011), 9–26 (pp. 25–26). For the *Navigatio* as bestseller, see e.g. Louis Kervran, *Brandan. Le grand navigateur celte du VIe siècle* (Paris: Éditions Robert Lafont, 1977), p. 20.

27 See, however, Swank, 'The Child's Voyage', p. 75. For Lewis's relationship with twentieth-century Irish literary tradition, see Christopher, 'Modern Literature', pp. 246–49. For his interest in Renaissance Italian literature see Derek Brewer, 'C. S. Lewis (1898–1963)', in *Medieval Scholarship. Biographical Studies on the Formation of a Discipline. Volume 2: Literature and Philology*, ed. by Helen Damico, with Donald Fennema and Karmen Lenz (New York and London: Garland Publishing, 1998), pp. 405–13 (pp. 405, 412).

scholars have paid serious attention to the medieval aspect of his opus and to his professional interests. Nevertheless, the identity of either author as a medievalist (an academic specializing in the study of the medieval period) is often entirely elided in discussions of their creative output, arguably partly because of the importance of their other identities, which tend to be emphasized in such discussions. There is a small number of notable exceptions to this trend, such as the analysis of Eco's *The Name of the Rose* by Theresa Coletti.[28] Coletti – a medievalist – reads Eco's *The Name of the Rose* in light of the novel's 'medievalism and its preoccupation with signs, focusing on the thorough grounding of its semiotic concerns in its representation of medieval culture'.[29] However, elsewhere Coletti also writes of Eco's *The Name of the Rose* as follows: 'The late twentieth-century mass-market appeal of a deeply erudite story set in a fourteenth-century Benedictine monastery has encouraged analysis of Eco's decision to render his central concerns as a theorist, journalist, and cultural critic in that narrative form.'[30] The term 'medievalist' is absent from the list. Yet, as Coletti also rightly points out, 'From the writing of his 1954 doctoral thesis on the aesthetics of Thomas Aquinas (*The Aesthetics of Thomas Aquinas*), the Middle Ages have been foundational to Eco's work as a theorist and critic, providing a textual and cultural resource for some of his most important concerns.'[31] The present study, without wishing to challenge or question these readings, offers a supplementary analysis, with emphasis on the two authors' academic identity and its influence on their work – an aspect that deserves more recognition than it has hitherto received.[32] As Coletti observes, 'in *The Name of the Rose* and *Baudolino*, the Middle Ages do not simply provide the intellectual architecture – or "theater" to use their author's metaphor – for Eco's ideas about history, language, and interpretation. What inevitably strikes the reader

28 One that I would like to highlight here is Theresa Coletti, *Naming the Rose: Eco, Medieval Signs, and Modern Theory* (Ithaca: Cornell University Press, 1988). C. S. Lewis as a medievalist is discussed in Jason M. Baxter, *The Medieval Mind of C. S. Lewis: How Great Books Shaped a Great Mind* (Downers Grove: IVP Academic, 2022).

29 Coletti, *Naming the Rose: Eco, Medieval Signs, and Modern Theory* (Ithaca: Cornell University Press, 1988), pp. 4–5; see also her comments on p. 11 of the book.

30 Theresa Coletti, 'Eco's Middle Ages and the Historical Novel', in *New Essays on Umberto Eco* ed. by Peter Bondanella (Cambridge: Cambridge University Press, 2009), pp. 71–89 (p. 71).

31 Coletti, 'Eco's Middle Ages', p. 72. The brackets are Coletti's.

32 A notable exception, making reference to both Eco's work as a medievalist and trends in academic thought on the Middle Ages relevant to Eco's novels, is Coletti, 'Eco's Middle Ages'.

who is also a serious student of the Middle Ages is the precision with which Eco represents even the most idiosyncratic elements of medieval life and culture'.[33] Indeed, as Coletti further points out, Eco's novels reflect the dominant trends in academic discourse on the Middle Ages in the decades of their respective publication – the 1980s and the early 2000s.[34] Similarly, Lewis can be read in the context of the academic discourse – and his own views on it – of the 1950s. The obvious academic context for both of these writers is also in other literatures of other periods, an intertextual relation shared also by other texts examined in this book.[35]

The most significant point of contact between the various narratives discussed in the following chapters is with the classical tradition of island narratives, a tradition deriving from and exemplified by Homer's *Odyssey*. The points of overlap between that tradition and the texts examined in this book are manyfold. Suffice it to mention Swift's reliance on Lucian, whose text is best described as a spoof on Homer.[36] Joyce's *Ulysses*, which will be mentioned in connection to the texts in our corpus, sits (un)comfortably between the Classical and the Irish traditions, insofar as these can be satisfactorily pried asunder.[37] The tendency to conflate the two island-hopping genres – the Classical and the medieval Irish – is evident in the occasional references to the *immram* genre as the Irish 'odyssey tales' in modern scholarship.[38]

The connection between the Old Irish *immram* genre as a whole and Lewis's adaptation of an overtly Christian Latin version of it is reinforced by Lewis's professed liking for Irish 'mythology': 'If Christianity is only a mythology, then I find the mythology I believe in is not the one I like best. I

33 Coletti, 'Eco's Middle Ages', p. 74.

34 Coletti, 'Eco's Middle Ages', p. 77.

35 See further the discussion of intertextuality below, pp. 32–42.

36 See below, pp. 15, 19, 123.

37 See discussion in Robert Tracy, '"All Them Rocks in the Sea": *Ulysses* as *Immram*', *Irish University Review*, 32 (2002), 225–41.

38 The term 'odyssey tale' is used for the *immram* in Michael Cronin, *Translation in the Digital Age* (London and New York: Routledge, 2013), p. 15, for instance. Note that the story of Ulysses was known in medieval Ireland, through an Irish narrative that was composed around 1200, a much later period than that of the composition of *immrama*; for discussion, see Barbara Hillers, 'Medieval Irish *Wandering of Ulysses* Between Literary and Orality', in *Classical Literature and Learning in Medieval Irish Narrative*, ed. by Ralph O'Connor (Cambridge: D. S. Brewer, 2014), pp. 83–97.

like Greek mythology much better: Irish better still: Norse best of all'.[39] The liking for Irish myth (which we know in the form of medieval Irish literary texts) shows through in the Narnia books, and particularly in Lewis's own *immram* narrative.[40] The roots of Lewis's *Voyage of the Dawn Treader* are sometimes incorrectly drawn as lying in Homer's *Odyssey*.[41] But the similarities to the Brendan narrative are too close to be ignored.[42]

The discussion of *Star Trek* in this book draws primarily on *Star Trek: The Original Series* (1966–1969); *The Next Generation* (1987–1994); *Voyager* (1995–2001); and *Enterprise* (2001–2005).[43] This corresponds to the first and

---

39 C. S. Lewis, 'Is Theology Poetry?', in *They Asked for a Paper. Papers and Addresses* (London: Bles, 1962), p. 152; quoted and discussed in Andrew Lazo, 'A Kind of Midwife. J. R. R. Tolkien and C. S. Lewis – Sharing Influence', in *Tolkien the Medievalist*, ed. by Jane Chance (London and New York: Routledge, 2003), pp. 36–49 (p. 41). See also comments on the passage in Michael Ward, *Planet Narnia. The Seven Heavens in the Imagination of C. S. Lewis* (Oxford: Oxford University Press, 2008), p. 27.

40 For a discussion of Irish mythology and its transmission in medieval texts, see Mark Williams, *Ireland's Immortals. A History of the Gods of Irish Myth* (Princeton: Princeton University Press, 2016).

41 Lazo, 'A Kind of Midwife', p. 46, citing John Lawlor, *C. S. Lewis. Memories and Reflections* (Dallas: Spence, 1998), p. 78, and Paul Ford, *A Companion to Narnia* (New York: Harper Collins, 1994), p. 272. No mention is made of Brendan, though Lazo does mention medieval narratives, focusing on Arthuriana (pp. 47–49). *Immrama* and the *Navigatio* are not mentioned in Devin Brown, *Inside the Voyage of the Dawn Treader: A Guide to Exploring the Journey Beyond Narnia* (Nashville: Abingdon Press, 2013), nor in Baxter, *The Medieval Mind* or Harry Lee Poe, *The Completion of C. S. Lewis (1945–1963): From War to Joy* (Wheaton: Crossway, 2022), p. 117 (he mentions the *Odyssey* only). The link with the Brendan story, is, however, well-established. See, for instance, David C. Downing, *Into the Wardrobe: C. S. Lewis and the Narnia Chronicles* (San Francisco: Wiley, 2005), p. 43.

42 See discussion in Lawyer, 'Three Celtic Voyages', pp. 329–36. See also comment in Helen Cooper, *The English Romance in Time: Transforming Motifs from Geoffrey of Monmouth to the Death of Shakespeare* (Oxford: Oxford University Press, 2004), p. 74; stated but not discussed also in Daniel VanderKolk, 'C.S. Lewis, Celtic Mythology, and Transatlantic Travel: the Story of Brendan the Voyager', conference paper *Translatlantic Connections Conference* 2015, p. 9 n. 33 <https://www.academia.edu/download/36327580/TransAtlSpch.pdf> [accessed 24 March 2024]. See also the discussion in Anne-Frédérique Mochel-Caballero, '"Where the Waves Grow Sweet": From Sea Adventure to Transcendence in The Voyage of the Dawn Treader by C.S. Lewis', *Fantasy Art and Studies*, 11 (2021) <https://u-picardie.hal.science/hal-03784545> [accessed 14 March 2024]. Ward sees the text as the result of a combination of influences, including both the *Odyssey* and the *immrama*, as well as *The Seafarer*, Mandeville, and Milton; Ward, *Planet Narnia*, pp. 108, 234.

43 For brief introductions to each series mentioned, see, respectively, the following chapters in *The Routledge Handbook of Star Trek*, ed. by Leimar Garcia-Siino, Sabrina

second iterations of *Star Trek*, before the long hiatus which preceded the reintroduction of new *Star Trek* series to the (home) screens in 2017, with *Star Trek Discovery*. Among the earlier generation of live-action series, my analysis largely excludes *Star Trek: Deep Space Nine* (1993–1999) because, since it is set on a space station, travel does not form a central part of the plot. Rather, I limit my analysis to the shows that 'follow the tired and trusted format of classic *Star Trek*: one ship, one crew, on one long journey through the cosmos'.[44] The main reason why *Star Trek Discovery* (2017–) and *Star Trek Picard* (2020–2023) are not included in this discussion is that both have committed fully to single-story-arc seasons which are not focused primarily on the journey process or a voyage of discovery, thus following a narrative form which does not correspond to the island-hopping definition of the *immram*.[45] My argument, therefore, is that *Star Trek* can be classed as *immram* only in relation to its original conception as 'Wagon Train to the Stars', and only in relation to the 1960s Original Series and to those of the subsequent series that imitated its format.[46]

Mittermeier, and Stefan Rabitsch (New York and London: Routledge, 2022): Ina Rae Hark, 'Star Trek: The Original Series' (pp. 9–17); A. Bowdoin Van Riper, 'Star Trek: The Next Generation' (pp. 28–36); Leimar Garcia-Siino, 'Star Trek: Voyager' (pp. 46–55); Zaki Hasan, 'Star Trek: Enterprise' (pp. 56–64).

44 Andy Lane and Anna Bowles, *Star Trek. The Adventure. Stardate 18.12.02. Hyde Park, London* (London: Titan Publishing Group, 2002), p. 30.

45 Mittermeier, 'Star Trek: Discovery', p. 67; see also Justice Hagan, 'Star Trek: Picard', in *The Routledge Handbook of Star Trek*, ed. by Leimar Garcia-Siino, Sabrina Mittermeier, and Stefan Rabitsch (New York and London: Routledge, 2022), pp. 74–79. Indeed, all of the new *Star Trek* series are also released in a form that is different from the previous generation: rather than a television release, the new media are online platforms. Expanding the discussion to include these, therefore, as with the inclusion of animated series, of the movies and other extensions such as games, would unnecessarily complicate the type of 'text' examined in this book, without necessarily adding to the argument being made. An additional reason why I have decided not to engage with *Star Trek: Discovery* (2017–), and *Star Trek: Strange New Worlds* (2022–) is partly because they are, at the time of writing, still running. The decision to exclude still-running series is made not on the basis of a medievalist's aversion to analysis of objects too current, but rather because the limitations of a chapter and unity of argument require that a line be drawn somewhere, and continuity is a good a place as any. Published work on the still-running series, includes, for instance, Sabrina Mittermeier and Marieke Spychala, ed., *Fighting For the Future. Essays on* Star Trek: Discovery (Liverpool: Liverpool University Press, 2020); see also Sabrina Mittermeier, 'Star Trek: Discovery' in *The Routledge Handbook of Star Trek*, ed. by Leimar Garcia-Siino, Sabrina Mittermeier, and Stefan Rabitsch (New York and London: Routledge, 2022), pp. 65–73.

46 Hark, 'Star Trek', p. 10; M. Keith Booker, 'The Politics of Star Trek', in *The Essential Science Fiction Television Reader*, ed. by J. P. Telotte (Lexington: University Press of Kentucky, 2008), pp. 195–208 (p. 196).

Similarly, my discussion of *Stargate* is selective and focuses primarily on the two of major television spin-offs: *Stargate SG-1* (MGM, 1997–2007) and *Stargate: Atlantis* (MGM, 2004–2009), with some reference to the original *Stargate* film (1994) and to *Stargate: Universe* (MGM, 2009–2011).[47] For the purposes of the present discussion, *Stargate*, including the initial movie directed by R. Emmerich (1994), the original television series, *Stargate SG-1*, and its first spin-off *Stargate: Atlantis*, I classify as belonging to the genre of the *echtra*, commonly glossed as 'otherworld journey', but more accurately (and importantly, for the purposes of my analysis of this text) rendered as 'otherworld visit'.[48] I largely exclude *Stargate: Universe* from the analysis in the chapter dedicated to the other *Stargate* series for the simple reason that, due to its primary structure as a series of jumps between (not entirely) random locations by means of a starship, it belongs to the *immram* rather than *echtra* genre. In the course of the series it also transpires that the ship is itself on a journey of discovery, like Brendan and his companions, and is following a pre-ordained path in seeking the secrets of the universe by assembling a puzzle. This is highly reminiscent of the search for the Land of Saints in the *Navigatio* and the 'Utter East' in *The Voyage of the Dawn Treader*.[49] It is also different in tone from the other series in the same manner that later *Star Trek* series differ from the first and second generation series of the franchise. Though a discussion of this series would serve well as an additional illustration the fuzziness of the genre sets, including it would in my opinion unnecessarily complicate the base outline of the book. Furthermore, this particular off-shoot of the Stargate franchise, much like *Discovery* and the initial seasons of *Picard* in *Star Trek*, alters the overall mood of the series considerably, and cannot be discussed without an extensive treatment of the increasing dystopian tendencies observed in science fiction in the recent decades.[50] I suggest that dystopian science-fiction can

---

47 My reasons for excluding the 2018 online mini-series *Stargate: Origins* is that it involves no travel. Like the more recent installments of *Star Trek* it breaks with the particular tradition which is the focus of this book. Unlike *Star Trek: Voyager*, *Stargate Universe* is more about travel away from home, and unlike the *immram* both *Voyager* and *Universe* are unintentional travel-tales. For further discussion, see Chapters 5 and 6 below.

48 See below, p. 27 for discussion of the concept of 'otherworld'.

49 See above, p. 5.

50 Indeed, arguably the new series of *Star Trek* have all taken a distinctly dystopian turn, thus marking yet another stylistic break from the earlier generation; see Hagen, 'Star Trek: Picard', p. 75, 76. For a rationalization of prevalence of dystopian over utopian narratives in visual entertainment media, see Simon Spiegel, 'Utopia', in *The Routledge Handbook of Star Trek*, ed. by Leimar Garcia-Siino, Sabrina Mittermeier, and Stefan

be treated as a separate fuzzy set, which I leave outside this enquiry.[51] My justification lies partly in the necessity to limit the corpus to proportions manageable within the scope of the present book, and partly in the thematic tension between utopia and the search for the better on the one hand, and dystopian despair on the other.[52] A focus dictated by the Irish literary tradition, to my mind, is best served by privileging the former. In this, I follow the analysis of the utopian topos in the Irish literary tradition (medieval and modern) presented by Tom Moylan, who observes that 'there is a tendency in the Irish imaginary that brings to people's social dreams a *topos* wherein those dreams can be located and, more or less, fleshed out, so that they can function as distanced (estranged) re-visions of what life could possibly bring'.[53]

To take the texts chosen for our corpus together is a relatively uncontroversial approach, since they might all be characterised as 'fantastic journey narratives', and as such belong to an old tradition. However, they also cut across contemporary conventional genre distinctions as well as the notional hierarchy of literariness, with only Swift and Eco's novels fulfilling the requirements of the category of 'high-art literariness', to quote David Matthews' discussion of Eco.[54] The re-classification of these texts resulting in parallel readings that highlight a new network of intertextualities, marks genre analysis not only as 'significant part of both writing and reading' texts, highlighted by Ann Rigney, but also of the meta-level analysis of their reception and its reading.[55] My choice of this particular combination of texts is dictated by three considerations:

Rabitsch (New York and London: Routledge, 2022), pp. 467–75 (p. 468, p. 471). The older Star Trek series, by contrast, are known for their optimism and general positive outlook; Booker, 'The Politics', pp. 195–96 and below, pp. 135, 143–45, 147–151. For a discussion of the concepts of dystopia, utopia, and heterotopia, see below, pp. 126–27.

51 For academic engagements with the increasingly dystopian tendencies in science-fiction over the past couple decades, see, for example, Lynette Porter, *Charming Villains and Modern Monsters: Science Fiction in Shades of Gray on 21st Century Television* (Jefferson: McFarland, 2010). The normalization of the dreary hopelessness of dystopia is to my mind best articulated by the emergence of such terminology as 'realist dystopian science fiction'; see Wei Lu, 'Sci-Fi Realism and the Allegory of Dystopia: With Kazuo Ishiguro's Never Let Me Go as an Example', *Comparative Literature Studies*, 57 (2020), 702–14.

52 For more on utopias and dystopias, see also below, pp. 27–29 and 120–29.

53 Moylan, 'Irish Voyages', p. 300. We will return to the presence of utopian otherworlds in *Stargate* narratives in Chapter 6.

54 Matthews, *Medievalism*, p. 127.

55 Ann Rigney, 'The Many Dimensions of Literature' in *The Life of Texts. An Introduction to Literary Studies*, ed. by Kiene Brillenburg Wurth and Ann Rigney (Amsterdam: Amsterdam University Press, 2019), pp. 43–76 (p. 63).

1) to show that old taxonomies can have new uses, and that Old Irish literature is not irrelevant to the study of contemporary cultures;
2) to show that there is a family of texts produced in the post-medieval period that are heirs of the Old Irish literary tradition of fantastic voyage narratives;
3) to illustrate a point about intertextuality succinctly made by Umberto Eco more than twenty years ago: when one finally comes to read a book purchased long ago and left unread since then on one's bookshelf, sometimes one finds the information in it is already known.[56]

The reason for the phenomenon mentioned in the third item above, according to Eco, is that in the interim, other books that had relied on it would have been read, so with the result that 'even that book you had not read was still part of your mental heritage and perhaps had influenced you profoundly'.[57] Intertextuality is thus a major theme in my book, and I will return to this point further in the introduction.

Despite the apparently eclectic nature of the selection, this is hardly a controversial mode of reading the texts. The debt of Eco and Lewis to medieval travel narratives is widely acknowledged.[58] Swift is usually read in the context of the classical tradition – Lucian's *True History* in particular – but will be shown to also represent a stage in the reception of the medieval fantastic voyage, and Irish medieval literature as well.[59] *Star Trek* famously abounds with intertextual references, and the world of *Stargate* is constructed almost entirely on the basis of reception of ancient mythologies and pre-modern legends (usually viewed through the prism of their early-modern retellings). The texts discussed in this book will be shown to belong to the same broad intertextual matrix, sharing and exerting on each other multiple layers of influences.

---

56 Eco, 'Borges and My Anxiety of Influence', in Eco, *On Literature*, trans. by Martin McLaughlin (London: Random hours Vintage, 2006), pp. 118–35 (pp. 131–32).

57 Eco, 'Borges', pp. 132–33. Eco's views on the interaction between innovation and building on previous works are also applied by Stan Beeler to the analysis of Stargate; '*Stargate SG-1* and the Quest for the Perfect Science-Fiction Premise', in *The Essential Science Fiction Television Reader*, ed. by J. P. Telotte (Lexington: University Press of Kentucky, 2008), pp. 267–82 (pp. 267, 277, 279).

58 It is even present in popular writing. See John Mullan's review of *Baudolino* in the *London Review of Books*, for instance; John Mullan, 'Catching the Prester John Bug', *London Review of Books*, 25 (2003) < https://www.lrb.co.uk/the-paper/v25/n09/john-mullan/catching-the-prester-john-bug > [accessed 6 March 2024].

59 For Lucian's influence on Swift, see in particular Richard Edward Compean, 'Swift and the Lucianic Tradition', Unpublished PhD Dissertation, University of California Davis, 1976; see also references in n. 78 below.

The act of viewing these texts through the lens not of modern, but of medieval genre categories and expectations yields new and striking patterns, in turn allowing connections to emerge that would otherwise have been lost.[60] It also allows to avoid the problems posed by the subjective and culturally defined nature of definitions (sic) of fantasy, for instance, which are as Gomel and Gurevitch point out, 'different in different cultural contexts'.[61] The decision to use Old Irish voyage narrative categories *immram* and *echtra* as classificatory devices instead of more modern generic terms (such as 'adventure tales', 'island narratives', 'fantasy' or 'science fiction') creates a counterpoint to the two common approaches to genre, which either take a modern genre and trace its origins, or take a modern genre and attempt to define its characteristics.[62]

Without seeking to replace generic categories in current use, this book experiments with an alternate way of categorizing texts, based on a diachronic view of reception of a dual 'genre'-type – the Old Irish travel narratives, composed of the *immram* and *echtra* 'genres'. In this, I follow the notion of dialogic engagement with predecessors based loosely on the theories of Mikhail Bakhtin and, to a small extent also Yuri Lotman, as a way of looking at intertextuality (and genre) diachronically.[63] As Clive Thomson points out, Bakhtin never wrote a single treatment of genre.[64] Thomson's

60 For a similar approach, in seeking to analyse contemporary educational challenges through the prism of Old Irish learning practices, see Marie Martin, *Learning by Wandering. An Ancient Irish Perspective for a Digital World* (Oxford and Bern: Peter Lang, 2010).

61 Gomel and Gurevitch, 'What is Fantasy and Who Decides?', p. 4. The categories used in *Modern Afterlives of Old Irish Travel Narratives* are not intended to replace the labels currently in use, but rather to provide a complementary view.

62 Elena Gomel and Danielle Gurevitch, 'What is Fantasy and Who Decides?', p. 4; with reference to Alastair Fowler, *Kinds of Literature. An Introduction to the Theory of Genres and Modes* (Oxford: Clarendon Press, 2002). To the second type belongs, for instance Brian Attebery, *Strategies of Fantasy* (Bloomington: Indiana University Press, 1992), cited by the authors on p. 6.

63 I use Lotman's theories of dialogic culture in my analysis of Lewis in Chapter 2; see pp. 49–54, 64, 70–72. For Bakhtin's ideas on genre see the helpful summary and discussion in Clive Thomson, 'Bakhtin's "Theory" of Genre', *Studies in Twentieth-Century Literature*, 9 (1984), 29–40 <https://doi.org/10.4148/2334-4415.1150>. As Massimiliano Bampi points out, discussions of genre theory frequently omit the medieval period altogether and otherwise are often limited to the application of established views on genre to the medieval material (rather than vice versa); Bampi, 'Genre', in *A Critical Companion to Old Norse Literary Genre*, ed. by Massimiliano Bampi, Carolyne Larrington, and Sif Rikhardsdottir (Cambridge: D. S. Brewer, 2020), pp. 15–30 (p. 16).

64 Thomson, 'Bakhtin's "Theory of Genre"', p. 33.

own digest based on the critic's various writings provides a useful starting point. Thomson summarises the traditional view of genre (and this still holds today) as follows: 'to classify two given texts from the same historical period in the same generic mode is to imply that the two texts have an element in common, or that the second text has repeated or reproduced an aspect of the first'.[65] By contrast, in Bakhtin's view as summarized by Thomson, 'the operative factor is transformation' even in cases where an individual reproduces a text, and certainly so in the diachronic reproduction of 'generic' features.[66] The importance of the role of the individual doing the reproducing links this diachronic and dialogic theory of genre to reception.

Particularly poignant in the context of reception is Bakhtin's statement that: 'Genre is a representative of creative memory in the process of literary development.'[67] In this instance we can understand 'creative memory' as the internalised dialogic stage of transmission: 'memory', as cultural memory, being elements that are inherited, while the 'creative' aspect is the contribution of new interpretation or new form to the inherited component.[68] Genre is thus conceived in *The Modern Afterlives of Old Irish Travel Nar-ratives*, 'as means of a communication strategy', 'understood primarily as instruments of communication and social interaction,' to borrow Massimiliano Bampi's apt turns of phrase.[69] Bampi anchors his discussion of genre in the theory of systems, and in particular polysystems theory.[70] This is an extremely fruitful approach, but a full exploration of the implications

65 Thomson, 'Bakhtin's "Theory of Genre"', p. 32.

66 Thomson, 'Bakhtin's "Theory of Genre"', p. 32.

67 Mikhail Bakhtin, *Problems of Dostoyevsky's Poetics*, ed. and trans. by Caryl Emerson (Minneapolis and London: University of Minnesota Press, 1984), p. 106. Quoted in Thomson, 'Bakhtin's "Theory of Genre"', p. 34.

68 I am conscious that such a use of Bakhtin in itself constitutes an act of creative memory. The articulation of differences, and of my (re-)definitions of the concepts involved also represent, however, a dialogic engagement with the theory. Perhaps this discussion itself may be analysed in the context of a study of the reception history of Bakhtin's theory. Reinterpretation, alteration and re-purposing, whether intentional or not, does appear to be the general fate of literary theories and of theoretical ideas in general. For a thought-provoking discussion of this issue, see Edward Said, 'Travelling Theory', in *The Selected Works of Edward Said. 1966–2006*, ed. by Moustafa Bayoumi and Andrew Rubin (London and Dublin: Bloomsbury Publishing, 2021), pp. 197–219, originally published in *Raritan Quarterly* in 1982. The dialogic aspect of reception plays a major role in the discussion of Lewis's engagement with the medieval *Navigatio sancti Brendani* as source for *The Voyage of the Dawn Treader* in Chapter 2 below.

69 Bampi, 'Genre', pp. 18, 20.

70 Bampi, 'Genre', p. 25.

of fitting the present book into that framework would require a theoretical discussion that would outstrip the length of the book itself. Suffice it to say here that the dialogic framework used to think about reception in the present book implies a view of literature as a dynamic evolving system and is not at odds with the prevailing views of polysystems theory based on the influential work of Itamar Even-Zohar and others.[71]

One final note needs to be added on the matter of genre and reception. One cannot discuss reception and genre without a reference to the work of Hans Robert Jauss, and in particular his treatment of medieval literature.[72] Jauss's discussion hinges on genre as a mediating tool in the 'horizon of the expectable', conditioning an audience's response to the text.[73] A crucial difference between the approach taken here and Jauss's analysis of medieval genres is that Jauss attempts to escape a normative and classificatory system, whereas this study embraces the medieval Irish system of classification in order to group texts and examine them in new combinations.[74] Similarly, Jauss's understanding of the medieval genre system is that it is a 'testimony for the ideal *and* reality of a unique political as well as cultural historical-world closed in itself', whereas the medieval Irish literary world examined in this book is seen as a radically open world which can help us understand today's cultural phenomena.[75]

I examine intertextual echoes between the selected works in light of a single medieval tradition, that of the medieval Irish travel narratives. This represents an exercise in 'strategic essentialism': I neither negate nor ignore the more complicated framework of references and influences within which each of the works examined originates, but rather choose to pick out a

71 Itamar Even-Zohar, 'Polysystem Theory', *Poetics Today*, 11 (1990), 9–94; see also literature cited in Bampi, 'Genre', p. 25 nn. 27, 28. For an effective application of polysystems theory to the study of reception as well as translation within a literary corpus, see, for example Haidee Kruger, *Postcolonial Polysystems: The Production and Reception of Translated Children's Literature in South Africa* (Amsterdam: John Benjamins, 2012).

72 Hans Robert Jauss, *Toward an Aesthetic of Reception* (Brighton: Harvester Press, 1982), pp. 76–109.

73 Jauss, *Toward an Aesthetic of Reception*, p. 79.

74 Jauss, *Toward an Aesthetic of Reception*, p. 80.

75 Jauss, *Toward an Aesthetic of Reception*, p. 109. The words 'radically open' purposefully echo the concept of the margin as place of 'radical openness', coined by Bell Hooks. Her concept of the margin as a place of possibility rather than exile seems appropriate in translation in the world of scholarly enquiry also to the 'niche' study of Old Irish literature; Bell Hooks, 'Choosing the Margin as a Space of Radical Openness', *Framework: The Journal of Cinema and Media*, 36 (1989), 15–23.

single thread in order to explore its importance and to argue for its potential as a unifying category framework.[76] A full intertextual exploration of all travel narratives examined here without the organizing principle of the *immrama* and *echtrai* genres would result in a sprawling construction reminiscent of Borges's dreams of the labyrinth of a universal library.[77] As it is, references to the world beyond the texts examined here will bring into the remit of the present book works as widely ranging as Lucian's *Ἀληθῶν Διηγημάτων* (*True History*), Marco Polo's and Mandeville's travel narratives, Sir Arthur Conan Doyle's *The Lost World*, and Italo Calvino's *Le città invisibili* (*The Invisible Cities*).[78]

The alternative way of classifying texts proposed in this book is not intended as a definitive or permanent, or as the only solution (or indeed even as *a* solution) to the genre problem. Rather, it illustrates the potential of the material to be understood differently. Classification is, in many ways, interpretation. The implications of genre labels for how a text is understood, and

---

76 Strategic essentialism was originally proposed by Gayatri Spivak as a tool for activist feminism, it 'simultaneously recognizes the impossibility of any essentialism and the necessity of some kind of essenialism for the sake of political action'; Ian Buchanan, *A Dictionary of Critical Theory*, 1st edn (Oxford: Oxford University Press, 2010) s.v. strategic essentialism; <https://www.oxfordreference.com/view/10.1093/acref/9780199532919.001.0001/acref-9780199532919-e-669> [accessed 6 November 2024]. In medieval studies, the concept has been used effectively as the starting point of discussion in the edited volume *Marco Polo and the Encounter of East and West*, edited by Susanne Conklin Akbari and Amilcare Ianucci, with John Tulk (Toronto, Buffalo and London: University of Toronto Press, 2008); see Susanne Conklin Akbari, 'Introduction', p. 3.

77 The most poetic and complex articulation of this idea is found in his 'La Biblioteca de Babel' ('The Library of Babel'). See Jorge Luis Borges, *Ficciones* (Madrid: Alianza Editorial, 1999), pp. 86–99.

78 Lucian, *True History. Introduction, Text, Translation, and Commentary*, ed. and trans. by Diskin Clay, and ed. by James H. Brusuelas (Oxford: Oxford University Press, 2021); Sir Arthur Conan Doyle, *The Lost World: Being an Account of the Recent Amazing Adventures of Professor E. Challenger, Lord John Roxton, Professor Summerlee and Mr. Ed Malone of the 'Daily Gazette'* (London: J. Murray, 1966 [1912]); Italo Calvino, *Le città invisibili* (Turin: Einaudi, 1972); *Invisible Cities*, trans. by William Weaver (New York: Harcourt Brace Jovanovich, 1974); According to Kingsley Amis, Lucian is named among the precursors of science fiction; Amis, *New Maps*, pp. 27–28. For Mandeville and Marco Polo, see below, p. 39. Calvino is less engaged with the Middle Ages than Eco, but also draws on medieval traditions; see Martin McLaughlin, 'Calvino, Eco and the Transmission of World Literature', in *Transmissions of Memory. Echoes, Traumas, and Nostalgia in Post-World War II Italian Culture*, ed. by Patrizia Sambuco (Vancouver, Madison, Teaneck and Wroxton: Fairleigh Dickinson University Press, 2018), pp. 3–19 (pp. 7–10).

what company it is read in, are apparent, for instance, is Margaret Atwood's resistance to the 'science fiction' label for her novels, embracing rather the label 'speculative fiction'.[79] Atwood associates the label 'science fiction' in particular with H. G. Wells' *War of the Worlds* and with the Martians, and 'speculative fiction' with Jules Verne.[80] Atwood's resistance to the former label might be seen as an indication of the straight-jacketing effect of contemporary genre distinctions. Multiple definitions of 'science fiction' exist, and the term is ambiguous. Kingsley Amis, while noting that a definition of 'science fiction' as a genre 'is bound to be cumbersome rather than memorable', proposes the following definition: 'Science fiction is that class of prose narrative treating of a situation that could not arise in the world we know, but which is hypothesized on the basis of some innovation in science of technology, or pseudo-science and pseudo-technology, whether human or extra-terrestrial in origin'.[81] A counterpoint for this definition is provided for the genre of fantasy by William Robert Irwin, who defines it as 'a story based on and controlled by an overt violation of what is generally accepted as possibility'.[82] The tug of war between the genres of fantasy and science fiction today is an important subject in itself, but poses a genre-definition problem which I would argue is a problem of how one cuts the literary cake. Ultimately, the definitional difficulty, and the related difficulty of straight-jacketing a work of literature into one or other of the two 'genres', is a problem of perspective. The present book experiments with a different way of cutting the cake.

In the approach adopted in *Modern Afterlives of Old Irish Travel Narratives*, rather than focusing on the teleology of the two genres of science fiction and fantasy (in conjunction with the sub-category of voyage literature),

79 See her discussion of the issue in 'The Road to Ustopia', *The Guardian*, October 14, 2011 <www.theguardian.com/books/2011/oct/14/margaret-atwood-road-to-ustopia> [accessed 18 February 2024]. The concept of 'ustopia' is further discussed below, pp. 126–27.

80 Atwood, 'The Road to Ustopia'. One wonders where Bradbury's philosophical take on Martian society might fit in this dichotomy – I would be inclined to place it alongside George Orwell, Kurt Vonnegut and Atwood herself, in the group headed by Voltaire, termed 'philosophical fable'.

81 Amis, *New Maps*, p. 18.

82 William Robert Irwin, *The Game of the Impossible* (Urbana: University of Illinois Press, 1974), p. 4; quoted and discussed in Gomel and Gurevitch, 'What is Fantasy and Who Decides?', p. 7. Gomel and Gurevitch introduce the term 'consensus reality' to their discussion, but for our purposes in the contrast to science fiction, reality has little to do with consensus, since we are dealing with the physical reality studied by physicists and mathematicians, which is independent of a reader's views or opinions.

I examine the post-medieval texts as witnesses to the after-life – a continuation of the tradition – and thus to the reception history of the Old Irish voyage tales. This approach is the result of a slight shift in perspective in looking at the picture presented by Sebastian I. Sobecki in the context of his discussion of the Latin *Navigatio*, the Anglo-Norman French *Voyage de Saint Brendan*, and Irish vernacular voyage narratives (*immrama*): 'In the literature set on the open sea of the Western *Ocean* (itself a name for the West), this mélange of the barely possible with the undiscovered generated an early mirror-image of what is now called "science-fiction": dazzling tales of the seafaring exploits of saintly heroes and heroic saints such as Alexander and Brendan that were even more daring than their Mediterranean counterparts, Odysseus and Sindbad'.[83] Sobecki's point is valid, but he inverts the narrative chronology by privileging the modern genre (science fiction), of which the pre-modern becomes the mirror image or antecedent. If we give precedence to the pre-modern as the starting point of the comparison, the result is the kind of intertextual matrix centred on the *immram* and *echtra* genres discussed in the following section of this book.

Jan Johnson-Smith provides a helpful template for looking at contemporary science fiction in a historical context: 'if we consider a broader spectrum and include early speculative fictions and fantasies, such as the tales of Gilgamesh or Odysseus – all of which include discoveries and advances of knowledge – we find ourselves in worlds of myth, magic and non-technological possibilities. It seems that the science of today is the magic of yesterday, the magic of today is the science of tomorrow'.[84] While I do not use the term 'speculative fiction' in relation to the Old Irish *echtrai* and *immrama*, the taxonomic principles employed in the present book echo Johnson-Smith's observation of the 'parallels' between early narratives and 'modern fictions of exploration and discovery' in both content and in storytelling modes and techniques.[85] Some of these modes and techniques were inherited by the modern texts discussed in these books. They are often combined by these new texts with techniques and themes taken from other traditions and other sources. Both Eco and Lewis, for instance, draw on the 'Marvels of the East' tradition. Lewis combines this with the

83 Sebastian I. Sobecki, 'From the *désert liquide* to the Sea of Romance: Benedeit's *Le voyage de Saint Brendan* and the Irish *immrama*', *Neophilologus*, 87 (2003), 193–207 (p. 194). Italics and brackets Sobecki's.

84 Jan Johnson-Smith, *American Science Fiction TV: Star Trek, Stargate and Beyond* (London: I.B. Tauris, 2012), p. 17, and cf. also comments on pp. 26–27.

85 Johnson-Smith, *American Science Fiction TV*, p. 34.

island-hopping tradition of the westward journeys, and notes both the St Brendan legend and Homer's *Odyssey*, as his models.[86]

As John Rieder points out, 'science fiction and the other genres usually associated with so-called genre fiction, such as the detective story, the modern romance, the western, horror, and fantasy, collectively compose a system of genres distinct from the preexisting classical and academic genre system that includes the epic, tragedy, comedy, satire, romance, the lyric, and so on; and […] this more recently formed genre system is an important historical phenomenon'.[87] If, as according to Rieder, this new system widely used in mass media, bookstores, and to use Rieder's words, 'mass-scale commercial production and distribution', constitutes a new development in terms of how we categorise 'texts' (broadly defined as subject of cultural production) building on, overlapping with, but not quite replacing the 'traditional' categories, then it simply represents an alternative way of cutting the cultural cake. We cut our genres one way. Others before us did it differently. The fact that we come later in chronological terms does not automatically mean our way is necessarily more helpful on all occasions and for all purposes (though it might be for some).

With this as background, the procedure I propose in this book should not seem excessively radical: to use a yet older way to cut the new cake by applying Old Irish taxonomies to modern texts, reading a selection of works of literature, fantasy and science fiction in terms of varied degrees of membership of the textual families of *echtrai* and *immrama*. Doing so has the additional advantage of cutting across what Rieder defines as the divide that runs between the 'mass cultural genre system and the contemporary academic-classical genre system'.[88] Rieder's call that the two systems 'are best understood in relation to one another, so that twenty-first-century literary history needs to recognize and study both' is thus answered in this book by virtue of taking an entirely different genre system and applying it to

86 Downing, *Into the Wardrobe*, p. 43, with reference to Lewis's notes. Cf. also discussion in P. Andrew Montgomery, 'Classical Literature', in *Reading the Classics with C. S. Lewis*, ed. by Thomas L. Martin (Grand Rapids, MI: Baker Academic, and Carlisle: Paternoster Press, 2000), pp. 52–71 (pp. 63–64), reading the *Voyage of the Dawn Treader*, like the *Odyssey*, as a quest for home. There is also an explicit reference to Ulysses (Odysseus) in the text; Lewis, *Voyage*, p. 247. For the discussion of the Greek classic in the context of medieval Irish (and Norse) voyage narratives, see Matthias Egeler, *Islands in the West. Classical Myth and the Medieval Norse and Irish Geographical Imagination* (Turnhout: Brepols, 2017), for example pp. 134–40, 246, 262.

87 John Rieder, *Science Fiction and the Mass Cultural Genre System* (Middletown, Connecticut: Wesleyan University Pess, 2017), p. 1.

88 Rieder, *Science Fiction*, p. 1.

material that would otherwise be found on two sides of the divide.[89] Umberto Eco and Jonathan Swift in Rieder's two modern genre systems are within the 'academic genre system', and while there might be some argument about whether C. S. Lewis should be categorized as 'merely' an author of 'children's fantasy', *Star Trek* and *Stargate* would be unequivocally termed science-fiction and entertainment, within the 'mass cultural genre system'. These texts would not appear to all 'belong' together. In this book, however, I will show that they can be taken as members of two intersecting fuzzy sets of *immrama* and *echtrai*, and once we examine them within that scheme, a new intertextual matrix begins to emerge which throws new light both on the texts themselves and on the interconnections between them.[90]

1.1 The Old Irish 'Genre System', Otherworlds, and Utopias

The two Old Irish genres (or rather more accurately labels for textual categories as recognised and practiced in medieval Ireland), which provide the reference point for the present exploration of the reception and transformation of fantastic voyages are: *immram* (lit. 'rowing-about'; pl. *immrama*) and *echtra* (lit. 'adventure'; pl. *echtrai*).[91]

Immram is usually translated as 'voyage' but comes from the verb *imb·rá / imm·rá* 'row-about'.[92] David Dumville's description of the *immrama*

89 Rieder, *Science Fiction*, p. 1.

90 For the notion of interconnections emerging after the process of intertextual analysis is undertaken, see Eco, 'Borges', p. 133. 'Fuzzy sets' are a concept borrowed from mathematics, and are discussed in more detail in section 1.3 of the Introduction, pp. 32–42. The notion of overlap between the two genres is widely acknowledged; see, for instance, Séamus Mac Mathúna, *Iceland and the Immrama: An Enquiry into Irish Influence on Old Norse-Icelandic Voyage Literature*, Münchner Nordistische Studien, 48 (München: utzverlag, 2021), pp. 20–21; Leonie Duignan, *The Echtrae as an Early Irish Literary Genre* (Rahden: Verlag Marie Leidorf, 2011), p. 6, and nn. 91, 105 and 137 of this book.

91 Electronic Dictionary of the Irish Language, s.v. *imram* <dil.ie/28025> [accessed 5 November 2024]; and s.v. *echtra* <dil.ie/19563> [accessed 5 November 2024]; and for a brief description of the genres, John T. Koch's entries on '*Echtrai*' and '*Immrama*', in *Celtic Culture: A Historical Encyclopedia*, ed. by John T. Koch (Santa Barbara: ABC-CLIO, 2006), pp. 646, 959. It is worth noting that as Koch points out, 'The *echtrae* genre continued into the later Middle Ages and modern times, becoming influenced by the international chivalric romance'('*Echtrai*', p. 646), and there is thus also a direct line of descent in the *echtra* genre to the modern period, alongside the more indirect reception routes charted in the present book.

92 Koch, '*Immrama*'.

will provide a useful guide to the analysis of all material examined in the following chapters, and thus merits quotation in full:

> These are all frame-tales. That is to say that the 'rowing about', as one may literally interpret the term *immram*, provides the means by which all manner of incidents may be secured and joined within the story. In this kind of tale episodes may be added or subtracted at will, as long as the frame itself is not damaged. Occasional internal inconsistencies sometimes reveal that such processes of addition and subtraction have indeed been at work. In the frame one must expect to find a motivation for the events of the tale, a satisfactory conclusion, and some material which will link very clearly with specific episodes within the narration of the circumnavigation itself.[93]

The quotation addresses aspects of this genre, and the importance of the rowing-about as the frame for the narrative in particular, that we will encounter in the texts examined in this book. Another important element in the definition is that these frame-tales accumulate episodes that contain encounters with all sorts of wonders. As Dumville points out, surviving *immrama*, vernacular as much as Latin (the *Navigatio*) are not particularly 'Celtic' in tone, and indeed 'Many of the episodes contained in the *immrama* are (even leaving aside theological material) of an origin which cannot be described as Celtic, and which must rely on bestiaries, lapidaries, and other compilatory works deriving ultimately from the learning of the world of classical antiquity'.[94] This combinatory aspect of the genre is also a feature of the more modern texts examined in this book.[95] The key component of the *immram* type of narrative is thus specifically a sea-voyage, with multiple stopping points, some or all of which might be at supernatural islands or locations where supernatural things happen, and which in some cases might be defined as 'otherworldly'.[96] The core surviving *immrama* are:

---

93 Dumville, '*Echtrae and Immram*', p. 75.

94 Dumville, '*Echtrae and Immram*', p. 75. The notion that the *immrama* are not an 'native' Irish genre is accepted by John Carey, 'The Location of the Otherworld in Irish Tradition', *Éigse*, 19 (1982–83), 36–43 (p. 36), reprinted in Wooding, ed., *The Otherworld Voyage*, pp. 113–19. I refer to the page numbers of the reprint edition throughout my discussion.

95 See also the section on 'intertextuality' below, pp. 32–42.

96 Wooding, 'Introduction', p. xi. Note that islands have a tendency to be associated with otherworlds; see Aisling Byrne, *Otherworlds: Fantasy and History in Medieval Literature*

Immram Curaig Maíle Dúin (The Voyage of Máel Dúin's Coracle), *Immram Curaig Ua Corra* (The Voyage of the Uí Chorra's Coracle), and *Immram Snedgusa agus Maic Riagla* (The Voyage of Snedgus and Mac Riagla).[97] The three tales are given here in chronological order, as their presumed approximate dates are ninth, tenth, and twelfth centuries (although *Immram Snedgusa* might be based on a lost Old Irish version).[98] A fourth narrative, *Immram Brain mac Febail* (The Voyage of Bran Son of Febal), also carries the label, but as we shall see below, does not fit comfortably into the genre and has been argued in previous scholarship to belong rather to the *echtra* tale-type.[99]

The *echtrai*, meanwhile, specifically concern a voyage to the 'otherworld', with a heavy focus on the adventures in the otherworld itself, and have been defined as narratives that 'usually involve a lone hero encountering supernatural or otherworldly challenges'.[100] This type includes the Old Irish tales *Echtra Nerai*, *Echtra Láegaire*, and *Echtrae Chonnlai* among others.[101]

(Oxford: Oxford University Press, 2015), pp. 141–42 and further references provided in her discussion.

97 For the texts, see Whitley Stokes, ed. and trans., 'The Voyage of Mael Duin (Part I)', *Revue Celtique*, 9 (1988), 447–95, continued in 'The Voyage of Mael Duin (Part II)', *Revue Celtique*, 10 (1989), 50–95; Whitley Stokes, ed. and trans., 'The Voyage of the Húi Corra', in *Revue Celtique*, 9 (1988), 22–69; Whitley Stokes, ed., 'The Voyage of Snedgus and Mac Riagla', *Revue Celtique*, 9 (1988), 14–25; Hans Pieter Atze Oskamp, ed., *The Voyage of Máel Dúin. A Study in Early Irish Voyage Literature followed by an Edition of Immram curaig Máele Dúin from the Yellow Book of Lecan in Trinity College, Dublin* (Groningen: Wolters-Noordhoff, 1970); Anton Gerard van Hamel, ed., 'The text of *Immram curaig Maíldúin*', *Études Celtiques*, 3 (1938), 1–20, and Anton Gerard van Hamel, ed., *Immrama*, Mediaeval and Modern Irish Series, 10 (Dublin: Dublin Institute for Advanced Studies, 1941). For discussions, see, for instance, Barbara Hillers 'Voyages Between Heaven and Hell: Navigating the Early Irish *Immram* Tales', *Proceedings of the Harvard Celtic Colloquium*, 13 (1993), 66–81 and Caoimhín Breatnach, 'The Transmission and Structure of *Immram curaig Ua Corra*', *Ériu*, 53 (2003), 91–107.

98 Mac Mathúna, *Iceland and the Immrama*, p. 19, n. 23.

99 See Kuno Meyer, ed. and trans., *The Voyage of Bran Son of Febal to the Land of the Living* (London: Nutt, 1895) and Séamus Mac Mathúna, ed., *Immram Brain – Bran's Journey to the Land of the Women*, Buchreihe der Zeitschrift für celtische Philologie, 2 (Tübingen: Max Niemeyer Verlag, 1985); for discussion and further references, see below, pp. 33–37.

100 Koch, '*Echtrai*'.

101 For the texts, see Kuno Meyer, ed. and trans, 'The Adventures of Nera', *Revue Celtique*, 10 (1889) 212–228; Kenneth Jackson, 'The Adventure of Laeghaire mac Crimhthainn', *Speculum* 17 (1942), 377–389; Kim McCone, ed. and tr., *Echtrae Chonnlai and the Beginnings of Vernacular Narrative Writing in Ireland*, Maynooth Medieval Irish Texts, 1 (Maynooth: Department of Old and Middle Irish, National University of

Typical features of these tales are the hero's involvement with an otherworldly woman (who sometimes invites him to the otherworld); a marked difference between the otherworld and the hero's world, such as riches and youth of otherwoldly inhabitants; sometimes, though not always, the hero's ultimate return to the otherworld at the end.[102]

In terms of our corpus of texts, such an *echtra*-type 'otherworld' in *Baudolino* is represented by the exotic Orient, filtered through the narrator's unreliable fantasy. In *Gulliver's Travels* the 'otherworld' is constituted by the various islands visited, and in *Stargate* it is represented by the various planets.[103] Crucially, Gulliver and the heroes of *Stargate* can be described as engaging on an *echtra* rather than *immram* voyage because after every (or almost every) island encounter they return home. In an *immram*, by contrast, the island-hopping, without the intermission at home, from strange place to strange place, is the driving characteristic. The 'otherworldly' elements of travel, in the sense of going beyond the boundaries of this world, are inherent in the etymology of *echtra*, which entails the 'sense of "going outside" or "outing"', and sometimes also involves alterations in the rate of the passing of time.[104]

The 'otherworld' forms a crucial element of both *immram* and *echtra* narratives. Since the two tale types have such elements in common, the

Ireland, 2000). The list is not exhaustive and focuses on texts which feature the most in the discussion below. Other medieval tales belonging to this genre also survive, although in their current form they cannot be dated as far back as the Old Irish period, including *Echtra Airt*, *Echtra Cormaic*, and *Echtrae mac nEchach Mugmedóin*. For the texts, see Richar Irvine Best, ed. and tr., 'The Adventures of Art son of Conn, and the Courtship of Delbchaem', *Ériu* 3 (1907), 149–173; Whitley Stokes, ed. and trans., 'The Irish Ordeals, Cormac's adventure in the Land of Promise, and the Decision as to Cormac's sword', in Whitley Stokes and Ernst Windisch, ed., *Irische Texte mit Wörterbuch*, 3.1 (Leipzig: Hirzel, 1891), pp. 183–221; Whitley Stokes, ed. and trans., 'The Death of Crimthann son of Fidach, and the Adventures of the Sons of Eochaid Muigmedón', *Revue Celtique* 24 (1903), 172–207 (pp. 191–203). For further discussion of the tales belonging to the *echtra* 'genre', see Duignan, *The Echtrae*.

102 See Duignan, *The Echtrae*, pp. 6, 8, 37–68.

103 See Chapters 4 and 6 below. For science fiction planets as islands, see also Amis, *New Maps*, pp. 30–31.

104 Koch, '*Echtrai*'. A thought-provoking traversal of the distance between the modern scientific and medieval literary conceptualisations of the world, specifically in relation to space-time and in contrast of the Newtonian absolute framework of the Early Modern work has been recently provided by Aled Llion-Jones in a paper which he labeled as 'comparative literature' with a tint of 'comparative hermeneutics'; Aled Llion Jones, 'Good Time(s), Bad Time(s): Myth and Metaphysics in Some Medieval Literature?', *Proceedings of the Harvard Celtic Colloquium*, 38 (2018), 47–74 (p. 52).

exact distinction between them has been a matter of some debate. For the purposes of the discussion in this book, we can zoom in on a selection of characteristics which seem to belong to a greater degree to one or to the other. When it comes to the otherworld, in the *immram*, a desirable (utopian) form of the otherworld is frequently the goal of the journey, a goal that is not always reached. It is present in the frame of the narrative, but the focus is on the process of getting there. Semi-otherworlds, in the form of strange lands, visited in the course of the journey, form the core of the narrative itself. In the *echtrai*, the otherworld is the central part of the narrative. One might think of the key generic distinction between the two as follows: without the journey there is no *immram* narrative; without the destination, there is no *echtra*.[105]

The term 'otherworld' is thus key to the present discussion.[106] I follow the use of the term conventional in discussions of medieval Irish material.[107] This use has been usefully and cogently described by Matthias Egeler, together with the term 'otherworldly', 'as metalinguistic scholarly generic terms which designate a world with marked supernatural and frequently (but not necessarily) paradisiacal attributes which is distinct, but not entirely separate, from the normal human world'; allowing crucially for a co-existence of a plurality of such otherworlds.[108] This approximates most closely the terminological range utopia-eutopia-dystopia and will provide a base for the discussion of utopian qualities of the imaginary lands

105 As mentioned above, a degree of overlap between the two categories of text already in the early period has been generally acknowledged in current scholarship. In both of the two genres, grouped under the common label of voyage literature, Carey observes that there is a similarity in the depiction of the location of the otherworld with 'an "overseas" rather than an "immanent" view, and a concomitant tendency to give an ecclesiastical colouring to the narrative' ('Voyage Literature', p. 1743).

106 There is some variation in the practice of capitalization of this term in secondary scholarship; in the present discussion I do not capitalise 'otherworld', unless quoting from a scholar who does so.

107 It is worth noting that, as Carey has shown, the notion of the 'overseas otherworld' is not as common a topos as it is often assumed to be in medieval Irish narratives, and does not appear to be a stable feature of the native tradition; Carey, 'The Location', pp. 116, 119. Rather, to quote Carey, 'Otherworld beings are depicted as living within hills, beneath lakes or the sea, or on islands in lakes or off the coast; there are also tales of halls chanced upon in the night, which vanish with the coming of day' (pp. 116–17).

108 Egeler, *Islands*, p. 2 n. 1. See also John Carey, 'Otherworlds and Verbal Worlds in Middle Irish Narrative', *Proceedings of the Harvard Celtic Colloquium*, 9 (1989), 31–42 (p. 31).

visited by the characters in the narratives under consideration, particularly in the extended discussion of utopias in Chapter 4.[109] The notion of the otherworld across the sea translates easily also into the otherworld across the interplanetary space in the three-dimensional (and multi-dimensional) travel mode of two of the modern narratives discussed in this book. The concept of the 'otherworlds' is thus also useful for thinking about the function of planets (conceived of as planetary otherworlds in Chapters 5 and 6) in modern works of space-faring science-fiction. The concept of the physical existence of geographically-positioned 'other worlds'/otherworlds in pre-modern thought created an intersection between worlds of literary imagination and worlds of cartographic imagination which is continued in planetary fantasies of the space-faring age.[110]

In each of these works the otherworld is either better, worse, or different. Thus, utopia and its contingent concepts are important also in discussion of the narratives examined in this book, both in utopia's pure form as the representation of an actualised idealised world, and in its implied existence when the worlds depicted to not quite match up to this – presumed – ideal.[111] Within the narrative worlds of the *immram* and *echtra* texts here examined, utopias can be both real and fictional. Eco's inveterate liar Baudolino, for example, according to Sabine Mercer, 'creates a utopia by his use of the power of hope and then sustains it by possibility for as long as possibility is contingent'.[112] Similarly, utopias and dystopias provide ways to comment on the reader's/audience's world for Swift, but also for the authors of *Stargate* and *Star Trek*. In line with the centrality of Swift's text to the present book (explained in the section 1.4 on structure below), the concept of utopia is treated in the 'Gulliver'-dedicated Chapter 4.[113] This concept of

---

109 See below, pp. 126–28.

110 See, for instance, discussion in W. G. L. Rundles, 'Le Nouveau Monde, l'autre monde et la pluralité des mondes' in *Actas do Congresso Internacional de História dos Descobrimentos*, IV (Lisbon: Oficinas Gráficas da Papelaria Fernandes, 1961), pp. 347–82; reprinted as Chapter XV in *Geography, Cartography and Nautical Science in the Renaissance* (Aldershot and Burlington: Ashgate Variorum, 2000), pp. 1–39.

111 Utopia is also a major theme in discussions of (the history of) science fiction; Amis, *New Maps*, p. 31.

112 Sabine Mercer, 'Truth and Lies in Umberto Eco's *Baudolino*', *Philosophy and Literature*, 35 (2011), 16–31 (p. 18). Note that to Mercer, 'Baudolino is not a liar, rather a borrower from the past who continues the tradition of medieval writers' (p. 25). See also discussion in Chapter 3 of this book.

113 See pp. 42–46 for the structure of the book and pp. 126–28 for the discussion of utopia in Chapter 4.

utopia (and related varieties of conceptualized and judged otherworlds), relates to the tropological (=moral) message of the narrative, specifically in relation to its treatment of the otherworld(s)/island(s) visited.

1.2 The Tropological Mode

A crucial distinction between *immrama* and *echtrai* that is intricately tied to the notion of utopia lies not only in the heavy focus of the former on the process of the journey itself (that journey being specifically a sea-voyage), but also in the heavy dose of moral/religious meaning, which I designate as the 'tropological aspect' in the discussion below.[114] Notable in this regard is the fact that elements of the *immrama* also occur in saints' lives, thus allowing for overlap between these genres.[115] Indeed, it has been suggested that the *Navigatio* had served as a prototype for the *immrama*, and that the term *immram* itself applied to this type of text may be a translation of the Latin term *navigatio*.[116]

The order of the interdependence of the Latin and the Irish vernacular texts has recently been questioned by Sobecki, who suggests that though they do belong to the same genre, the Latin may not be the source of the Irish but rather vice versa, or at least that they might have had a common ancestor.[117] It is possible that the positioning of the *Navigatio* as the source of *immrama* is conditioned by its dominant manuscript tradition and the

114 Wooding, 'Introduction', p. xi.

115 Wooding, 'Introduction', p. xiii. For more on genre overlap, see below, pp. 30, 36–37.

116 Wooding, 'Introduction', p. xiv, points out that voyage tales in saints' lives pre-date the vernacular *immrama*. See also Moylan, 'Irish Voyages', pp. 303, 304. He also suggests that the possibility that both had been influenced by Virgil's *Aeneid* may need to be revisited; we will return to this issue below in the context of the issue of Lucian's influence on Swift's *Gulliver's Travels*; Wooding, 'Introduction', p. xvi, see also below, p. 60. Wooding suggests the *Navigatio* is ninth-century in date; Wooding, 'The Date'. For further comments on knowledge of the *Aeneid* in medieval Ireland, with further references, see Ralph O'Connor, 'Irish Narrative Literature and the Classical Tradition, 900–1300', in *Classical Literature and Learning in Medieval Irish Narrative*, ed. by O'Connor (Cambridge: D. S. Brewer, 2014), pp. 1–22 (pp. 2, 4, 5, 14, 18, 19) and Erich Poppe, '*Imtheachta Aeniasa* and its Place in Medieval Irish Textual History', in *Classical Literature and Learning in Medieval Irish Narrative*, ed. by Ralph O'Connor (Cambridge: D. S. Brewer, 2014), pp. 25–39.

117 Sobecki, 'From the *désert liquide* to the Sea of Romance', pp. 196, 197–98.

presence of a multitude of vernacular translations.[118] The pattern of assuming that the numerically dominant tradition, particularly when it gives rise to a large number of vernacular translations and adaptations, is the source of *all* its vernacular equivalents is also seen elsewhere in medieval studies.[119] Regardless of whether the tropological aspect found in the *immrama* (and some *echtrai*) derives from saints' lives, or whether it was the reason why such journeys were incorporated into the *vitae sancti* in the long run, the importance of this feature to the Irish voyage narrative tradition is clear. It is also a feature shared by the various texts in this book.

To some extent, each of the texts here discussed addresses questions of 'human potential', which, as Johnson-Smith observes, 'is a continual fascination for us'.[120] Johnson-Smith refers to 'superpowers', as explored in super hero comics and films, but the observation is valid also for the more internal (ethical, spiritual or mental) self-improvement, which to a large degree is the concern of most, if not all of the texts under discussion.[121] The relevance of this feature is most marked in the case of Lewis's *The Voyage of the Dawn Treader*. In this narrative, the self-improvement is a spiritual journey in parallel to the physical journey, and is represented by the challenges and moral transformation of the children who visit Narnia.[122] In *Stargate*, the superpowers – in the more usual sense of the word – are associated with the process of 'ascension', the attainment of a higher, non-corporeal, state of existence, which also requires moral growth.[123] The tropological aspect is famously a feature of the original *Star Trek*, of which 'each story is a morality tale'.[124] Indeed, as Johnson-Smith further observes in the context of a brief

118 As Sobecki points out, the Latin *Navigatio* 'boasts over one hundred and twenty extant manuscripts and is translated into all major vernaculars' (of medieval Western Europe); Sobecki, 'From the *désert liquide* to the Sea of Romance', p. 196.

119 The same fallacy has governed the dominant scholarly view of the medieval Welsh narrative *Historia Peredur vab Efrawc* in relation to the numerically dominant grail narrative tradition arising from the romance of Chrétien de Troyes; Natalia I. Petrovskaia, *This is Not a Grail Romance. Understanding Historia Peredur vab Efrawc* (Cardiff: University of Wales Press, 2023), pp. 1–2.

120 Johnson-Smith, *American Science Fiction TV*, p. 8.

121 Johnson-Smith, *American Science Fiction TV*, p. 28.

122 Eustace and Lucy in particular, since Edmund had already had his moral transformation in a previous book of the Narnia series; see discussion below, pp. 64–70.

123 See discussion below, pp. 160–61, 167.

124 Johnson-Smith, *American Science Fiction TV*, p. 58. The tropological aspect of science fiction is not necessarily religious, although in some works of science fiction, as in those of C. S. Lewis, for instance, the two come together; see discussion in Amis, *New Maps*, pp. 82–83. For the utopian element in *Star Trek*, see for instance, Booker, 'The

discussion of the *Star Trek: Voyager* two-part episode 'Equinox' (Season 5 Episode 26; Season 6 Episode 1) which poses a conflict between an unethical solution to the stranded ship's situation, and an ethical path that would require sacrificing a chance to return home quickly: 'The values implicit in much science fiction are those of our own culture, sometimes idealised, sometimes extrapolated, but firmly recognisable: honour, duty, loyalty, all those things which create integrity are illuminated as the aspects of humanity most valued even in future societies'.[125] The self-improvement is part of a general positive view of humanity's progress as a species in the franchise and is thus a large part of the background canvas for most of the *Star Trek* series, and it can be characterised using Amis's term 'admonitory utopia', which he characterised – in the mid-twentieth century – as 'virtually the leading form of contemporary science fiction'.[126] The presence of the tropological element in some form both in the *immram*-type texts (more strongly) and in *echtra*-type text (less so), provides another instance of slight overlap between the two genres. Such overlap is best articulated in terms of fuzzy sets, a topic to which we will return in the following section of the introduction.

All texts examined here concern extraordinary voyages. They belong to a wider tradition, of which usually only the 'epic' examples are examined.[127]

Politics', p. 195; see also Sebastian Stoppe, *Is* Star Trek *Utopia? Investigating a Perfect Future* (Jefferson: McFarland, 2022), originally published in German as Sebastian Stoppe, *Unterwegs zu neuen Welten: Star Trek als politische Utopie* (Darmstadt: Büchner-Verlag, 2014). See also Bruce Isaacs, 'A Vision of Time and Place: Spiritual Humanism and the Utopian Impulse', in *Star Trek and Myth. Essays on Symbol and Archetype at the Final Frontier*, ed. by Mathew Wilhelm Kapell (Jefferson: McFarland, 2010), pp. 182–96. For further discussion, see below, pp. 134–35, 143–45.

125 Johnson-Smith, *American Science Fiction TV*, p. 28.

126 Amis, *New Maps*, p. 48. In the twenty-first century one might argue that this has been supplanted by the unremitting dread of the 'admonitory dystopia'. For the utopianism of *Star Trek*, see for instance, Jeff Massey, '"On Second Thought, Let's Not Go To Camelot ... 'Tis a Silly Space": Star Trek and the Inconsequence of SF Medievalism', in *Medieval Science Fiction*, ed. by Carl Kears and James Paz (London: King's College London Centre for Late Antique & Medieval Studies, 2016), pp. 95–114 (p. 97). See also further references in the discussion in Chapter 5 below.

127 For instance, Johnson-Smith writes: 'The heroic or epic narrative generally follows the pattern of a quest and the emphasis lies upon encounter and illumination. Often an incredible journey or voyage is part of the tale (Gilgamesh, Odysseus), emphasising not only the experiences of the journey (Jason and the Argonauts, Sinbad), but the splendour and awe of remote, unknown places (Hercules, Aeneas)', *American Science Fiction TV*, p. 35; brackets Johnson-Smith's.

Yet the tropological aspect of the religion-infused narratives (*immrama* and Lewis's *Voyage* in particular) widens the field. In essence, as we have seen, these extraordinary voyages can be described as voyages to other worlds, or indeed otherworlds. To these applies with equal force Aisling Byrne's remark on the function of medieval otherworld journey accounts: 'Although they are among the most fantastical of medieval literary fictions, otherworld accounts could be enlisted by their authors and audiences to a variety of entirely serious ends'.[128] In the various texts discussed in this book, such a tropological message can be of the religious, social, ethical and political varieties. The nature of such shared features can be analysed as a fuzzy zone of overlap between the genres to which they belong, when these are conceived of as fuzzy sets. It is to the discussion of this concept that the following section of the introduction is devoted.

1.3 The Intertextual Matrix

In the theoretical notion of 'intertextual matrix' employed in this book I combine the conventional concepts of intertextuality with the conceptual model of fuzzy sets, derived from the work of Lotfi A. Zadeh.[129] A 'collection of items' constitutes the basic definition of a set.[130] Traditional sets are ones where there are no degrees of membership: an item either is in a set or it is not. A traditional set as an analytical tool has its limitations, particularly for fields such as history and literature, where it is difficult to reduce statements to absolutes. It is for this type of field that the type of set known as 'fuzzy' is particularly useful.[131] A fuzzy set is a set that allows for gradation of

128 Byrne, *Otherworlds*, p. 141.

129 The foundational text on fuzzy set theory is Zadeh, 'Fuzzy Sets', *Information and Control*, 8 (1965), 338–53.

130 An accessible definition is provided by Sir Roger Penrose: 'A *set* just means a collection of things—physical objects or mathematical concepts—that can be treated as a whole' in his inspirational *The Emperor's New Mind. Concerning Computers, Minds and The Laws of Physics*, Oxford Landmark Science, revised impression (Oxford: Oxford University Press, 2016 [1989]), p. 130 n.; see also the definition in Paul R. Halmos, *Naïve Set Theory* (Princeton: Princeton University Press, 1960), p. 1; and Eric Schechter, *Classical and Nonclassical Logics. An Introduction to the Mathematics of Propositions* (Princeton: Princeton University Press, 2005), §3.1b-3.5, pp. 66–70.

131 For the distinction between classical sets (with binary member/non-member division) and fuzzy sets, see, for example, Witold Pedrycz and Fernando Gomide, *An Introduction to Fuzzy Sets: Analysis and Design* (Cambridge, MA: MIT Press, 1998), pp. 3–8.

membership.[132] In practice this means that an item can be a member of a set to a certain degree. One item can be a member of a fuzzy set to a greater degree than another item, allowing for nuance and differentiation. Genre is a particularly illustrative case of a fuzzy set, and genre is precisely the concept for which fuzzy sets will be applied in this book.

The idea to use fuzzy sets for genres was proposed by Brian Attebery in 1992.[133] Objections to it were raised by Rieder, who argued that this was too cumbersome as it would require painstaking translation of literary qualities into mathematical terms to map these onto a coordinate system.[134] However, it is possible to use the concept of fuzzy sets as a shorthand way of visualizing the unclear and sometimes overlapping boundaries of genres, without reducing text to number, and without assigning numerical quantities to stylistic qualities.[135] Since fuzzy sets allow for marginal and overlapping membership, such conceptualization allows for texts belonging to multiple 'sets' and displaying characteristics belonging to multiple 'genres' to a lesser or greater degree. The medieval Irish narrative *Immram Brain*, for example, despite its title, is usually considered to belong rather to the *echtra* genre.[136] The problem lies in the text's seeming mis-match with its medieval taxonomic label *immram*.[137] The surviving tale appears to be incomplete and a conflation of several narratives, and Dumville's conclusion of his analysis is that 'affinities of the story, both as it stands at present and in the hypothetical unconflated form proposed by Nutt, are wholly with the *echtrae*-genre'.[138] The revision and conflation which led, in Dumville's reading,

132 Zadeh, 'Fuzzy Sets', p. 339.

133 Rieder, *Science Fiction*, p. 19, discusses and dismisses the approach, referring to Attebery, *Strategies of Fantasy*, pp. 12–13.

134 Rieder, *Science Fiction*, p. 19 (in context of a discussion of fuzzy sets in application to genre on pp. 18–19). Note that Rieder provides no references to mathematical literature.

135 See also the discussion of this type of use of fuzzy sets in Gillian Adams, 'A Fuzzy Genre: Two Views of Fantasy', *Children's Literature*, 28 (2000), pp. 202–14; R. B. Gill, 'The Uses of Genre and the Classification of Speculative Fiction', *Mosaic: An Interdisciplinary Critical Journal*, 46 (2013), 71–85.

136 Carey, 'The Location', p. 113; Proinsias Mac Cana, '*Mongán Mac Fiachna* and *Immram Brain*', *Ériu*, 23 (1972), 102–42 (p. 117, 121). See also discussion in Egeler, *Islands*, pp. 27–41.

137 Dumville, '*Echtrae and Immram*', p. 83. See also Duignan, *The Echtrae*, pp. 32–34.

138 Dumville, '*Echtrae and Immram*', p. 86, with reference to Kuno Meyer ed. and trans., *The Voyage of Bran Son of Febal*, vol. 1, p. 137, which is quoted and discussed earlier in Dumville's article (p. 85).

to the assignation of the label *immram* to the tale, was the result of tenth-century growth of the *immram* tradition.[139]

Dumville's outline of the relative chronology of the *immram* tradition, specifically relation to the *echtra*, is relevant to the following discussion and thus worth quoting in full:

> The elements of this story-type were developing by the end of the seventh century. Their inspiration was essentially the wanderings involved in the 'clerical sea pilgrimages', but it may be that the possible borrowings by the *immrama* from the *echtrae*-tradition presuppose the existence of the *echtrai* and their influence on the growth of the new genre.[140]

This represents a diachronic view, with reference in particular to the influences of the earlier genre on the later one as the latter came to prominence. The influences, articulated as 'borrowings' can be seen to represent a transfer of characteristics from one clearly defined group (or genre) to another. Before proposing another way of representing this situation, I must emphasise that my proposed alternative is in no way intended as disagreement with Dumville's reading, or even as an adjustment to it. It is explicitly intended as an alternative representation or projection, much in the same way that an aerial photograph, a topographic map, a planning map, and a schematic representation of a street network might all represent the same city but look different and convey different types of information. An apt illustration of the point I am making here is provided by the various maps produced by the Municipality of Amsterdam (Figure 1.1).[141]

The two maps in Figure 1.1 represent the same area of the city of Amsterdam, the Museumplein, in green on the top map, surrounded by (in pink, counter-clockwise) the Rijksmuseum in the north-east, the Van Gogh Museum and the Stedelijk Museum of modern art on the West, and the

139 See also above, p. 25, and below, p. 36.

140 Dumville, '*Echtrae and Immram*', p. 89.

141 The maps are screenshots taken from the *Interactieve Kaarten* (interactive maps) website of the *Gemeente Amsterdam* <maps.amsterdam.nl>, (City of Amsterdam, 2023) [accessed 7 December 2024]. The two maps used in Figure 1.1 can be accessed via the following links: 'Bestemmingsplannen' <https://maps.amsterdam.nl/bestemmingsplannen?C=52.358099,4.883347&Z=16.75&T=1&L1=4> [accessed 7 December 2024] and 'Wat zegt een straatnaam?' (What's in a Streetname?) <https://maps.amsterdam.nl/straatnamen/?LANG=en> [accessed 7 December 2024].

FIGURE 1.1 Maps of the Museumplein area. 'Bestemmingsplannen' (above) and 'Wat zegt een straatnaam?' (below)
SOURCE: <MAPS.AMSTERDAM.NL> *INTERACTIEVE KAARTEN* GEMEENTE AMSTERDAM

Concertgebouw on the south-west. The buildings are not visible on the street chart on the bottom map, but are nevertheless still there. Similarly, my proposed synchronic schematisation of the situation outlined in relation to *immrama* and *echtrai* by Dumville, is merely an alternative representation, aimed to bring into visibility some features which are not the focus of a diachronic reading.

Immram Brain in Dumville's diachronic reading is an *echtra* narrative that was altered and re-labelled due to the tenth-century rise of the *immram* genre. The *immrama* themselves potentially show influence of the *echtra* narratives, if those indeed represent an earlier literary stratum.[142] In terms of a synchronic snapshot of the surviving material this yields two fuzzy sets with a significant area of intersection (for texts which might 'belong' to one or the other genre by virtue of their label, like *Immram Brain*, while in practice exhibiting major features that are characteristic of the other). For the notion of 'intersection' I follow Zadeh's own definition: 'the intersection of *A* and *B* is the *largest* fuzzy set which is contained in both *A* and *B*', where A and B are fuzzy sets themselves.[143] In our case, let A be *immram*- and *B* be *echtra*-type narratives. The diagram below represents the two fuzzy sets and their intersection (Figure 1.2).[144]

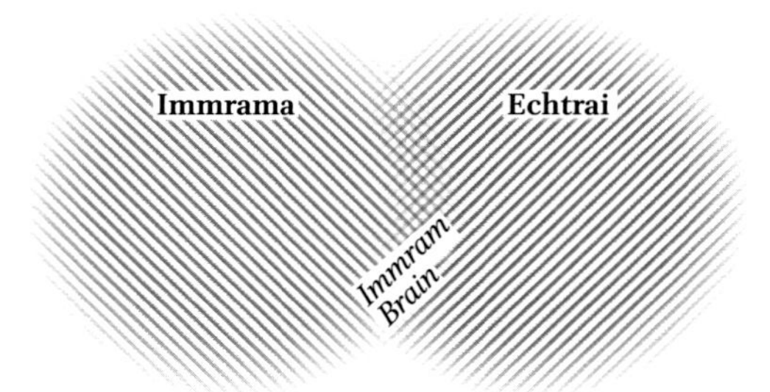

FIGURE 1.2 The *immram* and *echtra* genres as overlapping fuzzy sets, with *Immram Brain* on the intersection

142 See above, pp. 24–27.

143 Zadeh, 'Fuzzy Sets', p. 339, 341, for intersections. The italics are Zadeh's.

144 The diagram is mine. The overlapping visual representation is inspired by the idea of representing fuzzy sets as opacity-varying Venn diagrams in Lifeng Zhu, Weiwei Xia, Jia Liu, and Aiguo Song, 'Visualizing Fuzzy Sets Using Opacity-Varying Freeform Diagrams', *Information Visualization*, 17 (2017), 146–60.

As Figure 1.2 shows, *Immram Brain* belongs to some degree to both sets. The figure is not mathematically generated, and is approximate. While it is almost certainly possible to assign numerical values to the different aspects and characteristics of the tale as they relate to the *echtra/immram* genre division and thus provide a set of precise coordinates for the text within this system, I do not believe sufficient mileage is to be gained for the purposes of the present argument from the resulting increased precision to justify the time expenditure. The approximation suffices to be able to say that taking the genres as fuzzy sets allows us to formally describe *Immram Brain* as it stands in its current form as 'a bit of both'. This is no comment on what it was to start with, nor on its development and textual history, but merely on the resulting combination of features. The notion of these 'genres' as intersecting fuzzy sets is also close to Hans Pieter Atze Oskamp's evaluation of the relative difficulty in establishing a distinction between the two, though he did not express it in mathematical terms.[145] This is an important distinction because it will allow us to place Swift's *Gulliver's Travels* in a similar position on the intersection of the fuzzy sets represented by the *immram* and *echtra* genres, and thus justifies that text's centrality in the structure of this book.

My insistence on the synchronicity of the approach proposed here is dictated by the need to underline that while this book argues for reading works examined here in light of the medieval Irish genres, it is not my purpose to imply that they were necessarily conceived in those terms. I would like to suggest, however, that it is useful to class, for the sake of discussion, *Gulliver's Travels*, *The Voyage of the Dawn Treader* and *Star Trek* (particularly *The Original Series* but also *The Next Generation*) as *immrama*. Whilst this might seem at first glance controversial and experimental, it is in fact no more and no less than a suggestion to experiment with a genre classification no more arbitrary – and certainly older – than that currently employed by Western literary criticism. If we can classify Murasaki Shikibu's *Tale of Genji* as the world's first 'novel' for the sake of analysis, why can we not equally usefully (and less problematically, as will be shown in Chapter 5) class *Star Trek: The Original Series*, *Star Trek: The Next Generation*, *Star Trek: Voyager*, and *Enterprise* as *immrama*?[146]

---

145 Oskamp, ed., *The Voyage of Máel Dúin*, p. 43; quoted and discussed in Duignan, *The Echtrae*, p. 6.

146 For the *Tale of Genji* as 'novel', see, for instance, Murasaki Shikibu, *The Tale of Genji*. Abridged, trans. by Royall Tyler (London: Penguin, 2006), p. ix.

As our discussion progresses, it will be seen that some patterns of development and influence begin to emerge, and the members of the corpus are not as unrelated as they might at first glance appear. Connections, even direct ones, become visible and become thematically reinforced and explicable within the new proposed framework. To give but one example, while *Gulliver's Travels* and *Star Trek* are not usually discussed together, and while the former is never mentioned as a major source of inspiration for the latter, Gene Roddenberry's original television series carried, for a brief moment, the title of Swift's work.[147]

Thus, as a conceptual tool, fuzzy sets are particularly suited to the study of genre as modern genres themselves have been shown to be fluid and ambiguous, and crucially, not a single uniform system. The overlap between the different genres allows us to take these as a complex system and investigate precisely these fuzzy areas of overlap and the emerging connections.

One such fundamental connection between various fantastic voyage narratives in the fuzzy genre system of fantasy-science-fiction-*immram-echtra* and contingent categories – both those discussed in this book and those beyond its narrow focus – is what one might describe as the persistent fascination of the remote, and the resulting activation of the human faculty of fantasy. Consider, for instance, the lyrical and almost impressionist description of the narrator, Marlowe's, impression of the Far East in Joseph Conrad's semi-autobiographical *Youth*:

> And this is how I see the East. I have seen its secret places and have looked into its very soul; but now I see it always from a small boat, a high outline of mountains, blue and afar in the morning; like faint mist at noon; a jagged wall of purple at sunset. I have the feel of the oar in my hand, the vision of a scorching blue sea in my eyes.[148]

Many of the images invoked in this quotation lie at the very heart of this project: 'secret places', 'small boat'; 'faint mist'; 'the feel of the oar'; 'a scorching blue sea'.[149] '[T]he vision of a scorching blue sea' is almost a

147 According to the brochure for the 2002 *Star Trek* Adventure event held in London's Hyde Park, it was 'renamed *Gulliver's Travels* for a few unfortunate days', Lane and Bowles, *Star Trek. The Adventure*, p. 18.

148 Joseph Conrad, 'Youth', in Joseph Conrad, *Youth. Heart of Darkness. The End of the Tether*, ed. by Owen Knowles (Cambridge: Cambridge University Press, 2010), p. 35.

149 For discussions of Conrad's engagement with the East, see, for example, Norman Sherry, *Conrad's Eastern World* (Cambridge: Cambridge University Press, 1966), and

premonition of the mystical journey outlined by Lewis (discussed in Chapter 2 of this book). The mysterious and almost mystical imagery opens up vistas of fantastic possibilities, reminiscent of those explored earlier by writers such as the twelfth-century encyclopaedist Honorius Augustodunensis, and travellers, both real such as Marco Polo and the armchair variety represented by John Mandeville.[150] The same quality is also found later, in a conscious echo of Mandeville by Umberto Eco in *Baudolino* (discussed in Chapter 3). The small boat reminds one of Gulliver's escape from Lilliput, and perhaps also contains echoes of Robinson Crusoe and all lonely seamen (Chapter 4). The sense of adventure and of new vistas and lands to explore – in space, since our own world is a little too familiar by that point – is echoed in the excitement of 'seeking out new worlds' in *Star Trek* (Chapter 5) and *Stargate* (Chapter 6). Conrad's landscape is real (insofar as memory is real). That of Gulliver is not real, but coloured by memories of (others') real-life travel, particularly in descriptions of sea voyages. That of Marco Polo is real, coloured by the fantastic reinterpretations of reality in Honorius's *Imago mundi* and similar texts.[151] That of Umberto Eco's *Baudolino* takes these and creates something that, as shall be seen in the discussion below, is both real and not, and forces

most recently essays *Joseph Conrad and the Orient*, ed. by in Amar Acheraïou and Nursel Içöz (Lublin: Maria Curie-Skłodowska University Press, 2012). For the role of mist, and fog, in the introduction of a passage to the otherworld in medieval Irish narratives, and in text that follow in their tradition, see below, p. 66.

150 The bibliography on these texts is extensive. For the texts, see, for instance, Marco Polo, *The Travels*, trans. by Ronald Latham (Harmondsworth: Penguin, 1958); M. C. Seymour, ed., *Mandeville's Travels* (Oxford: Clarendon Press, 1967); C.W.R.D. Moseley, trans., *The Travels of Sir John Mandeville* (Harmondsworth: Penguin, 1983). For a discussion of these two authors in the context of the traditions of marvels of the east, see, for instance, Suzanne M. Yeager, 'Marco Polo's *Le Devisement dou monde, The Book of Sir John Mandeville*, and Their Medieval Audiences', in *Marco Polo and the Encounter of East and West*, ed. by Suzanne Conklin Akbari and Amilcare Iannucci, with the assistance of John Tulk (Toronto, Buffalo and London: University of Toronto Press, 2008), pp. 156–81. For more on Honorius and his *Imago mundi*, see Valerie I. J. Flint, 'Honorius Augustodunensis', *Authors of the Middle Ages*, II, *Historical and Religious Writers of the Latin West*, 5–6, ed. by Patrick J. Geary (Aldershot, Hants: Variorum Reprints, 1995), pp. 89–183 and Natalia I. Petrovskaia, *Transforming Europe in the* Images of the World, *1110–1500. Fuzzy Geographies* (Amsterdam: Amsterdam University Press, 2025). See also discussion and further references in Chapter 3 below in the context of the analysis of the exotic in Eco's *Baudolino*.

151 For an edition of the *Imago mundi*, see Honorius Augustodunensis, *Imago mundi*, ed. by Valerie I. J. Flint, Archives d'histoire doctrinale et littéraire du Moyen Âge, 49 (1982).

the readers to question their own realities. Those of *Star Trek* and *Stargate* are probably not real in any meaningful way, but reflect an interpretation of what could be real if our technology permitted us to test our theoretical scientific hypotheses about what the universe is like out there, to 'look into its very soul'. In this respect all of these texts are fantastic in the broader, non-genre-specific sense of the term.

As Yi-Fu Tuan observes, 'fantasy merits serious study because it plays a key role in the enlivenment and transformation of culture'.[152] Tuan is referring not to the literary genre but to 'fantasy' as characteristic of human thought opposed to 'realism'.[153] In this discussion also I use the term 'fantasy' not in its modern, narrow, genre-specific sense, but rather following Tzvetan Todorov's haunting definition: *Le fantastique, c'est l'hésitation éprouvée par un être qui ne connaît que les lois naturelles, face à un événement en apparence surnaturel* ('The fantastic is the hesitation felt by a being who knows only natural laws, when faced with an apparently supernatural event').[154] This moment of disconcerted hesitation is manifest whenever, within the second of our courses on Medieval Welsh at Utrecht University, we read with the students the geographical treatise *Delw y Byd*, a thirteenth-century translation of the enormously popular twelfth-century encyclopedia *Imago mundi*.[155] In this text, there is a passage that does not fail to enthuse the students every year. The passage concerns

152 Yi-Fu Tuan, 'Realism and Fantasy in Art, History, and Geography', *Annals of the Association of American Geographers*, 80 (1990), 435–46 (p. 435). The term 'fantasy' is here used in a broad sense. The point is particularly poignant in relation to phenomena such as *Star Trek*, which has made a 'measurable cultural impact' not least in inspiring technological advances; Massey, 'On Second Thought', p. 97.

153 'Fantasy' as genre label is not used in this book. Although conventionally used as an organizational category label in bookstores and video streaming services, it is fluid and often imprecise; see above, p. 16. For a recent discussion of the issue, see Elena Gomel and Danielle Gurevitch, 'Introduction', in *The Palgrave Handbook of Global Fantasy*, ed. by Elena Gomel and Danielle Gurevitch (Cham: Springer and Palgrave Macmillan, 2023), pp. xv–xx (pp. xv–xvi); Gomel and Gurevitch, 'What is Fantasy and Who Decides?', in *The Palgrave Handbook of Global Fantasy*, ed. by Elena Gomel and Danielle Gurevitch (Cham: Springer / Palgrave Macmillan, 2023), pp. 3–13.

154 Tzvetan Todorov, *Introduction à la littérature fantastique* (Paris: Seuil, 1970), p. 29; my translation.

155 For editions of the Welsh text, see Henry Lewis, and P. Diverres, ed., *Delw y Byd (Imago Mundi)* (Cardiff: Cardiff University Press, 1928) and Natalia I. Petrovskaia, ed., *Delw y Byd. A Medieval Welsh Encyclopedia* (Cambridge: MHRA, 2020). For the Latin version, see reference in n. 151 above.

the marvellous beings who inhabit India according to this text, and it runs as follows:

> Yno y mae ryϬ bopyl, a rann yndunt o dynyon, a rann arall o anniueileit. Ac Ϭyth troet udunt. Ac eu gϬadneu yn uchaf. […] Yno y maent ryϬ bobyl vnllygeityaϬc, ac a elwir 'Arismapi', a 'Siclopes'. Ereill yssyd yno a seith troet udunt, ac o vntroet, buanach ynt, no'r awel wynt, a thra orffϬyssont ar y dayar, y dyrchauant yn wascaϬt udunt, gϬadyn vn oc eu traet. Ereill yssyd yno heb penn udunt a elwir 'Lemennii'. Ac eu llygeit yn eu dϬyvron. Ac yn lle trϬyn a geneu udunt, deu dϬll yn eu dϬyvron.[156]
>
> (There is a certain type of people, one part to them of men and another part of animals. And they have eight feet. And their foot soles above. […] There is another type of one-eyed people there, who are called 'Arismapi' and 'Cyclopes'. There are others there with seven feet to them, and of one leg, who are faster than the breath of the wind, and when they rest on the ground, they raise for shade above them the sole of one foot. There are others there without heads to them called 'Lemennii', and their eyes in their chests. And instead of nose and lips to them, two holes in their chests.)[157]

This, as the rest of the Welsh text, represents a thirteenth-century translation of an encyclopedic text written in Latin in the twelfth century by Honorius Augustodunensis, the *Imago mundi*. The *Imago mundi* enjoyed immense popularity in medieval Europe.[158] In particular, the section quoted above on the marvellous creatures inhabiting India seems to have exercised a particular fascination on medieval translators. This passage relates to a broader tradition concerning marvels of the east in medieval European literature.[159] This wider tradition exerted, and continues to exert, a tremendous influence on the creative imagination, not only inside the classroom, but via novels and via other visual media, on big international audiences. I quote it in extenso because an echo of it, via another

156 Petrovskaia, ed., *Delw y Byd*, p. 51.

157 My translation.

158 Petrovskaia, *Transforming Europe*.

159 For more on the medieval wonders of the East see, for example A. J. Ford, *Marvel and Artefact. The 'Wonders of the East' in its Manuscript Contexts* (Leiden: Brill, 2016), pp. 6–15; see also further discussion and references in Chapter 3 below, pp. 90–91.

branch of the same tradition, is recognizably present, as we will see in Chapter 3 below, also in Umberto Eco's *Baudolino*.[160] The one-footed people feature, of course, also in Lewis's *The Voyage of the Dawn Treader*, discussed in Chapter 2.[161]

The discussion of the travel narratives analysed in this book as a whole is constructed on the basis of a basic axiom articulated by Umberto Eco: 'books talk to each other'.[162] On this basis I propose the method used in this book: the use of an intertextual matrix, employed in combination with the application of medieval Irish taxonomies, or 'native categories of narratives' as an alternative to a modern genre system, to a selection of thematically interconnected texts.[163]

1.4 Structure and Route

The intertextual connections between the texts examined in this book allow for a number of possible configurations of the discussion: chronological, thematic, geographical, linguistic. There is no ambition in this book to follow a Hamiltonian circuit through my chosen intertextual network (a Hamiltonian circuit is a route that visits every vertex in a network only once).[164] Rather, there are multiple connections between the texts discussed, not all of which can be addressed within a single monograph. Some of those which seem more important for my argument I will revisit multiple times in different chapters.

An important second aspect of the book's structure is related to the use of space. While *Modern Afterlives of Old Irish Travel Narratives* engages with travel and thus with movement through space, I have not up to this point engaged with the theoretical notions of spatiality. Space, however, is key to both *immrama* and *echtrai*. As John Carey points out, Old Irish literature often presents cases of 'the transgression of our habitual ideas of human space'.[165] Such transgressions, whether in terms of flying ships (the subject of Carey's discussion), travel to the otherworld via a number of different means, or an altered sense of sea-space in voyage narratives, provide

---

160 See in particular pp. 91, 100–1.

161 See p. 63.

162 Eco, 'Borges', p. 122.

163 Koch, '*Immrama*', p. 959.

164 See Ernesto Estrada and Philip Knight, *A First Course in Network Theory* (Oxford: Oxford University Press, 2015), p. 7 for the definition.

165 John Carey, 'Aerial Ships and Underwater Monasteries: The Evolution of a Monastic Marvel', *Proceedings of the Harvard Celtic Colloquium*, 12 (1992), 16–28.

ample material for later re-enactments of spatial questioning. In her study of the spatial dimension of the Old Irish literary tradition Amy C. Mulligan observes that 'the medieval Irish did not only innovate significantly in developing geospatial literature. In simultaneously theorizing the process and its implications, medieval Irish thinkers also enacted a medieval "spatial turn", a focused and sustained literary consideration of what it means to be in a powerfully transformative landscape'.[166] I build here on Mulligan's argument that 'Irish placelore' and literature including the *Navigatio*, 'profoundly influenced other literature of the North Atlantic region' but that the Irish 'medieval spatial turn' postulated by Mulligan reverberates still in later travel narratives, which I bring together in this book.[167]

Issues of spatiality are relevant specifically to the structural organisation of the book. This is conceived as itself a progressive movement through different phases of spatial conceptualization. These are represented in Table 1.1 (the diagrams in the table are mine).

The narrative in this book thus moves through spaces of increasing dimensional complexity in each chapter. Chapter 2 deals with the imaginary flat Narnian world of C. S. Lewis. Chapter 3 with the 'real' medieval worldview of Baudolino. Eco's novel raises questions about the flatness or rotundity of the world, which the characters debate (but for their journey it is largely irrelevant).[168] In Chapter 4 Gulliver's world is that of globes and round-the-world travel. The analysis in Chapter 5 focuses on a selection of texts from the extended *Star Trek* franchise, taking the discussion into outer space. Chapter 6, while continuing to explore outer space, sometimes takes a shortcut via unknown dimensions with a wormhole or two in the *Stargate* narratives. *Star Trek* and *Stargate* also share both three-dimensional travel by spaceship and wormhole travel, but the balance in *Star Trek* leans heavily towards the former and in *Stargate* towards the latter.[169] In each instance, the imaginary lands are mapped onto spatial coordinates of the same world (the real world) occupied by the reader, but just out of reach.

---

166 Amy C. Mulligan, *A Landscape of Words: Ireland, Britain and the Poetics of Space, 700–1250* (Manchester: Manchester University Press, 2019), p. 5.

167 Mulligan, *A Landscape of Words*, pp. 5, 11, 20.

168 See pp. 93–94 below.

169 For *Star Trek* space (and some travel modes), see Andrew S. Fazekas, *Star Trek. The Official Guide to Our Universe. The True Science Behind the Starship Voyages* (Washington, DC: National Geographic, 2016), esp. pp. 10, 24–25, 62–5, 106, 107–09. For *Stargate* space and travel modes, see Kathleen Ritter, *Stargate SG-1. The Ultimate Visual Guide* (London, New York, Munich, Melbourne and Delhi: DK, 2006), pp. 10–11, 54–57, 92–93; see also Johnson-Smith, *American Science Fiction TV*, p. 173.

TABLE 1.1 Increasing dimensional complexity of spaces conceptualised in the texts discussed in this book

Space of travel	Text	Comment
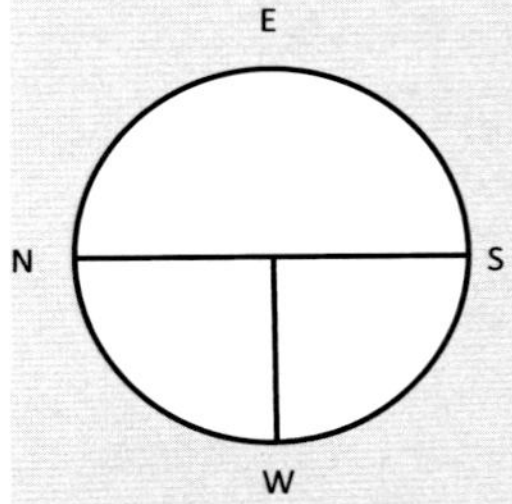 **2 dimensions**	Medieval *immram* and *echtra* narratives (this world); Lewis's *Voyage*; Eco's *Baudolino*	Lewis famously instructed the illustrator to draw the map of Narnia as a flat land; Eco's novel represents travel to the East in exactly the same terms as medieval accounts, and the novel plays with the idea that medieval maps make the world look flat (but do not represent a flat world). Both function in the T-O schematic tradition of representing the inhabited part of the spherical earth as a 2D image.
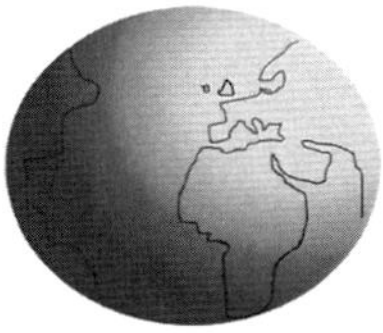 **2/3 dimensions**	Swift, *Gulliver's Travels*	Although the travel trajectory across the ocean is two-dimensional, the sphericity of the earth is present in the text, which reflects the travel traditions of the seventeenth and early eighteenth centuries. Gulliver's voyages take place on a globe.
 **3 dimensions**	*Star Trek*	Most of *Star Trek* travel takes place in the three-dimensional world of deep space.
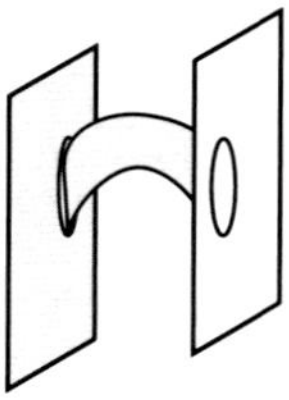 **?unknown dimensions**	*Stargate*	Although some travel through space in spaceship is present, in *Stargate,* the primary mode of travel to other worlds is through wormholes.

The movement is from the two-dimensional movement across a flat surface (of the inhabited ecumene, of course – the medieval mind did not conceive of the Earth as flat!), to the globe of the seventeenth- and eighteenth-century travel, to the three-dimensional travel through space in *Star Trek*, to the multi-dimensional time-space-defying wormhole travel through an imagined version of the Einstein-Rosen bridge in *Stargate*.[170] In each case we are dealing with fuzzy categories, since Lewis and Eco, though they themselves belong to a world post-round-the-world-travel, as does Swift, nevertheless represent in their fictional worlds smaller sections of the inhabited world, equivalent to (and inspired by) the T-O maps of the medieval world.[171] Swift's *Gulliver's Travels* occupies the central position in this book not only because it can be taken both ways: as *echtra* (if we take each 'travel' separately) or as *immram* (if we take the multi-episode narrative as an island-hopping whole) but also because of the influence this text has exerted on all the others (with the possible exception of *Stargate*).[172]

The progression of relative space in this book thus begins with the flat Narnian world (complete with an edge one might fall off) and continues through the two-dimensional immediate Eurasian landmass in the *immrama* and *Baudolino* through a more global scope of Gulliver (who visits Japan on his way home), through the Milky Way galaxy and beyond the known dimensions of space into wormholes. This sequence is partly

170 The Einstein-Rosen bridge, which later acquired the alternative name of 'wormhole', is named after Albert Einstein and Nathan Rosen, as the idea is described in their co-authored article 'The Particle Problem in the General Theory of Relativity', *Physical Review*, 48 (1935), 73–77. We return to the description of the bridge further below, p. 157. For a brief overview of the history of the idea of wormholes, the role of the Einstein-Rosen article, with its implications for and uses in science fiction, see David Lindley, 'The Birth of Wormholes' *Physical Review* Focus 15, 11 (2005) <https://link.aps.org/doi/10.1103/PhysRevFocus.15.11> [accessed 19 May 2023].

171 T-O maps are so called because of their shape: they represent the inhabited part of the world as a circle, separated into three parts (Asia, Africa and Europe) by a T shape; Petrovskaia, *Transforming Europe*, pp. 24–25. For more on medieval maps, see, for example, David Woodward, 'Medieval *Mappaemundi*', in *History of Cartography 1: Cartography in Prehistoric, Ancient, and Medieval Europe and the Mediterranean*, ed. by J. B. Harley and David Woodward (Chicago and London: University of Chicago Press, 1987), pp. 286–370.

172 For the relationship between *Baudolino* and *Gulliver's Travels* see, for example, Cristina Farronato, 'Umberto Eco's *Baudolino* and the Language of Monsters', *Semiotica*, 144 (2003), 319–42 (p. 336); and discussion below, pp. 94–95. Sabine Mercer points out that Baudolino's uncanny ability to pick up languages is also reminiscent of Gulliver; Mercer, 'Truth and Lies', p. 18.

inspired by the arrangement of relative spaces envisaged by Immanuel Kant, as charted by Michael Friedman in his introduction to his translation of Kant's *Metaphysical Foundations of Science*:

> In order to determine the true motions in the material, and thus empirically accessible universe, we begin with our parochial perspective here on earth, quickly move to the point of view of our solar system (where the earth is now seen to be really in a state of motion), then move to the perspective of the Milky Way galaxy (where our solar system, in turn, is itself seen to be in motion), and so on *ad infinitum* through an ever widening sequence of ever larger galactic structures serving as ever more expansive relative spaces.[173]

Kant's world, of course did not include the paradoxes later introduced by Einstein and thus did not loop back into wormholes. Before travelling through 'an ever-widening sequence of ever larger galactic structures' on the rowing-about journey of this book – if the rather obvious metaphor may be permitted – we will explore the very flat world of Narnia and its eastern seas, exploring C. S. Lewis's dialogic response to the Irish Saint Brendan's medieval westward journey.

173 Michael Friedman, 'Introduction', in Immanuel Kant, *Metaphysical Foundations of Science*, trans. by Michael Friedman, Cambridge Texts in the History of Philosophy (Cambridge: Cambridge University Press, 2004), p. xiii.

CHAPTER 2

C. S. Lewis, the *Dawn Treader*, and St Brendan

Our journey from the two-dimensional towards the hyper-dimensional begins, as promised, with Lewis's *The Voyage of the Dawn Treader* (henceforth: *Voyage*). The position of this text in relation to the Old Irish voyage tales is, perhaps, the least ambiguous of all the texts examined in this book. Not only is the frame of the narrative heavily indebted to the *Navigatio*, but it follows the conventions of the *immram* genre closely also. As with all *immrama*, without the description of the journey itself, without the sea and the islands, Lewis's story is an impossibility. (By contrast, without the description of the journey, Eco's *Baudolino* would be a different novel, but it would still exist.) As mentioned in the introduction above, the *Navigatio* stands in a close-knit relationship with the vernacular tradition of Irish voyage tales, and can itself be assigned to the *immram* genre. It in turn also generated a large pan-European literary tradition, with translations and adaptations in various European vernacular languages circulating in a large number of manuscripts.[1] A version thereof was even integrated into the French branch of the encyclopedic *Imago mundi* tradition mentioned in the introduction.[2] Lewis seems to have had an interest in the Brendan legend, as he acquired a copy of Ashe's *Land to the West*, published in 1962.[3]

The argument I present in this chapter, in favour of reading the *Voyage* both typologically as an *immram* narrative, and as an adaptation of the *Navigatio* (as member of the Old Irish voyage tradition), is not proposed in opposition to existing interpretations of the text. Rather, it builds on Michael Ward's suggestion that Lewis's Narniad has multiple layers of meaning.[4] Ward, in his convincingly argued *Planet Narnia*, outlines the first two: a literal and a spiritual (Christological) reading, previously adopted by scholars,

---

1 See the 'Introduction' above, p. 29 n. 116.

2 Petrovskaia, *Transforming Europe*, p. 125, n. 82. For discussions, see, also for instance, Paul Meyer, '*L'Image du monde*, rédaction du MS. Harley 4333', *Romania*, 21 (1892), 481–505 (pp. 482–83, 498) <https://doi.org/10.3406/roma.1892.5743>; Oliver Herbert Prior, ed., *L'Image du monde de maitre Gossuin. Rédaction en prose* (Lausanne and Paris: Payot, 1913), pp. 4, 7, 13.

3 Geoffrey Ashe, *Land to the West: St. Brendan's Voyage to America* (London: Collins, 1962); owned by Lewis according to Downing, *Into the Wardrobe*, p. 45.

4 Ward, *Planet Narnia*, pp. 10, 221, 245.

 | DOI:10.1163/9789004734548_003

and suggests he has found a third, metaphorical one.[5] As a starting point to the next step of the argument I take Ward's observation that Lewis was a medievalist through-and-through who conveyed both medieval form and medieval meaning through his works, and was in addition an admirer of Dante.[6] If that is so, there must be four levels of meaning to Lewis's opus, not three, because the medieval theory of meaning allowed formally for four methods of interpretation.[7]

The discussion of Lewis's work can fruitfully draw on his own attitudes to reception and interpretation (we will see this also in the following chapter in our discussion of Umberto Eco). In Peter J. Shackel's discussion of his conception of the imaginative faculty, an image emerges of Lewis positioned precariously between New Criticism and Reception Theory, while at the same time emphatically distancing himself from both.[8] While maintaining the idea of an independent reality of the artistic work (and the significance it carries), Lewis also acknowledged the need for an active engagement with it on the part of the reader, using the faculty of the imagination. In Schakel's words, Lewis 'loved imagination and realized its importance to a rich and full life, but he resisted subjectivity in imaginative experience, engaging in futile efforts to keep imagination grounded in objectivity'.[9] The classification of the effort at 'futile' is of course in itself a subjective reading. With Schakel we here read Lewis with a post-modernist perspective caught in the whirlwind world of Ecoean instability.

The following discussion takes Lewis's engagement with his sources, particularly in this text, as a dialogue. He is, as Jason M. Baxter has observed, a '"populariser" of ancient wisdom', engaged in the transmission of earlier material to new audiences.[10] Baxter analyses Lewis's engagement with Boethius specifically, but he also points out that this is a general trend in Lewis's work.[11] I take my cue in this chapter from Baxter's observation that 'it was habitual for him [=Lewis] to put ancients in dialogue with Christians and medieval Christians in dialogue with Romantics, despite the intervening

5 Ward, *Planet Narnia*, p. 245. For a critique of Ward's reading, see Poe, *The Completion of C. S. Lewis*, pp. 122–26.

6 Ward, *Planet Narnia*, pp. 19–20, 41.

7 See below, p. 54.

8 Peter J. Schakel, *Imagination and the Arts in C. S. Lewis: Journeying to Narnia and Other Worlds* (Columbia and London: University of Missouri Press, 2002), p. 21.

9 Schakel, *Imagination and the Arts*, p. 21.

10 Baxter, *The Medieval Mind*, p. 21.

11 Baxter, *The Medieval Mind*, pp. 21, 24, 28, 52–54.

millennia, in a way that recalled Dante's own blending of various eras'.[12] I argue that Lewis's active engagement with the reception of his medieval sources and models can be conceptualised as a dialogue, continuing the conversation started by the medieval writers.[13]

The generation of meaning through dialogic engagement with preceding utterances is also a key concept in Yuri M. Lotman's theory of cultural communication.[14] It is interesting to read Lotman's theory alongside Bakhtin's discussion of dialogism, and particularly internal dialogism as the two discussions address the issue of (artistic) meaning creation on similar lines.[15] We will return to Bakhtin's theory at the beginning of the following section, as in our discussion his idea of dialogic engagement with a preceding text will constitute the next step in approaching Lewis's work, after setting out the broader theoretical context with Lotman's theory of communication.

According to Lotman, all communication, and thus all artistic texts, can be described as a transfer of information within either an 'I–HE' or an 'I–I' system, or a combination of both, thus always arising from a process of communication, whether external (self-other) or internal (self-self).[16] Crucially, his conclusion is as follows:

> culture itself can be regarded as the sum of messages exchanged among various addressers (each of whom, to an addressee, is the "other," "he"), and as the single message that the collective "I" of humanity is sending to itself. From this perspective, the culture of humanity is a colossal example of autocommunication.[17]

---

12 Baxter, *The Medieval Mind*, p. 17.

13 As Baxter points out, echoes of medieval thought and medieval sources are 'everywhere in Lewis's writing, just beneath the surface', *The Medieval Mind*, p. 23.

14 See Lotman, *Universe of the Mind. A Semiotic Theory of Culture*, trans. by Anna Shukman (London: Tauris, 1990). In the discussion that follows I quote mainly the essay 'Autocommunication: "I" and "Other" as Addressees (On the Two Models of Communication in the System of Culture)', from *Culture and Communication. Signs in Flux. An Anthology of Major and Lesser-Known Works by Yuri Lotman*, ed. by Andreas Schönle, trans. Benjamin Paloff (Boston: Academic Studies Press, 2020), pp. 4–33.

15 Mikhail M. Bakhtin, *The Dialogic Imagination. Four Essays*, ed. by Michael Holquist, trans. by Caryl Emerson and Michael Holquist (Austin: University of Texas Press, 1981), pp. 282–83.

16 Lotman, 'Autocommunication', p. 21.

17 Lotman, 'Autocommunication', p. 21.

Ultimately, therefore, the reception processes in literature can be conceived of in dialogic, communicative terms as Lotman's 'I–HE', where the recipient becomes the new 'I' but also, when we conceive of the pair as belonging to the same 'culture', as an 'I–I' process. It is useful to think of Lewis's engagement with the *Navigatio* in the latter terms, as it allows us to incorporate Lotman's insights into autocommunication. In particular, in Lotman's view the 'I–HE' system is composed only of information communication, whereas the 'I–I' system is enriched by additional codes, drawn into the message of 'extratextual associations of varying degrees', encoded in the message sometimes by syntagmatic reorganisation.[18]

In the analysis of Lewis's dialogic engagement with the *Navigatio* that follows, I also refer to what now will be considered outdated editions and translations of the medieval text, on the principles that these would have been available to Lewis, and belong to the era, and thus the language, of the time. By 'language' here I mean the type of discourse, language and style that Bakhtin describes in the *Dialogic Imagination* as 'language of the day' – where to each 'day' (historical moment) corresponds 'another socio-linguistic semantic "state of affairs", another vocabulary, another accentual system'.[19] Following Lewis's own periodization placing the dividing line at the twentieth century, the 'language of the day' used by Lewis corresponds to the academic language of the late-nineteenth century, and thus is shared with Denis O'Donoghue's 1893 translation and discussion of the Brendan legend.[20]

2.1 C. S. Lewis's Dialogic Imagination

The title of this section derives from that of Bakhtin's essay collection.[21] Bakhtin's observation that a novel is usually regarded 'as if it were a hermetic and self-sufficient whole, one whose elements constitute a closed system presuming nothing beyond themselves, no other utterances', is

18 Lotman, 'Autocommunication', pp. 15, 17.

19 Bakhtin, *The Dialogic Imagination*, p. 291.

20 Lewis, '*De descriptione temporum*' in *20th Century Literary Criticism. A Reader*, ed. by David Lodge (Harlow: Addison Wesley Longman, 1972), pp. 443–53; originally published in *They Asked for a Paper. Papers and Addresses* (London: Bles, 1962). Denis O'Donoghue, *Brendaniana. St. Brendan the Voyager in Story and Legend* (Dublin: Browne and Nolan, 1893). Reference is also made where relevant to the more recent editions and discussions.

21 Bakhtin, *The Dialogic Imagination*.

particularly poignant for works such as the *Voyage*, which build on, and respond to, pre-existing traditions.[22] Bakhtin's remarks relate to his discussion of stylistics, but can be extended to other types of analysis. In all cases, our understanding of the text will change if it is addressed, to quote Bakhtin again, 'as a rejoinder in a given dialogue'.[23] In Bakhtin's reading all discourse is dialogical, engaging with previous discourses on the same subject, and 'all this may crucially shape discourse, may leave a trace in all its semantic layers, may complicate its expression and influence its entire stylistic profile'.[24] In a Bakhtin-informed reading, therefore, the *Voyage* can be regarded as a response to the *Navigatio*, uttered within a dialogic system inscribed by the *immram* genre.[25] We can also go further and read Lewis's engagement with his predecessors in Bakhtin's terms as 'active understanding'.[26]

Bakhtin defines 'active understanding' as 'one that assimilates the word under consideration into a new conceptual system, that of the one striving to understand, establishes a series of complex interrelationships, consonances and dissonances with the word and enriches it with new elements'.[27] If we take the text as a whole as the 'word'/utterance, then this describes Lewis's process of internalizing the Cristian philosophy of the original text and transforming it into modern discourse of a novel for children. This harks back to Baxter's view of Lewis as populariser, discussed above.[28] The idea of an 'assimilation into a new conception system' also helps understand why Lewis, in a letter to a reader, named 'spiritual life' as the novel's main idea.[29] In this instance, we must understand 'spiritual life', not merely as self-improvement or even as the religious aspect of existence, but as the

22 Bakhtin, *The Dialogic Imagination*, p. 273.

23 Bakhtin, *The Dialogic Imagination*, p. 274.

24 Bakhtin, *The Dialogic Imagination*, p. 274.

25 This also builds on the broad conception of genre as a dynamic system, also ultimately grounded in Bakhtinian theory, outlined in the introduction above, pp. 16–18.

26 The application of Bakhtin's dialogic idea to reception studies is explored, for instance, in relation to classical reception, in Lorna Hardwick, 'Aspirations and Mantras in Classical Reception Research: Can There Really Be Dialogue between Ancient and Modern' in *Framing Classical Reception Studies. Different Perspectives on a Developing Field*, ed. by Maarten De Pourcq (Leiden and Boston: Brill, 2020), pp. 15–32 (pp. 21–29). A dialogic model (not bound to Bakhtin), is insightfully and effectively applied to classical reception in, for instance, Emily Greenwood's *Afro-Greeks: Dialogues between Anglophone Caribbean Literature and Classics in the Twentieth Century* (Oxford: Oxford University Press, 2010).

27 Bakhtin, *The Dialogic Imagination*, p. 282.

28 See p. 48.

29 C. S. Lewis, *The Collected Letters of C. S. Lewis. Volume III. Narnia, Cambridge, and Joy, 1950–1963* ed. by Walter Hooper (New York, Harper Collins, 2007), p. 1245.

spiritual journey, on the model of the development outlined in such works as Bunyan's *Pilgrim's Progress* as well as the *Navigatio*.[30] Lewis's letter singles out Reepicheep because he is the only one who actually reaches the goal of his journey in the novel – the promised land in the Utter East. His is thus the only story, and only (earth/Narnia-bound) life completed in the voyage (and *Voyage*). By contrast, the protagonists (the children of Lewis's and the reader's 'real' world) and even King Caspian, are instructed by Aslan to go back to their respective worlds and live out their lives (=continue their individual journeys) first.[31]

The Pevensie children, and Eustace, not only enter a different (other) world as they enter Narnia, but they enter an otherworld, which borrows much from its medieval Irish predecessors. The flow of time, in particular, is different in Narnia from that of the real world, but there is no consistent pattern to the relative speed of the passage of time.[32] The observation made by John Carey in relation to the Celtic otherworld, therefore, is equally valid for Narnia: 'Otherworld time is not only out of alignment with mortal time, but [...] it is fundamentally different in kind'.[33] The extra emphasis given in *echtra* narratives to the stay in the other world allows a for a somewhat better point of comparison here than with the *immrama*. One thinks in particular of the adventure of Nera, who leaves his world for the otherworld of the *síd* mound, but returns briefly to warn his people of an impending attack by the otherworldly army. When he does so, he finds that time had passed more quickly in the otherworld, and none had passed in his world since he had left, as his otherworldly wife informs him: *'Atat immon caire cetno beus, 7 ni tallad in lucht don tinig cuse.' Sech bao hairem tri laa ocus teoro n-aidqi leissium bui issin tsid* ('"They are still around the same cauldron and the charge had not yet been removed from the fire." Yet it had seemed to him three days and three nights since he had been in the sid').[34] That the parallels are easily drawn here with *echtrai* does not diminish the novel's debt to

30 Lewis analyses the *Pilgrim's Progress* on a number of occasions, and alludes to the work in the title of his own *Pilgrim's Regress*. The bibliography on this engagement is extensive and cannot be reproduced here within the space available. For a discussion see, for instance, Harry Lee Poe, *The Inklings of Oxford: C. S. Lewis, J. R. R. Tolkien, and Their Friends* (Grand Rapids: Zondervan, 2009), pp. 81–82.

31 Swank, 'The Child's Voyage', p. 88–89. See further discussion below, pp. 69–70.

32 Lewis, *Voyage*, p. 24.

33 John Carey, 'Time, Space and the Otherworld', *Proceedings of the Harvard Celtic Colloquium*, 7 (1987), 1–27 (p. 8).

34 Meyer, ed. and trans., 'The Adventures of Nera', pp. 220, 221.

the *immram* genre. The difference in the flow of time is a feature of Narnia and thus of Lewis's novel series rather than of this narrative alone. This emphasizes, however, the fuzzy nature of the genre distinctions. The *Voyage* belongs both to the Narnia set (which is about prolonged visits to the otherworld and thus *echtra*-like), and, equally, because of its own structure, to the fuzzy set of the island-hopping *immram* genre. Indeed, elements from elsewhere are also on hand. An allusion to medieval precedents/parallels is made explicit by Lewis in the passage, as he compares the Pevensie children's return to Narnia with the prophesied return of Arthur: 'when the Pevensie children had returned to Narnia last time for their second visit, it was (for the Narnians) as if King Arthur came back to Britain, as some people say he will. And I say the sooner the better'.[35] There are thus many more fuzzy sets involved, which cannot all be addressed within the limits of this discussion.

Lewis transmits elements of the *immram*, and of (Arthurian) chivalric society, to a new audience and a new age in the *Voyage*.[36] In this he follows the medieval translatory mode of narrative composition, following, as Baxter observes, the model of writers such as Chaucer and Malory.[37] Thus, Lewis is a distinctly un-modern writer in prioritizing not originality but engagement with, transformation and translation of pre-existing material.[38] Arguably, Lewis internalizes the material first, before reproducing it with the additional code attached to the message, to put this in Lotman's terms. The surface communicative meaning is intelligible to the reader, but the additional rich associations are not visible to the child reader or even the informed lay

35 Lewis, *Voyage*, p. 24. The brackets are Lewis's. For discussions of the legend of Arthur's return in medieval sources, see for instance, Françoise Le Saux, 'Wace's *Roman de Brut*' in *Arthur of the English. The Arthurian Legend in Medieval English Life and Literature*, ed. by W. R. J. Barron (Cardiff: University of Wales Press, 2001), pp. 18–22 (p. 20); and Le Saux, 'Laȝamon's *Brut*', in the same volume, pp. 22–32 (pp. 30–32), and Oliver Padel, *Arthur in Medieval Welsh Literature* (Cardiff: University of Wales Press, 2013), pp. 38, 47–48.

36 For Lewis's activity of cultural 'translation' of the medieval sources for new audiences, see Baxter, *The Medieval Mind*, p. 47; an argument might be made for employing Lewis's own terminology of 'transposition' in this context (pp. 28–29). However, I would suggest that Lewis used the term 'transposition' borrowed from music in the sermon that Baxter discusses because the idea he is representing, *translatio* (translation) in the broader medieval sense of 'transmission' (close to the modern 'cultural translation') would be unfamiliar to the broader audience he was addressing.

37 Baxter, *The Medieval Mind*, pp. 53–54.

38 Baxter, *The Medieval Mind*, pp. 55–58.

reader (but are visible in the autocommunication circuit within the culture of academic medievalists).[39] A case in point is in the conclusion to the novel, and the conversations that first Caspian, and then the children, have with Aslan.[40] The instructions to turn back to their own world, to which I have already referred in the context of the 'spiritual life' reference above, and the glimpse provided to the children of Aslan's country, echo the conclusion of Saint Brendan's voyage.[41] We will return to this scene once more later in this chapter.

2.2 The *Dawn Treader* and Fourfold Interpretation

The reference to the 'spiritual life' leads us to the tropological aspect of the narrative, already mentioned, which in turn falls within the medieval framework of the four methods of interpretation. This was ultimately based on the four modes of meaning presented by John Cassian in the fourth century.[42] Although subject to evolution and re-organisation in the course of the Middle Ages, the four methods of interpretation can be thought of as constituted by one literal (=historical) and three spiritual levels of meaning:[43]

- **literal**, also known as **historical**
- **allegorical**
- **anagogical**, referring to the afterlife and to things eternal
- **tropological**, also known as **moral**

---

39 The frequent references to the Odyssey rather than the *Navigatio* as Lewis's model attest to this.

40 Lewis, *Voyage*, pp. 248, 255.

41 O'Donoghue, *Brendaniana*, p. 174; Lewis, *Voyage*, pp. 254–55.

42 For an introduction to Cassian, see Owen Chadwick, *John Cassian*, 2nd edn (Cambridge: Cambridge University Press, 1968); a recent up-to-date bibliography on Cassian can be found in Niki Kasumi Clements, *Sites of the Ascetic Self: John Cassian and Christian Ethical Formation* (Notre Dame, Indiana: Notre Dame University Press, 2020).

43 The summary and definitions given below are based on Robert S. Sturges, *Medieval Interpretation: Models of Reading in Literary Narrative, 1100–1500* (Carbondale and Edwardsville: Southern Illinois University Press, 1991), p. 13 (for further discussions of medieval multiplicities of interpretation, see his pp. 1–31) and Umberto Eco, *The Limits of Interpretation* (Bloomington and Indianapolis: Indiana University Press, 1994), p. 12. For more Dante and the four levels of meaning, see also Eco, *The Limits*, pp. 16–17; and earlier work by Charles S. Singleton, 'Dante's Allegory', *Speculum*, 25 (1950), 78–86 (p. 78). For a more recent general overview, see Jeremy Tambling, *Allegory* (London and New York: Routledge, 2010), p. 25.

Of these four, allegory has exercised particular fascination, on both medieval and modern imagination and scholarship.[44] Lewis, who, as Baxter points out, was a proponent of metaphorical discourse and influenced through and through by his identity as medievalist, is almost certainly analysable from this medieval perspective.[45] One might map the three modes of reading the Narnia books identified by Ward onto these four as follows.[46] The literal meaning is the same, the anagogical we can read as the traditional Christological reading of the Narnia books and the allegorical is Ward's new analysis. To this we can add the tropological – the moral of the story. All four interact on the model of a medieval text. In this instance, the fourfold interpretation is invited by the text because it is built on the pattern of the *Navigatio*.

As Harry Lee Poe points out in his critique of Ward's book, Lewis himself objected to allegorical readings of his work.[47] However, the point of fourfold interpretation is not that a work was *designed* with it in mind, but that it was created within a tradition where works subject to fourfold interpretation are the norm. Because Lewis belongs to the medieval narrative mode, and because of his engagement in dialogue with medieval texts, the four layers of meaning are an inescapable part of his creative world. Indeed, in a letter Poe quotes, Lewis – in what we shall see is a strikingly Eco-like mode – suggests that perhaps works are given additional meanings by readers which were not intentionally intended by the original writer at all.[48] If, as J. S. Mackley points out, Lewis sees the voyage of Brendan as 'a means to explore principal ecclesiastical issues without confronting them directly',

---

44 For a general introduction to allegory, see Tambling, *Allegory*. For an overview of the early modern fascination with allegory, see Jason Crawford, *Allegory and Enchantment. An Early Modern Poetics* (Oxford: Oxford University Press, 2017), with discussion of the exegetical roots of allegorical interpretation on pp. 10–11 and in his Chapter 1. Crawford refers, amongst other texts, to Lewis, *The Allegory of Love. A Study in Medieval Tradition* (Oxford: Oxford University Press, 1958 [1936]). We will return to Lewis's work on allegory and to possible readings of Swift's *Gulliver's Travels* as allegory, below, pp. 114–16 and 181.

45 Baxter, *The Medieval Mind*, pp. 158–59. We will see that this is also the case for Dean Swift in the discussion below, pp. 115–16.

46 Ward, *Planet Narnia*, p. 245.

47 Poe, *The Completion of C. S. Lewis*, p. 125. This has not deterred commentators, however. See, for instance, Lawyer, 'Three Celtic Voyages', p. 331.

48 C. S. Lewis, *The Collected Letters of C. S. Lewis. Volume III. Narnia, Cambridge, and Joy, 1950–1963* ed. by Walter Hooper (New York, Harper Collins, 2007), p. 1116; quoted and discussed in Poe, *The Completion of C. S. Lewis*, p. 126; compare the opening passages of Eco's 'Borges'.

then an allegorical reading may be inescapable.[49] Mackley points out that in Lewis's reading, 'the allegorical Earthly Paradise does indeed belong to the Otherworld, but it is an Otherworld of imagination rather than of religion'.[50] However, since the role of religion in Lewis's writings has been so well studied, it is not my goal here to provide an allegorical reading of the *Voyage* on the model of interpretations of the *Navigatio*. Instead, my purpose is, by drawing on the similarities and the apparent influence of the medieval text on Lewis, to show how the genre category of *immram* can be fruitfully applied to the twentieth-century text.[51] I am therefore not reading the work through the four methods of interpretation, but rather wholistically as a narrative that belongs to the same tradition which used these methods and constructed narratives accordingly. The approach of taking the narrative as a whole, rather than individual details (though details will be mentioned), is also a response to Lewis's own view that scholars tend to ignore narrative in narrative poems (but also, one suspects, in prose).[52] Medieval literature affected the form not only of the *Voyage* and Lewis's other Narnia books, but also of his science-fiction novels, particularly in the framework of journey narratives, as Poe observes.[53]

As we will see in the next chapter, in *Baudolino* Eco builds on several different traditions, in kaleidoscopic arrangement, thereby also following the model of the patchwork makeup of the original Prester John legend. One of the components of Eco's kaleidoscopic picture is composed of the Brendan legend and Irish island-hopping narrative traditions, though he sends his characters not westwards across the sea but eastwards across the desert. Such re-interpretation and re-application of the legends he is transmitting follows Eco's postmodern sensibilities. Lewis, on the other hand, produces a much more straightforward adaptation (comparatively speaking). He, too, combines several distinct influences and traditions in the *Voyage*.[54] Although his heroes, like those of Eco, travel eastwards, Lewis's

---

49 Mackley, *The Legend*, p. 28.

50 Mackley, *The Legend*, p. 28. Note that the otherworld of Old Irish travel narratives is also not necessarily 'of religion'; see above, p. 27.

51 See, for instance, Lawyer, 'Three Celtic Voyages', for a reading of the Lewis-Brendan connection from a religious and spiritual perspective.

52 Lewis, letter to Dorothy L. Sayers, *The Collected Letters of C. S. Lewis. Volume II. Books, Broadcasts, and the War, 1931–1949*, ed. by Walter Hooper (New York, Harper Collins, 2004), pp. 654–55, quoted in Poe, *The Completion of C. S. Lewis*, p. 21.

53 Poe, *The Completion of C. S. Lewis*, p. 87.

54 Ward, *Planet Narnia*, p. 108.

island-hopping *Voyage* has less in common with Marco Polo's travel account than with the westward-directed *Navigatio*, and the Old Irish *immrama* (such as the *Immram Curaig Maíle Dúin*). The *immrama* also connect to an illustrious predecessor of Lewis's, Jonathan Swift's *Gulliver's Travels*, discussed in Chapter 4.

As David C. Downing points out, parallels between the *Navigatio* and the *Voyage* are plentiful and easily apparent:

> As in Brendan's voyage, there are three latecomers – late indeed, as Edmund, Lucy, and Eustace join the *Dawn Treader* after it is already under way. One of the three latecomers, Eustace, is caught stealing. There is an island mostly inhabited by sheep, Felimath, and an island of sleep – or the worst part of sleep, nightmares. There is also an island with what seems a great empty house until its owner, the magician Coriakin, appears. And Ramandu, with his long white hair and beard, looks just like the hermit Paul. His island has a "dim, purple kind of smell," which reminds us of the island covered with grape trees. And here, birds prepare Aslan's Table every day, blending several incidents in the *Navigatio* – the Paradise of Birds, the supernatural feeding by a bird of brilliant plumage, and the animal who brings food to Paul every day.[55]

This brief descriptive passage shows that there are many surface parallels demonstrating that the *Navigatio* provided the framework for Lewis's story. One might add others. For instance, the transparency of the sea in which Lucy sees an undersea land and inhabitants, is also present in the *Navigatio*, in the episode of the encounter with the crystal column (probably an iceberg).[56] The encounter with the sea serpent echoes the encounter with the sea-monster (defeated by another one in the *Navigatio* rather than by the travellers).[57] The island of sheep, and the white birds who sing hymns in a human tongue (though unintelligible in Lewis's version) are examples of *Navigatio*-derived elements that, taken in isolation, could have been

55 Downing, *Into the Wardrobe*, p. 46; for his summary of the *Navigatio sancti Brendani*, see pp. 43–45.

56 O'Donoghue, *Brendaniana*, p. 158.

57 O'Donoghue, *Brendaniana*, p. 147–48; translation in John J. O'Meara and Jonathan Wooding, 'The Latin Version', in *The Voyage of Saint Brendan. Representative Versions of the Legend in English Translation*, ed. by W. R. J. Barron and Glyn S. Burgess (Exeter: University of Exeter Press, 2002), pp. 13–64 (p. 47).

perceived as coincidental.[58] Islands used entirely as pastures are attested in real life.[59] Some of the elements might also have come from other sources, and including medieval Irish ones.[60] A number of shared elements are found also with *Immram Curaig Maíle Dúin*, a vernacular narrative which is usually considered to be based on the *Navigatio*. Like Brendan, Máel Dúin is joined by three latecomers, whom he picks up as they swim after him, as Caspian picks up the Pevensie siblings and Eustace, to rescue them from drowning.[61] Ramandu the retired star, and his daughter, with whom Caspian falls in love, are reminiscent of Prospero and his daughter in *The Tempest*.[62] The comparison is perhaps not so fanciful given the presence of an explicit reference to Shakespeare's other magic play, *Midsummer Night's Dream*: one of the spells which Lucy reads in the magician's book is 'how to give a man an ass's head (as they did to poor Bottom)'.[63] The cumulative evidence, however, is in favour of Downing's point – Lewis uses the *Navigatio* as a framework. The *Voyage* is thus an *immram* narrative.

Lewis's debt to the *Navigatio* can be described in the same terms he uses for medieval intertextuality. In that sense – the use of previous authorities to mould a new text – Lewis himself is a thoroughly medieval author. This echoes also Bakhtin's concept of 'creative memory' discussed above.[64] In mode of continuing creative memory of the past Lewis also, as he himself indicates in his inaugural lecture at Cambridge, positions himself on the

58 Lewis, *Voyage*, pp. 212, 226; O'Donoghue, *Brendaniana*, p. 173.

59 The 'sheep island' of Saint Brendan is sometimes identified as Streymoy, while the 'bird island' as Mykines, both in the Faroes; Donnchadh O'Corráin, 'Irish and Nordic Exchange. What They Gave and What They Took', in *Heritage and Identity. Shaping the Nations of the North*, ed. by J. M. Fladmark (London: Routledge, 2002), pp. 61–72 (p. 66).

60 A recent investigation of the Eastern references in the Narnia books shows that despite the amount of ink already spilt on the subject of influences and source, more remains to be discovered; Warwick Ball, *East of the Wardrobe. The Unexpected Worlds of C. S. Lewis* (Oxford: Oxford University Press, 2022).

61 Stokes, ed. and trans., 'The Voyage of Mael Duin (Part 1)', pp. 460–61. See the discussion in Mackley, *The Legend*, pp. 86–88, 92–94.

62 A similar echo of the *Tempest* is present in the *Enterprise* Season 1 Episode 19 'Oasis', as the father and daughter alien survivors of the crashed ship. The daughter, Liana, the episode's version of Shakespeare's Miranda, had never seen real people, let alone humans, and forms a romantic bond with the first human she sees, the Enterprise's chief engineer, Charles 'Trip' Tucker.

63 Lewis, *Voyage*, p. 161. The brackets are Lewis's.

64 See above, p. 17.

medieval-renaissance continuum rather than as part of 'modern civilisation', which he posits to be something of a breakaway phenomenon.[65]

One might usefully compare Lewis's creative work with the following passage, where he describes the sources of the description of the spirits inhabiting the air in Laȝamon's *Brut*:

> But Laȝamon is not writing thus because he shares in any communal and spontaneous response made by the social group he lives in. [...] He takes his account of the aerial daemons from the Norman poet Wace (*c.*1155). Wace takes it from Geoffrey of Monmouth's *Historia Regum Britanniae* (before 1139). Geoffrey takes it from the second-century *De Deo Socratis* of Apuleius. Apuleius is reproducing the pneumatology of Plato. Plato was modifying, in the interests of ethics and monotheism, the mythology he had received from his ancestors.[66]

A similar genealogy can be constructed for Lewis's own creative work, and in particular for the *Voyage*, within the continuum of the texts' (and crucially their ideas') reception history. Lewis's work also similarly connects multiple previous traditions. As Ward points out, in relation to the origins and inspiration behind the *Voyage*, 'In constructing this picaresque romance, Lewis had many sea-voyage stories to draw upon, such as Homer's *Odyssey*, the Irish tradition of *immram*, the Anglo-Saxon poem *The Seafarer*, the *Voyage of St. Brendan*, and Mandeville's *Voiage and Travaile*.'[67] Ward's argument is that Lewis's journey narrative is a 'sun-voyage' rather than 'sea-voyage', for which a model is provided by Milton's *Paradise Lost*, and I do not propose to argue against the reading, because my point about the

65 Lewis, 'De descriptione'; Baxter, *The Medieval Mind*, esp. p. 76.

66 Lewis, *The Discarded Image. An Introduction to Medieval and Renaissance Literature* (Cambridge: Cambridge University Press, 1994 [1964]), p. 2. Cf. discussion in Baxter, *The Medieval Mind*, p. 55.

67 Ward, *Planet Narnia*, p. 108. In 1928, Edwin George Ross Waters (1890–1930), published his edition of the Anglo-Norman poem concerning the voyage of St Brendan, composed by Benedeït, a secularised adaptation of the Latin *Navigatio sancti Brendani*; Edwin George Ross Waters, *The Anglo-Norman Voyage of St.Brendan by Benedeit. A Poem of the Early Twelfth Century* (Geneva: Slatkine, 1974 [Oxford: Clarendon Press, 1928]), pp. lxxxi–cv for the relationship with the Latin version. For a discussion of this adaptation see Sobecki, 'From the *désert liquide* to the Sea of Romance', esp. p. 195 for comments on its secularized nature. Waters had been appointed to a Research Fellowship in Oxford in 1925, the same year as Lewis was appointed to his permanent fellowship; Waters, *The Anglo-Norman Voyage*, p. v.

Voyage is not what it 'is' but rather what type of text we can usefully interpret it as.[68]

For that purpose it is illustrative that the *immram* despite only being mentioned by name once, in actual fact features twice in Ward's description, because the *Navigatio* of Saint Brendan is widely – and fairly uncontroversially – accepted as a member of the *immram* genre.[69] Downing also suggests that Lewis's 'utter East may be an echo from a William Morris story, "The Land East of the Sun and West of the Moon"'.[70] It is worth noting in this regard that Lewis's early reading included Morris's *The Earthly Paradise* (1868–1870), a multi-story narrative, modelled on the *Canterbury Tales* but framed as tales told at the culmination of a voyage by Norsemen in search of an Earthly Paradise in the West, where failing to find this place, the travellers settle for an unknown island 'where the ancient Greek gods are still worshiped'.[71] Although supposedly based on Chaucer, Morris's text is markedly different, because as David Lyle Jeffrey points out, 'Chaucer's pilgrims make their Lenten pilgrimage not in search of an earthly paradise but rather the completion of an act of penance and communal reconciliation'.[72] This text might thus be seen as a step in the line leading from the *Navigatio* to Lewis (but Lewis also used the *Navigatio* directly).

In analysing Lewis as a creative writer it is also salubrious to keep in mind his comments on the Christian element in the medieval European tradition:

> When we speak of the Middle Ages as the ages of authority we are usually thinking about the authority of the Church. But they were the age not only of her authority, but of authorities. If their culture is regarded as a response to environment, then the elements in that environment to which it responded most vigorously were manuscripts. Every writer, if he possibly can, bases himself on an earlier writer,

68 Ward, *Planet Narnia*, p. 108.

69 See, e.g. Dumville, '*Echtrae* and *Immram*', p. 75. That the *Navigatio* is intricately connected to the vernacular *immrama* is also highlighted in Wooding, 'The Date', pp. 25–26. See also above, pp. 29–30, 47.

70 Downing, *Into the Wardrobe*, p. 46. For Morris's influence on Lewis, see Poe, *The Completion of C. S. Lewis*, p. 112; Matthews, *Medievalism*, p. 127.

71 David Lyle Jeffrey, 'Medieval Literature', in *Reading the Classics with C. S. Lewis*, ed. by Thomas L. Martin (Grand Rapids, MI: Baker Academic, and Carlisle: Paternoster Press, 2000), pp. 72–86 (p. 73).

72 Jeffrey, 'Medieval Literature', p. 74.

> follows an *auctour*: preferably a Latin one. This is one of the things that differentiate the period almost equally from savagery and from our modern civilisation.[73]

In this passage one could replace medieval authors with Lewis himself as the object of discussion, and the observations made will remain largely valid. This passage is closely followed by remarks on the contrast between twentieth-century modernity and the Middle Ages: 'In our own society most knowledge depends, in the last resort, on observation. But the Middle Ages depended predominantly on books'.[74] The view appears to have been shared by Umberto Eco, as we will see in the next chapter that Baudolino and his companions first discover faraway lands through books.[75] Indeed, books feature in the background as source of knowledge and preparation for the journey(s) and alien encounters also in *Stargate SG-1*, as the resident archaeologist/linguist/culture, legend, mythology and history expert (the humanities conflated into one person) Dr Daniel Jackson, regularly briefs the team on the alien cultures they are about to encounter, based on his knowledge of Earth-bound legends and mythologies (and sometimes armed with a leather-bound tome as a prop).[76]

Lewis's comments both in '*De descriptione temporum*', and on the 'modernity' of Eustace's (Cambridge-based!) parents in the opening passages of the *Voyage* betray his distrust of an excessively utilitarian and empirical modernity.[77] In the *Voyage* this is opposed to the power of belief and of the magic

73 Lewis, *The Discarded Image*, p. 5.

74 Lewis, *The Discarded Image*, p. 5.

75 See below, p. 99.

76 Sometimes he also (mis-)represents medieval history, following the established view familiar to the general public; see in particular the comments on the 'Dark Ages' quoted in Steven John Gil, '"Remember the Nox": *Stargate: SG-1*'s Narrative Structure and the Changing Form of Television Fiction', *New Review of Film and Television Studies*, 12 (2014) 178–202 (p. 192); see also Vincent Van Bever Donker and Stephanie Yorke, 'Re-Imagining the Colonial Encounter in *Stargate: SG-1*: Discourses of Linear Progress and Separate Development', *Interventions* 20. *Violence in a Global Frame* (2018), 734–49 (p. 737).

77 Note, however, that Eustace's (and his parents') obsession with numbers and 'facts', seems to correspond to what Lewis describes in *The Discarded Image* as characteristics of a 'medieval man': 'At his most characteristic, medieval man was not a dreamer, nor a wanderer. He was an organiser, a codifier, a builder of systems. He wanted "a place for everything and everything in the right place". Distinction, definition, and tabulation were his delight', Lewis, *The Discarded Image*, p. 10; cf. Lewis, *Voyage*, pp. 13, 37, 256.

of imagination. Indeed, Eustace illustrates the opposition between fantasy and realism which Tuan charts in the discussion cited in the introduction above: 'One common notion of a realist is that he or she is a stickler for facts'.[78] Eustace also matches Tuan's description of a realist in his disdain for fantasies 'unworthy of an adult's serious attention because they depart too far from what the world is really like'.[79] In Lewis's own work, I would argue, this dry practical empiricism of modernity is also opposed to the magic of tradition and written authority. Eustace's preference for 'books of information' in the opening of the novel sets the tone for the whole.[80] He fails to recognise a dragon or its treasure cave because he had been reading 'none of the right books'.[81] By contrast, the implied/intended (child) reader, one imagines, would have read the 'right books' and would snigger knowingly or cry out excitedly recognizing the dragon and the treasure before Eustace does.

The mode of description is defamiliarizing – rather than refer to the objects as they are known to the reader, they are described through the experience of someone unfamiliar with them. This is a textbook example of the literary technique labelled by the formalists as 'defamiliarisation' (also known as 'estrangement').[82] In the interests of maintaining some semblance

78 Tuan, 'Realism', p. 435.

79 Tuan, 'Realism', p. 436.

80 Lewis, *Voyage*, p. 13; see also comments in Lawyer, 'Three Celtic Voyages', p. 331.

81 Lewis, *Voyage*, pp. 92, 95. The reader is reminded of this again later on in the story, p. 204. See comments in Dabney Adams Hart, *Through the Open Door. A New Look at C. S. Lewis* (Tuscaloosa: University of Alabama Press, 1984), pp. 90–91.

82 Eco, 'Borges', p. 127. The literary device of defamiliarisation is primarily derived from Viktor Shklovsky's *ostranenie* (остранение), and its contemporary *Entfremdung* and *Verfremdungseffekt* 'estrangement effect' coined by Bertold Brecht refer to a literary technique whereby the familiar reality is shown to the reader in such a way as to make it possible to see aspects of it which are usually invisible because they too familiar. See discussion in of alternative translations of остранение as 'alienation', 'defamiliarisation' and 'estrangement' in Erik Martin, 'Alienation/Defamiliarisation/Estrangement (*ostranenie*)', in *Central and Eastern European Literary Theory and the West*, ed. by Michał Mrugalski, Schamma Schahadat and Irina Wutsdorff (Berlin: De Gruyter, 2022), pp. 881–86; Виктор Борисович Шкловский, (Viktor Borisovich Shklovsky), 'Искусство как приём' (Art as Device) in *О теории прозы* (*O Teorii Prozi*) (Moscow: Krug, 1925), pp. 23–55; Viktor Shklovsky, 'Art as Technique' in *Russian Formalist Criticism: Four Essays*, ed. by Lee T. Lemon, Marion J. Reis, and Gary Saul Morson (Lincoln and London: University of Nebraska Press, 1965), pp. 5–24. For a comparative discussion of Shklovsky's and Brecht's concepts, see Douglas Robinson, *Estrangement and the Somatics of Literature: Tolstoy, Shklovsky, Brecht* (Baltimore: John Hopkins University Press, 2008). The term 'cognitive estrangement' is found also

of remaining within the already broad intertextual matrix described in this book, I quote the elegant definition provided by Umberto Eco: 'the poetics of "defamiliarisation", which the Russian formalists describe as representing something in such a way that one feels as if one were seeing it for the first time, thus making the perception of the object difficult for the reader'.[83] The reader's perception of reality is thereby altered, with the effect that the previously mundane acquires a feeling of strangeness.

The same mode is used later on in the description of the monopods (to be renamed dufflepuds later on in the story) when Lucy first sees them. Because she had not read about them before, she does not recognise them, and each feature is gradually revealed in the description.[84] One might argue whether 'defamiliarisation' is quite right if the reader is not familiar with the object described, but we must remember that Lewis the medievalist was. In this instance, the descriptive sleight of hand, which ends up an in-joke for other medievalists, is probably best seen as an example of Lotman's 'I–I' communication mode, referred to above.[85] Indeed, the entire story can be read as a doubly encoded message, where the reader is aware of the message content (this is in Lotman's terms 'I–HE'), but only Lewis can read the additional code within the 'I–I' communication.[86] With some effort, and reference to Lewis's medieval models and literary allusions, it may be possible to crack some of that code (though probably not all). The only explicit reference, in the 'I–I' mode, and for those in the know, is the 'little skin boat, or

in MacKinnon's quotation from the definition of science fiction as genre in M. K. Booker and A. M. Thomas, *The Science Fiction Handbook* (Chichester: Wiley Blackwell, 2009), p. 4; quoted and discussed MacKinnon, '*Stargate Atlantis*', p. 39. Brooker and Thomas chart the origins of the term via Suvin to Berthold Brecht's theatre (which they term Suvin's inspiration for the concept); *The Science Fiction Handbook*, p. 323. At the risk of appearing pedantic I feel the need to observe that Brecht also was a theoretician of estrangement, the exact relation of whose theory's to Shklovsky's presents its own intertextual conundrum; see Robinson, *Estrangement*, Part Three, esp. pp. 167–68.

83 Eco, 'Borges', p. 127. We will see in Chapter 3 that Eco himself practices a reverse technique—describing the unfamiliar so as to make it seem well-known to the reader; see pp. 89–90.

84 Lewis, *Voyage*, p. 174.

85 See above, pp. 49–50.

86 We will see in the following chapter that this is a feature of Eco's writing. Eco, however, also notes this himself in his several commentaries on his creative process; see above, p. 4.

coracle', the company finds, and that becomes Reepicheep's boat, since it is big enough only for the mouse.[87]

The alterations made by Lewis to the *Navigatio* narrative, however, speak to the difference between his (and his audience's) world(view) and that of his medieval predecessors. The most striking difference is the fate of the three late-comers. In the *Navigatio*, the thief is saved (but dies soon after) and one of the other late-comers is dragged off by demons.[88] The difference thus can be simply put as redemption. In Lewis's work – arguably because it is a book for children – no one is irrevocably lost, not even Eustace. The benevolent view of humanity as redeemable echoes that of his contemporary G. K. Chesterton. Indeed, Lewis acknowledged Chesterton's influence himself.[89] This is part of Lewis's dialogical engagement with those who came before.

In my view, Eustace's journey of redemption is central to the narrative (and to its tropological node) and constitutes part of Lewis's contribution to the continuing *immram*-based conversation.[90] It is notable that the story both opens and closes with Eustace, who is thus the focal character.[91] The redemption story-arc appears to frame the narrative as a spiritual journey, inherited from its medieval exemplars.[92] In the spiritual journey narrative

87 Lewis, *Voyage*, p. 122. The coracle itself is a nod to the *immrama*. Cf. comments in Oscamp, '*Echtra Condla*', p. 218: 'A boat in Irish literature is explicitly a curragh'. One thinks in particular of the *Immram Curaig Maíle Dúin* the 'Immram of the Coracle of Mael Duin' and the *Immram Curaig Ua Corra* 'The Voyage of the Uí Chorra's Coracle'; see above, p. 25. For a brief introduction to the latter tale, see Carey, 'Voyage Literature', p. 1745. Severin's journey reconstructed such a coracle; Timothy Severin, *The Brendan Voyage* (London: Hutchinson, 1978).

88 O'Donoghue, *Brendaniana*, p. 162.

89 See discussion in David Pickering, 'Chesterton, Lewis, and the Shadow of Newman. A Study in Method', *New Blackfriars*, 104 (2023), 142–60 (pp. 143, 153) and references to Lewis's correspondence and autobiography (nn. 5, 32). See also Benjamin Fischer and Philip C. Derbesy, 'Literary Catholicity. An Alternate Reading of Influence in the Work of C. S. Lewis and G. K. Chesterton', *Religion and the Arts*, 19 (2015), 389–410.

90 Swank, 'The Child's Voyage', pp. 93–94.

91 For students of Celtic Studies, the reference to Eustace in the opening sentence of the book may strongly evoke the opening of each of the Four Branches of the Mabinogi, three of which start with the reference to the main (now titular) characters; for discussion of these openings see, e.g. Patrick K. Ford, 'Branwen: A Study of the Celtic Affinities' *Studia Celtica*, 22–23 (1987–1988), 29–41 (p. 32). Another element suggestive of such influence is the turn of phrase 'it crept into their hearts' for the characters beginning to feel doubt; Lewis, *Voyage*, p. 139.

92 For Lewis's own description of the story as a 'spiritual life', see *The Collected Letters of C. S. Lewis*, III, ed. by Hooper, p. 1245.

the journeying character is often an everyman figure, representing the reader – though perhaps with some exaggerated faults to make his chastisement easier to swallow. Eustace the everyman starts his journey with a mindset reflected by the register of language he uses, marked by references to the British Consul, and use of terms such as 'lodge a disposition'.[93] He is anchored in the world of technological progress (and of idolization of technological progress as the ultimate good), as he is found 'boasting about liners and motor-boats and aeroplanes and sub-marines'.[94] His definition of 'civilization' is also technological: 'Machinery!' he exclaims at one point in the narrative, 'I do believe we've come to a civilized country at last!'[95] The entry in Eustace's diary in Chapter 2 illustrates this: his measure of comparison for the *Dawn Treader* is the *Queen Mary*, a reference that would have been picked up by Lewis's contemporaries, but perhaps increasingly less obvious to subsequent generations of readers.[96] The *Queen Mary* was a Cunard-White Star giant liner of over 80,000 ton, capable of carrying 2,139 passengers, launched in 1934, making her first transatlantic voyage in 1936.[97] Recognised as the world's fastest liner until 1952, the year of publication of Lewis's *Voyage*, reference to it by Eustace in the diary stands for the pinnacle of progress in sea-faring technology (the impressive luxury levels are also alluded to by Eustace).[98]

In the course of the diary entry Eustace also refers to other aspects of twentieth-century progress: democracy (as 'republicanism') and feminism. Both are subverted in his rendition. This is not to say that for Lewis the absurdity is inherent in the concepts themselves, but rather in Eustace's understanding of them. He claims to be a 'republican' to distance himself from what he sees as the others' 'buttering up' of King Caspian, and argues that according to Alberta (as he 'modernly' calls his mother) special treatment – here in Lucy receiving Caspian's cabin for sole use – 'is really lowering' girls.[99] Here and throughout – until his brief stint as a dragon – an underlying selfishness, justified through (mis-)application of modern terminology,

93 Lewis, *Voyage*, p. 37.

94 Lewis, *Voyage*, p. 39.

95 Lewis, *Voyage*, p. 144. Ironically, they had arrived at an island inhabited by monopods and ruled over by a magician.

96 Lewis, *Voyage*, p. 41.

97 William H. Miller, *Picture History of British Ocean Liners. 1900 to the Present* (Mineola, New York: Dover Publications, 2001), p. 43.

98 Miller, *Picture History of British Ocean Liners*, p. 44; Lewis, *Voyage*, p. 40.

99 Lewis, *Voyage*, p. 41.

and concepts, is visible in Eustace's diary entries, as in his speeches and internal monologue.[100] Eustace's claim to be a 'pacifist' who does not 'believe in fighting' in the face of Reepicheep's challenge to draw his sword is particularly jarring given his unprovoked attack on Reepicheep earlier (apparently, 'pacifism' in Eustace's reading allows for picking up the mouse by the tail and swinging him about mercilessly, in the assumption he would be helpless to resist).[101] A similar subversion of real-world concepts and discourse – also for selfish reasons – is on hand when the heroes encounter his corrupt Sufficiency, governor Gumpas of Doorn. Gumpas represents an unsettling view of the potential future towards which Eustace at that point is headed. If Eustace's (mis-)use of 'republican', 'pacifist' and feminist discourses harms no one except himself (Reepicheep pierces his hand in self-defence), Gumpas uses the terms 'economic development' and 'present burst of prosperity' to justify slavery.[102]

Eustace seems to constantly need to exculpate himself in his diary, but it is not entirely clear why (or to whom) he is justifying himself.[103] One possible interpretation would be to suggest that he is grappling with his own internal conscience – the implied presence of which in these passages foreshadows his redemption on Dragon Island. His self-delusion is emphasized at the beginning of his adventure on that island through the presence of fog, associated with the otherworld in medieval Irish (and Welsh) narratives.[104] The internal debate is not exclusive to Eustace. A more explicit example of justification against internal conscience is present in Lucy's struggle against the temptation of magic spells in Coriakin's house, also marked by a context of limited visibility (Coriakin is supposed

100 Lewis, *Voyage*, pp. 40–41, 72, 79–84, 86–88. In some cases it remains unclear whether Eustace is bending reality to his selfish needs through mis-representing 'facts', or whether his analytical skills are letting him down, leading to cases of spectacularly faulty logic, as in his explanation that 'perspiration really cools people down, so the men would need less water if they were working' (p. 81).

101 Lewis, *Voyage*, pp. 43–44.

102 Lewis, *Voyage*, p. 67.

103 See, for instance, his diary entry in Lewis, *Voyage*, p. 82.

104 Lewis, *Voyage*, pp. 88, 91; Swank, 'The Child's Voyage', p. 81; see also Carey, 'Time, Space and the Otherworld', pp. 2, 4–6 and earlier discussion in Howard Rollin Patch, 'Some Elements in Mediæval Descriptions of the Otherworld', *PMLA*, 33 (1918), 601–43 (p. 627) and list of source references (n. 91). Lewis may well have read Patch's article. For the discussion of the fog, 'mist barrier' in the *Navigatio*, see J. S. Mackley, 'Some Celtic Otherworld Motifs in Brendan's Voyage to Paradise', Paper presented to the International Medieval Congress, Leeds (2010), online archived version <http://nectar.northampton.ac.uk/4949/> [accessed 24 March 2023].

to be invisible, as are the dufflepuds).[105] We will return to this scene in the discussion below. The foregrounding of such an internal voice of conscience is also, arguably, Lewis's new modern addition to the tropological aspect of the *immrama*.

Returning to Eustace's first diary entry, an important element provides context – the additional 'code' of Lotman's reading – for understanding the entire message of Eustace's text. This is in the reference to, and capitalization of, the term 'Fact'.[106] This distinctly echoes the famous opening of Charles Dickens's *Hard Times*: 'Now, what I want is, Facts. Teach these boys and girls nothing but Facts'.[107] I would argue that the reference to the mispurposing of education represented in Dickens's novel echoes in this passage Lewis's own concerns as educator. The additional code carried in the I–I message within the text refers back to Lewis's role as supervisor at Cambridge and his concern with students who are in it for the grades only, like Eustace, who 'didn't care much about any subject for its own sake, he cared a great deal about marks'.[108] Eustace's reality is based on jargon only and is otherwise hollow.[109] A similar negative impression is given by the reference to 'statistics' by corrupt governor Gumpas when challenged, and removed from power, by King Caspian.[110] (Gumpas is, once again, the projection of warning against the future towards which Eustace in his then state of mind and soul, was headed.)

The probable echo of *Hard Times* is one of many intertextual elements in Lewis's book. Among the others, the most obvious is the explicit reference to Shakespeare's *Midsummer Night's Dream*, referred to already.[111] The three sleepers in Chapter 13 are a reference to the legend of the Seven Sleepers.[112]

105 Lewis, *Voyage*, p. 163. For comments on Eustace's and Lucy's educational arcs in the narrative, see also Lawyer, 'Three Celtic Voyages', pp. 331–32; Swank, 'The Child's Voyage', p. 83.

106 Lewis, *Voyage*, p. 40; compare the capitalization of 'Magic' (p. 13).

107 Charles Dickens, *Hard Times*, in Charles Dickens, *Great Expectations and Hard Times* (Bloomsbury: Nonesuch Press, 1937, republished in 2005), p. 489.

108 Lewis, *Voyage*, p. 40. For a discussion of Lewis's teaching, see Poe, *The Completion of C. S. Lewis*, pp. 46–57.

109 There is evidence from Lewis's former students that he was particularly opposed to the use of jargon, and demanded that terminology be defined and explained in layman's terms; Poe, *The Completion of C. S. Lewis*, p. 51.

110 Lewis, *Voyage*, p. 67.

111 Lewis, *Voyage*, p. 161. The brackets are Lewis's.

112 It may be fanciful to see in the lords' names a reference to their (enchanted) fates: Revilian (*reveiller* 'to wake up'); Argoz (seems to echo the Argonauts); Mavramorn (morn = morning). For the medieval legend of the Seven Sleepers, see, for instance,

Like the sleepers in Lewis's tale, who had set out for the distant East on the orders of (and to escape) a tyrannical ruler, the Seven Sleepers of medieval legend had fallen asleep for a miraculously long time as escape from Roman persecution of Christians.[113] Thus, Lewis builds on the *immram* framework with a polyphony of intertextual references. This is also a feature we will see returning throughout the discussion of the other texts in this book. The selected matrix thus intersects with other textual matrices in the ever-evolving (poly)system of literature and culture.

Eustace is not the only one of the three late-comers who goes through a process of education in the story. Edmund had already had his moment of redemption in an earlier Narnia book, where he had played the role filled in the *Voyage* by Eustace.[114] Lucy, however, still has something to learn on the 'Island of the Voices', as she reads the magic book on the request of the unionized monopods in the scene with the internal monologue mentioned above.[115] She resists the temptation of making herself look beautiful, while the reader is treated to a passage describing the possible outcome of the spell.[116] The idea of extraordinary beauty leading to war in Lewis's description invokes the Helen of Troy legend:

> In the third picture the beauty beyond the lot of mortals had come to her. […] She saw herself throned on high at a great tournament in

Hugh Magennis, 'The Anonymous Old English Legend of the Seven Sleepers and its Latin Source', *Leeds Studies in English*, 22 (1991), 43–56; R. M. Liuzza, 'The Future is a Foreign Country: The Legend of the Seven Sleepers and the Anglo-Saxon Sense of the Past', in *Medieval Science Fiction*, ed. by Carl Kears and James Paz (London: King's College London Centre for Late Antique & Medieval Studies, 2016), pp. 61–78; and most recently Megan G. Leitch, *Sleep and its Spaces in Middle English Literature: Emotions, Ethics, Dreams* (Manchester: Manchester University Press, 2021), pp. 47, 58–60, 69, 251.

113 The legend is summarized in Liuzza, 'The Future', pp. 66–67, and analysed from the perspective of the history of time-travel science fiction narratives.

114 Even Edmund, however, has a moment of temptation and recovery (together with Caspian), at the island of the golden water. Edmund's major fall and redemption arc is in *The Lion, the Witch and the Wardrobe*, the first (in order of writing) of Lewis's Narnia novels; for discussion, see, for instance, Jill Ogline, 'Edmund Pevensie and the Character of the Redeemed', *Inklings Forever*, 2 (1999), 48–53. Jeanne Murray Walker describes Edmund in that novel as 'the skeptic, the child of a modern industrial society', words which could be used to describe Eustace also at the beginning of his trajectory; '*The Lion, The Witch and The Wardrobe* as Rite of Passage', *Children's Literature in Education*, 16 (1985), 177–88 (p. 180).

115 Lewis, *Voyage*, pp. 139–83 (pp. 160–68).

116 Lewis, *Voyage*, pp. 161–63.

> Calormen and all the kings of the world fought because of her beauty. After that it turned from tournaments to real wars, and all Narnia and Archenland, Telmar and Calormen, Galma and Terebinthia were laid waste with the fury of the kings and dukes and great lords who fought for her favor.[117]

Although Helen of Troy is not named here, the allusion to beauty causing war is unambiguous.[118] Shocked by the images of war and destruction, Lucy manages not to fall into the temptation, but the following spell proves impossible to resist, and she eavesdrops on two classmates to know what they think of her.[119] As her conversation with Aslan later shows, however, it was not what they thought about her that she learned, but what they said only.[120] Like that of beauty, this spell does not reach beyond the surface. Like Eustace, Lucy makes mistakes but is forgiven. She also, like Eustace, already carries within the potential for improvement, marked by the internal dialogue with her conscience. All three, with Reepicheep, arrive at their destination, the Utter East, the equivalent of Saint Brendan's Promised Land of Saints. The narrator assures the reader of his belief that Reepicheep ultimately reaches Aslan's country, though this is not shown in the book.[121] This is in line with the narrator, on the whole, knowing only as much as he could have learned from the children's eyewitness accounts.[122] The children, as we have already seen, turn back for their spiritual life/journey to continue at home.[123]

The journey of spiritual development, key to the *Navigatio*, is also key to Lewis's story. The sequence of dangers and temptations, urging and facilitating personal growth, accompanied by encouragement (and the occasional chastisement) on the part of Aslan, creates a spiritual journey within the *Voyage* that runs parallel to and is intertwined with the physical progress

117 Lewis, *Voyage*, p. 162.

118 For a discussion of Helen of Troy, and her associations with beauty and conflict, see Ruby Blondell, *Helen of Troy. Beauty, Myth, Devastation* (Oxford: Oxford University Press, 2013). For a discussion of allusions to Helen and her beauty in Lewis's other work, see Ian Storey, 'Classical Allusion in C. S. Lewis' *Till We Have Faces*', *The Chronicle of the Oxford University C. S. Lewis Society*, 4 (2007), 5–20 (p. 8).

119 Lewis, *Voyage*, pp. 163–64.

120 Lewis, *Voyage*, pp. 167–68.

121 Lewis, *Voyage*, p. 252.

122 For echoes of this in *Star Trek*, see below, p. 130.

123 See above, pp. 52, 54.

towards the Utter East. Here, I would argue, Lewis engages in dialogue with the *Navigatio*, which, too, has a similar narrative of challenge-based spiritual development.[124] Lewis's dialogic engagement with his exemplar precludes slavish repetition. Rather, his response to the unforgiving medieval monk is to give his late-comers, the children, a chance to thrive. They stand, in the book, not as an unreachable model like Saint Brendan or the heroic Reepicheep, or warning of punishment like those of the Irish saint's weaker companions, but rather as everyman figures, avatars of the real-life children reading, or being read-to.[125]

Ultimately, the arrival of the *Dawn Treader* at its destination, and the explanations provided by Aslan in the closing sections of the narrative, echo closely the conclusion of Brendan's seven-year voyage at the holy island that he and the monks had set out to find.[126] Here, too, Lewis's engagement with his medieval models is dialogic. A feature of the earlier work translated by Lewis here is the light thrown on the journey itself at its conclusion. Mulligan's summary of the conclusion in the *Navigatio* strikingly applies equally to the *Voyage of the Dawn Treader*: 'Much is illuminated in this conclusion. God does not deliver them to this land until they have witnessed, experienced and learned from the ocean's mysteries. One must study, contemplate and be transformed by the seascape before gaining a view and knowledge of (if not complete access to) the Land of Promise'.[127] One of the echoes of Brendan's *Navigatio* thus found in the conclusion of Lewis's story is the reference to the river isolating the Promised Land of Saints which Brendan and his companions cannot cross, transformed into the river that Aslan says needs to be crossed to arrive at his country.[128] Brendan and his company have to return to their own land first, as do the children in Lewis's book, but whereas Brendan only has the final trip to heaven to look forward to at the end of his life, the children in the *Voyage* must, in Lewis's response, discover Aslan first in his guise in our world, and thus discover Christianity.[129] The response, again, enfolds the reader.

---

124 Moylan, 'Irish Voyages', p. 307.

125 Cf. comments in Swank, 'The Child's Voyage', p. 80.

126 Lewis, *Voyage*, pp. 253–55; see also Mulligan, *A Landscape of Words*, pp. 47–48 for a brief discussion of the arrival at the holy island in the *Navigatio*.

127 Mulligan, *A Landscape of Words*, p. 48.

128 O'Donoghue, *Brendaniana*, p. 174; Lewis, *Voyage*, p. 255. Discussed in Swank, 'The Child's Voyage', pp. 88–89.

129 Compare the discussion of the closing passages of the Brendan narrative, in Moylan, 'Irish Voyages', pp. 308, 314–15. As Moylan points out, the *Navigatio*'s engagement with its readership is originally didactic, gradually shifting in the process of reception

This dialogic engagement exemplifies Lewis's medievalism, which is usually discussed in conjunction with his Christianity and the intentionality of his creative work. Charles Connell, for instance, describes it as follows:

> Lewis clearly offers us a form of medievalism that is both selective and powerful. He does so in an attempt to offer hope for a future that is built upon positive medieval values regarding order in the universe and the spiritual connection between religion, man, and nature. This process of medievalism, of "recreating" the Middle Ages, of helping his readers to walk by starlight through a myth which helps man to understand the "indescribable," is a process that involves "cultural adaptation".[130]

I would like, here, however, to place the accent in the analysis of Lewis's work, as I will also in the following chapter in my analysis of Eco's, on his identity as professional academic medievalist, and as a scholar.[131] Unlike Eco, however, Lewis is usually described primarily as a Christian author and secondly as the author of fairy tales (often interpreted in the much narrower sense as fantasy books for children).[132] His adaptation of the medieval *immram/navigatio* model thus focuses on the tropological (educational) aspect

towards an entertainment function, 'informed by the more open mode of the fantastic' (pp. 309, 311).

130 Charles Connell, 'Reading the Middle Ages: The "Post-Modern" Medievalism of C. S. Lewis', *Sehnsucht: The C.S. Lewis Journal*, 1 (2007), 19–28 (pp. 27–28).

131 Note that Tolkien, for instance, considered Lewis's capacity as a 'critic', at least, a hindrance to his writing; see Lazo, 'A Kind of Midwife', p. 39.

132 See, however, Ward, *Planet Narnia*, pp. 19–20, 26. Edward James, 'Tolkien, Lewis and the Explosion of Genre Fantasy', in *The Cambridge Companion to Fantasy Literature*, ed. by Edward James and Farah Mendehlson (Cambridge: Cambridge University Press, 2012), pp. 62–78 (p. 62). The work of Lewis's contemporary fellow fantasy writer J. R. R. Tolkien, by contrast, is frequently discussed in light of his academic interests. See, for instance, Jane Chance, ed., *Tolkien the Medievalist* (London and New York: Routledge, 2003); Kelly Ann Fitzpatrick, *Neomedievalism, Popular Culture, and the Academy. From Tolkien to Game of Thrones* (Cambridge: D. S. Brewer, 2019), pp. 52–60. A discussion of Tolkien's work remains outside the scope of the present book, but it is worth noting that Kris Swank has argued that Tolkien's *Roverandom* was constructed based on Old Irish *immrama*; 'The Irish Otherworld Voyage of *Roverandom*', *Tolkien Studies*, 12 (2015), 31–57. Tolkien also composed a poem entitled 'Imram' and based explicitly on the Brendan legend; for more, see Norma Roche, 'Sailing West: Tolkien, the Saint Brendan Story, and the Idea of Paradise in the West', *Mythlore*, 17 (1991), 16–20. As Baxter observes, Lewis himself objected to the classification of fairy-tales as stories for children; Baxter, *The Medieval Mind*, p. 84; but see also Poe, *The Completion of C. S. Lewis*, pp. 102, 106.

and adds, in dialogic engagement with his source, a note of hope for individual growth. Lewis the medievalist updates the medieval source with a positive message encoded by Lewis the Oxbridge supervisor (=educator) and Lewis the Christian thinker.[133]

The fictional world in which Lewis sets his journey – as his vision of the world in which the reader experiences it – is a stable and reassuring one, in line with his preference for the medieval 'discarded image' over the disturbing and unstable literary world of modernity and modernism.[134] By contrast with Lewis, as we will see in the following chapter, Eco's postmodern sensibilities allow him to discern the inconsistencies in the fabric woven by the medieval sources and employ these in new combinations so as to amplify these cracks in the textual reality (and in the reader's sense of their own reality as a side-effect).[135] I use the term 'postmodern' in relation to Eco in full cognizance of the fact that the label carries with it a significant amount of cultural baggage, not all of which goes well with Eco's novels. As has been pointed out by Rocco Capozzi, the label 'postmodern' has been used for Eco's opus rather for the sake of 'convenience or for lack of any other definition' than for any fundamental generic reason.[136] Capozzi's own term, 'encyclopedia superfictions' fits the multivalent and sprawling erudition of Eco's novels much better.[137] My use of the term 'postmodern' throughout the discussion therefore relates rather to the conceptual gulf that Lewis draws between pre-modern and modern works. Lewis belongs to the medieval world-view, with its stable reality, while Eco, discussed in the following chapter, engages in a counter-intuitive activity of not so much world-building in the novel as world-deconstructing outside it.[138]

---

133 For the importance of Lewis's role as educator to his creative output, see Hart, *Through the Open Door*, pp. 74–120.

134 Lewis, 'De descriptione'; see above, pp. 58–62.

135 First published as Umberto Eco, *Baudolino* (Milan: Bompiani, 2000); trans. William Weaver (London, Vintage, 2003). From this point onwards when referring to or quoting this work, I refer to the Italian edition as Eco, *Baudolino*, followed by reference to the English translation as 'trans. Weaver'.

136 Rocco Capozzi, 'Knowledge and Cognitive Practices in Eco's Labyrinths of Intertextuality', in *Literary Philosophers. Borges, Calvino, Eco*, ed. by Jorge J. E. Garcia, Carolyn Korsmeyer and Rudolphe Gasché (New York and London: Routledge, 2002), pp. 165–84 (p. 177).

137 Capozzi, 'Knowledge', pp. 167, 177.

138 A contrastive reading of Lewis and Eco is also invited by the title of one of the chapters in Coletti's book on Eco's *Name of the Rose*, 'Allegory of Love', which echoes Lewis's book of the same name; Coletti, *Naming the Rose*, pp. 39–72; Lewis, *The Allegory of Love*.

CHAPTER 3

Umberto Eco, 'Reality' and Prester John

Umberto Eco's *Baudolino* has been discussed from a variety of perspectives, but not yet hitherto as an heir to, or as an example of the reception of, the Old Irish travel narratives. Nevertheless, though lacking a sea-journey and therefore less obviously indebted to the *immram* framework, it can be categorised as an heir of the tradition, strongly leaning towards the *echtrai*, with elements of *immrama*.

As pointed out by Oskamp, *echtrai* do not have to involve travel on water, and thus both in terms of the focus on a single otherworld land, and in terms of the land-bound journey, the eastward journey in Umberto Eco's *Baudolino* is more of an *echtra* narrative.[1] While we know that Eco was heavily inspired by medieval travel narratives, and used a liberal helping of imagery derived from Marco Polo and from the medieval encyclopedic tradition, amongst the myriad of other sources that constitute *Baudolino*'s eclectic intertextual matrix, there is no direct evidence for Eco's use of Irish vernacular sources.[2] He is demonstrably, however, fascinated by the Latin *Navigatio*. My classification of *Baudolino* as an *echtra* narrative is, therefore, a largely taxonomic exercise. It will, however, within the frame of this book, as I hope to show, yield interesting results in bringing to light additional layers of meaning for this text and for the texts alongside which it is read.

An important starting point for this investigation is that *immrama* and *echtrai* are referred to in the narrative itself, making part of the rich intertextual tapestry woven by Eco the medievalist. I would like to begin this discussion by examining the most obvious reasons for seeing Eco's text as part of the reception history of Old Irish literary traditions. The evidence

1 Oskamp, *The Voyage of Máel Dúin*, p. 43.

2 A similar intertextual matrix, though involving a variety of other texts, can be posited for Italo Calvino's *Le città invisibili*. Marco Polo's influence on the text has been explored by Martin McLaughlin, but the invisibility theme also carries a strong echo of Lucian's invisible peoples; Martin McLaughlin, 'Calvino's Rewriting of Marco Polo: From the 1960s Screenplay to *Invisible Cities*', *Marco Polo and the Encounter of East and West*, ed. by Suzanne Conklin Akbari, and Amilcare Ianucci, with John Tulk (Toronto, Buffalo and London: University of Toronto Press, 2008), pp. 182–200.

 | DOI:10.1163/9789004734548_004

comes from a passage which, as an example of intertextual weave, is worth quoting *in extenso* for the purposes of analysis:

> Dunque il ragazzo si chiamava Abdul, come appunto un moro, ma era nato da una madre che veniva dalla Hibernia, e questo spiegava quei capelli rossi, perché tutti quelli che vengono da quell'isola sperduta sono fatti così, e la fama li vuole bizzarri e sognatori. Il padre era provenzale, di una famiglia che si era installata oltremare dopo la conquista di Gerusalemme, cinquanta e più anni prima. Come Abdul tentava di spiegare, questi nobili franchi dei regni d'oltremare, avevano assunto i costumi dei popoli che avevano conquistato [...]. Ragione per la quale un hibernico (a metà), coi capelli rossi, veniva chiamato Abdul, e aveva il viso bruciato dal sole di quella Siria dove era nato. Pensava in arabo, e in provenzale si raccontava le antiche saghe dei mari gelati del Nord, udite dalla madre sua.[3]
>
> (The boy's name was Abdul, a Moor's name, in fact, but he was born of a mother who came from Hibernia, and this explained the red hair, because all those who come from that remote island are like that, and according to report, they are bizarre, dreamers. His father was Provençal, of a family that had settled overseas after the conquest of Jerusalem, some fifty years before. As Abdul tried to explain, those Frankish nobles had adopted the customs of the peoples they had conquered. [...] For which reason a half-Hibernian with red hair, could be called Abdul and could have a face burned by the sun of Syria, where he was born. He thought in Arabic, and in Provençal he told the ancient sagas of the frozen seas of the north, which he had heard from his mother.)[4]

This passage is so multi-layered and multi-stranded that it is impossible to do full justice to its complexity within the space available here. I will therefore focus on the Irish strands. The term 'Hibernia' is used in line with Baudolino's tendency to use the 'international standard' medieval Latin names for locations, and is thus medieval. The reference to the Irish as, according to hearsay, 'dreamers', is a nod not to the medieval but to

3 Eco, *Baudolino*, pp. 73–74.
4 Eco, *Baudolino*, trans. Weaver, p. 69

(early) modern preconceptions.[5] Later on Abdul's chief characteristic becomes his love for a princess whom he had only seen in a dream – a feature familiar form medieval Irish narratives of the *aisling* genre.[6] In the Old Irish genre system, an *aisling* is a narrative wherein, to borrow Geraldine Parsons' description, 'an encounter with the supernatural that is initiated when a protagonist, invariably male, is dreaming or in a comparable state of altered consciousness'.[7] Usually, a (male) protagonist, while asleep (or in a differently-induced vision state, as Parsons points out), sees the vision of a beautiful woman.[8] He promptly falls in love with her, and the rest of the narrative, once he is in a waking state, is concerned with a search for this loved-one. Later, the reader learns that Abdul had first seen his love in a vision induced by drugs, thus in an altered mind-state, and has since become convinced that her existence is real. His entire life is dedicated to this love. The characterization as 'dreamer' echoes both modern preconceptions and medieval Irish literary tradition, and is reflected in Abdul's figure later in the narrative.

The phrase 'antiche saghe dei mari gelati del Nord' ('ancient sagas of the frozen seas of the North') in the first instance also seems to refer back to Irish literature, and specifically to the *immrama*, as the island-hopping narratives. Given the ambiguities in the delineation of the *immram/echtra*

---

5 For comments on the stereotyping of the Irish as 'dreamers', see, for instance, Richard Kerney, 'Poetry, Language and Identity: A Note on Seamus Heaney', *Studies: An Irish Quarterly Review*, 75 (1986), 552–63. The stereotypes in question date back to the nineteenth century. The topic is too extensive to be treated here, but see, for instance, Terence Brown, 'Cultural Nationalism, Celticism and the Occult', in *Celticism*, ed. by Terence Brown (Amsterdam and Atlanta: Rodopi, 1996), pp. 221–30; Gerard Carruthers and Alan Rawes, 'Introduction: Romancing the Celt', in *English Romanticism and the Celtic World*, ed. by Gerard Carruthers and Alan Rawes (Cambridge: Cambridge University Press, 2003), pp. 1–19.

6 For an introduction to the medieval genre, see Geraldine Parsons, '*Aisling* (Vision)', in *The Encyclopedia of Medieval Literature in Britain*, ed. by Siân Echard and Robert Rouse (Wiley Online Library, 2017), n.p. <https://doi.org/10.1002/9781118396957.wbemlb067>; and Jisca Harder, '"For As Often As He Slept": A Comparative Analysis of Medieval Insular Vernacular Dream-Narratives', unpublished RMA thesis, Utrecht University, 2022 <https://studenttheses.uu.nl/handle/20.500.12932/42282> [accessed 24 March 2024]. The genre is further discussed in Chapter 5 below, pp. 149–51.

7 Parsons, '*Aisling*'.

8 For more, see, for example, Nicole Johanna Bernartina Volmering, 'Medieval Irish Vision Literature: A Genre Study', unpublished PhD thesis, University College Cork, 2014. A typical example is the *Aislinge Óenguso* 'Dream of Oengus', discussed, for instance, in Sarah Michie, 'The Lover's Malady in Early Irish Romance' *Speculum*, 12 (1937), 285–419 (pp. 307–08). This is discussed further below in Chapter 5, p. 150.

genres discussed in the introduction above, it may also be taken as a generalized reference to both. Despite the dual reference to the vernacular (it is in Provençal that Abdul tells these stories which he heard from his mother presumably either in Provençal or in Irish) Eco here probably is thinking in particular of the Latinate branch of the tradition and the *Navigatio*, which was translated into multiple languages and to which he returned in multiple discussions.[9] In *Baudolino*, Saint Brendan is mentioned by name in a brief summary of the *Navigatio* given by Abdul: 'Quell'uomo virtuoso che visse nella mia isola e che fu San Brandano, ha navigato per mare sino agli ultimi confini della terra, e ha scoperto un'isola tutta coperta di uve mature, alcune azzurre, altre viola e altre bianche, con sette fontane miracolose e sette chiese …' ('That virtuous man who came from my island, Saint Brendan, sailed the seas to the farthest confines of the earth, and discovered an island all covered with ripe grapes, some blue, some purple, others white, with seven miraculous fountains and seven churches …')[10] Abdul proceeds to enumerate the precious stones from which these churches are made. Saint Brendan is mentioned again by Baudolino who recounts the giant fish island (Jasconius) episode to Deacon John when telling him about the marvels of the West.[11]

In this chapter, I argue that the Irish voyage narrative tradition, and the *Navigatio* specifically, is present in the background of *Baudolino* in multiple ways. I also argue that because of the translatory changes undertaken by Eco in transforming the influences of the Irish sea-voyage tale into his postmodern fantastic narrative of overland travel to the mythical East, the resulting novel shifts between the Old Irish genres, landing in the realm of the *echtrai*.

9 Eco discusses and quotes the *Navigatio*, for example, in *Storia delle terre e dei luoghi leggendari* (Milan: Bompiani, 2013), pp. 154–56, 173–75; Umberto Eco, 'Why the Island is Never Found' in Eco, *Inventing the Enemy and Other Occasional Writings*, trans. by Richard Dixon (Boston and New York: Houghton Mifflin Harcourt, 2012), pp. 192–216 (pp. 193, 198–99). Eco cites the discussion in Alessandro Scafi, *Il paradiso in terra. Mappe del giardino dell'Eden* (Milan: Bruno Mondadori, 2007), pp. 41–42, in the original English Alessandro Scafi, *Mapping Paradise. A History of Heaven on Earth* (Chicago: Chicago University Press, 2006), pp. 52–53.

10 Eco, *Baudolino*, p. 103; trans. Weaver, p. 98.

11 Eco, *Baudolino*, p. 411, trans. Weaver, p. 405; for the episode, see O'Meara's translation in O'Meara and Wooding, 'The Latin Version' pp. 34–35. Like the *aisling*, this, too, resurfaces in the *Star Trek* texts; see discussion of the reference in the *Star Trek: Voyager* episode below, pp. 154–55.

Before we begin the analysis itself, it is worth remarking that the Irish references in *Baudolino* are not limited to the modern stereotypes of the 'dreamy Celt' and the internationalized Brendan legend. In the context of the discussion of the languages of Babel, reference is made to the origin legend of the Irish language: according to Abdul, his mother had told him that:

> la lingua di Adamo è stata ricostruita nella sua isola, ed è la lingua gaelica, composta di nove parti del discorso, tante quante furono i nove materiali di cui era composta la torre di Babele [...]. Furono i settantadue saggi della scuola di Fenius a costruire la lingua gaelica usando frammenti di tutte le settantadue favelle nate dopo la confusione delle lingue, e per questo il gaelico contiene ciò che c'è di meglio in ogni lingua ...[12]

> (the language of Adam was reconstructed on her island, and it is the Gaelic language, composed of nine parts of speech, the same number as the nine materials from which the tower of Babel was built [...]. It was the seventy-two sages from the school of Phenius, who constructed the Gaelic language, using fragments of all the seventy-two tongues born after the confusion of tongues, and for this reason Gaelic contains what is best in every language ...)[13]

This discussion builds largely on Eco's own fascination with the idea of the perfect language. The legend recounted here is that preserved in the *Auraicept na nÉces* ('the scholar's primer'/'the poets' primer') – a text originating from the seventh century – and the *Lebor Gabála Érenn* ('book of invasions'/'book of the takings of Ireland'), amongst other sources.[14] The *Auraicept na nÉces* represents the earliest vernacular equivalent of a Latin grammar book.[15] In the introduction to this text, it contextualises the

12 Eco, *Baudolino*, p. 134.

13 Eco, *Baudolino*, trans. Weaver, p. 127.

14 For discussions, see, for instance, Caitríona Ó Dochartaigh, 'Language and Identity in Early Medieval Ireland', *Études Irlandaises*, 27 (2002), 119–31; Paul Russell, '"What Was Best of Every Language": the Early History of the Irish Language', in *A New History of Ireland 1: Prehistoric and Early Ireland*, ed. by Dáibhí Ó Cróinín (Oxford: Oxford University Press, 2005), pp. 405–50. Ó Dochartaigh refers also to an eleventh-century poem in the Book of Leinster, which cites the legend; 'Language and Identity' (p. 128). For more legendary language-creation material connected with the name of Fénius, see Roisin McLaughlin, 'Fénius Farsaid and the Alphabets', *Ériu*, 59 (2009), 1–24.

15 Ó Dochartaigh, 'Language and Identity', pp. 125–26.

study of the Irish language by presenting an account of its creation at the tower of Babel by Fénius Farsaid (erroneously rendered in the English translation of Eco's novel as *Phenius*) from *a mba ferr íarum do cach bérlu 7 a mba leithiu 7 a mba caímiu, is ed do·reped isin nGoídilc* ('what was best then of every language and what was widest and finest was cut out into Irish').[16] The aspect of 'linguistic confidence and pride' highlighted by Caitríona Ó Dochartaigh in her discussion of the passage, is also a significant aspect of Eco's rendering, in the context of the characters' discussion of the language of Adam.[17]

Eco also discusses the Irish case in *Serendipities* with explicit reference to the *Auraicept*, citing there in particular the passage that relates the parts of speech in the Irish language to the materials used in the Tower of Babel, which he picks up again in the *Baudolino* passage quoted above.[18] Eco's fascination with this story of the Irish language is visible in his wording, which carries some traces of the mystic perception of the 'Celt': 'This first-born and consequently supernatural language retained traces of its original isomorphism with the created world. As long as the proper order of its elements was respected, this ensured a sort of natural link between names and things'.[19] Whilst scholars of medieval Ireland usually see in this legend evidence for language-based identity creation, or concerns with language status (particularly in relation to Latin), and the positioning of Ireland in relation to Biblical history (in which it does not feature), Eco underlines the 'supernatural' aspect of this man-made language.[20]

In *Baudolino*, the dialogue between Rabbi Solomon and the Irishman Abdul from which the passage quoted above comes, represents the two alternatives formulated by Eco in *Serendipities* in terms of medieval attitudes to the lost ideal Adamic language. On the one hand, the ones who, like the medieval Irish, 'looked ahead, aiming to fabricate a rational language

16 Anders Ahlquist, ed., *The Early Irish Linguist: An Edition of the Canonical Part of the* Auraicept na n'Eces (Helsinki: Societas scientiarum fennica, 1982), pp. 47–48; text quoted from p. 48.

17 Ó Dochartaigh, 'Language and Identity'; Eco, *Baudolino*, pp. 133–35; trans. Weaver, pp. 126–28.

18 Eco, *Serendipities. Language and Lunacy*, translated by William Weaver (London: Phoenix, 1999 [1998]), pp. 36–37.

19 Eco, *Serendipities*, p. 37.

20 Ó Dochartaigh, 'Language and Identity', for example. See also Máire Ní Mhaonaigh, 'The Peripheral Centre: Writing History on the Western "Fringe"', *Interfaces: A Journal of Medieval European Literatures*, 4 (2017), 59–84 (p. 60) <https://doi.org/10.13130/INTERFACES-04-05>.

possessing the perfection of the lost speech of Eden', and on the other, those who 'tried to discover the lost language spoken by Adam'.[21] This duality also represents a duality in Eco's representation of the journey of Prester John, through re-construction (through Baudolino, and based on genuine medieval sources), and fictionalized creation (also through Baudolino, but in his capacity of creator of fables).

3.1 Creating and Following the Footsteps of Saint Brendan

Eco's work 'to reconstruct the visual atmosphere of that historical moment' in each of his novels, relies on a combination of tools and knowledge from the disciplines of translation, semiotics, and in the case of his medievalist novels *The Name of the Rose* and *Baudolino* also medieval studies.[22] *Baudolino* represents a form of reception (and transmission) of the Old Irish travel narratives in Eco's dual translation of the *Navigatio*.

It is something of a commonplace now to note the close link between the medieval Irish travel narratives, particularly the religious voyages of the *Navigatio* type, with real-life practice of *peregrinatio pro amore Dei* ('pilgrimage for the love of God').[23] The original Irish sea-voyages can be seen as

---

21 Eco, *Serendipities*, p. 38. Eco presents no hierarchy between the two options, either in *Serendipities*, or in *Baudolino*. By contrast, Paul Russell characterises Irish as a 'close second' to the 'language of Paradise'; Russell, 'What Was Best of Every Language', p. 405.

22 Eco, 'To See Things and Texts', p. 111. See also Thomas Stauder's interview with Eco about Baudolino: 'Un colloquio con Umberto Eco intorno a *Baudolino*', *Il lettore di provincia*, 110 (2001), 3–14; reprinted in Thomas Stauder, *Colloqui con Umberto Eco. Come nascono i romanzi* (Milano: La nave di Teseo, 2024).

23 See, most recently Angélica Varandas, 'The Sacred Space of Gods and Saints: Some Considerations About the Sea and Exile in Irish Mythology and Tradition' in *Creating through Mind and Emotions*, ed. by Mário S. Ming Kong and Maria do Rosário Monteiro (Boka Raton and London: CIC Press and Taylor and Francis, 2022), pp. 423–28. See also Kathleen Hughes, 'The Changing Theory and Practice of Irish Pilgrimage', *Journal of Ecclesiastical History*, 11 (1960), 143–51; Thomas M. Charles-Edwards, 'The Social Background to Irish *Peregrinatio*', *Celtica*, 11 (1976), 43–59 and Arnold Angenendt 'Die irische *Peregrinatio* und ihre Auswirkungen auf dem Kontinent vor dem Jahre 800', in *Die Iren und Europa im früheren Mittelalter*, ed. by Heinz Löwe, 2 vols (Stuttgart: Klett-Cotta, 1982), I, pp. 52–79; Sobecki, 'From the *désert liquide* to the Sea of Romance', pp. 195, 199–200; Carey, 'Voyage Literature', p. 1745. The fact that his discussion of the Irish pilgrims washed ashore at King Alfred's court Sobecki invokes the image of the Magi in itself forms another example of the cross-pollination of the different traditions.

anchoritic exercises, heavily inspired by the ascetic withdrawal from the world of the desert fathers, seeking *in mari herimum*.[24] Moylan sees the narratives of island-voyages as the precursors of an utopian discourse.[25] If, to borrow Michael Cronin's apt turn of phrase, 'By substituting the waves of the ocean for the wastes of the desert, the Irish were able to effect a geographical translation that legitimized an odyssey of exile and spiritual renewal in a very different setting', Eco re-translates the exercise by having Baudolino finish his journey(s) as a stylite (the pillar in the desert becoming in turn his island in the sea).[26]

In addition to the heremitic aspect, the importance of the process of the journey to the novel, discussed further below, also aligns *Baudolino* with *immram* narratives.[27] If read as an *immram*, *Baudolino*'s tropological aspect needs to be addressed. It is most obviously present in the discussion of difference and bias among the races inhabiting the Kingdom of Prester John. These people and their inability to see physical differences, coupled with disproportionate attention to differences in dogma and interpretation, hold up a curved mirror not only to Baudolino and his companions but to Eco's readers and their world.[28] Baudolino summarises this early on:

For more on the Magi, in the context of *Baudolino* and the voyage into the land of Prester John, see below, pp. 104–5.

24 See, for instance, in Charles-Edwards, 'The Social Background', and Westley Follett, 'An Allegorical Interpretation of the Monastic Voyage Narratives in Adomnán's *Vita Columbae*', *Eolas. The Journal of the American Society of Irish Medieval Studies*, 2 (2007), 4–27 (pp. 12–14) for discussion of medieval Irish authors' terminology borrowed from the earlier eremitic practice in descriptions of Irish sea-voyages.

25 Moylan, 'Irish Voyages', pp. 301–02. For more on utopias, see below, pp. 122–29.

26 Cronin, *Translation*, p. 15. The text quoted here is part of Cronin's discussion of a fourteenth-century Venetian translation of the *Navigatio*, which, like Eco in the journey to the land of Prester John, shifts the focus of the journey narrative by expanding the description of the place of arrival (p. 16). Baudolino becomes a stylite in Chapter 39 of Eco's novel. For a brief introduction to the stylites, see Simon Yarrow, *Saints. A Short History* (Oxford: Oxford University Press, 2016), pp. 29–30. In connection to the Irish precursors of *Baudolino* it is significant that Yarrow maps medieval pilgrimage practices generally, and crusading in particular, as belonging to the afterlife of the Irish pilgrimage traditions (p. 60).

27 See below, pp. 98–109.

28 See, for instance, Eco, *Baudolino*, pp. 376, 381–82; trans. Weaver, pp. 369, 374–75. For discussion, see, for instance, Merecer, 'Truth and Lies', pp. 21–23; Hannah Priest, '"Oh, the funnies, the funnies": The Medieval Monstrous Races in *The Voyage of the Dawn Treader* and *Baudolino*', in *Our Monstrous (S)kin: Blurring the Boundaries Between Monsters and Humanity*, ed. by Sorcha Ní Fhlainn (Oxford: Interdisciplinary Press, 2009). See also Farronato, 'Umberto Eco's *Baudolino*'.

> Amici, [...] Mi pare evidente che le varie razze esistenti in questa provincia non danno alcuna importanza alle differenze del corpo, al colore, alla forma, come facciamo noi [...] E invece, come d'altra parte molti dei nostri sapienti, danno molta importanza alle differenze delle idee sulla natura del Cristo, o sulla Santissima Trinità...[29]
>
> ('Friends [...] it seems obvious to me that the various races existing in this province give no importance to bodily differences, to color or shape, as we do [...] But instead, like many of our learned men, for that matter, they attach great importance to the difference of ideas about Christ, or the Most Holy Trinity ...')[30]

This constitutes a defamiliarised view both of the emphasis of the physical difference and that of religious differences of opinion. Such techniques are attested also in other texts in our corpus, most notably in *Star Trek*.[31] The otherworldly inhabitants, like *immram* islands, function as moralising messages for the reader.

One can also playfully assign to Baudolino's journey to the East the label of *echtra*, defined by Dumville as '"(an) outing" [...] a human excursion into supernatural territory'.[32] An important addition to this definition that is relevant to *Baudolino* is: 'Otherworld music, a fairy-woman, the magic branch, and the journey to the otherworld, not to mention the description of the pleasures of this supernatural land, are all features of the *echtrai* and occur variously elsewhere in the Irish secular literary tradition. It is the secular literature of which the *echtrai* are a part.'[33] The only crucial distinction between Eco's novel and the Old Irish narratives is that the quite solidly 'real' (in the narrative world) Irish otherworld is replaced in *Baudolino* with the fantastical world of the main character's imagination. Whether it exists or not is unclear, and the boundaries between the real and the imaginary are blurred (not only for the reader, but for both Baudolino the narrator and for

29 Eco, *Baudolino*, p. 376.

30 Eco, *Baudolino*, trans. Weaver, p. 369.

31 One thinks in particular of the much-discussed example of the bi-coloured aliens in the 1969 *Star Trek: Original Series* episode 'Let That Be Your Last Battlefield' (Season 3 Episode 15).

32 Dumville, '*Echtrae* and *Immram*', p. 73. Dumville discusses in detail the distinction between *echtrae* and *immram*. This distinction is also drawn by Vivien Mercier, *Irish Comic Tradition*, p. 16, citing Miles Dillon, *Early Irish Literature*, p. 104.

33 Dumville, '*Echtrae and Immram*', p. 74.

his in-story audience Niketas). It is still a fantasy world, and in that sense an 'other' world, but it is no longer an independently existing realm. It represents, in Eco's own analysis, his pervasive interest in 'narrative universes' which 'constitute an *Ersatz*, or rather, a substitute for the world' and thus permit us to explore the processes of understanding the world in which we live.[34]

A health warning is necessary when drawing such parallels. As John Carey points out, the invitation to the otherworld issued by a fairy woman in the *echtrai* tradition is found in two tales: *Immram Brain* and in *Echtrae Chonnlai*, which might share a source for this feature.[35] In other words, this might not be a general feature of the tradition, but rather belong to a small branch, ultimately deriving from one text. In Eco's novel, the invitation is not issued by a fairy woman, though there are two figures who fulfil parts of the function she has in the *echtrai*: Abdul's imaginary princess calls to him from the Orient and this love motivates him to seek the kingdom of Prester John, and Baudolino finds an otherworldly love at the end of that journey in Hypatia.[36] In the case of the medieval Irish *echtra* narratives one has to consider issues of direct influence, borrowing, and possible common sources. In the case of *Baudolino*, the issue of influence is complicated by the author's own views, which feed into both his creative work and its possible interpretations.

Any analysis of Eco's work that places it within an intertextual matrix and therefore touches, even tangentially, on the vexed issue of literary inspirations, must take into account Eco's own views on the matter of influence, also in light of his responses to analyses of his own work.[37] For Eco, influences can be direct, indirect, and even unconscious, and the study of influence of one author or work on another would have to take into account also 'culture, the chain of previous influences' and 'the Zeitgeist', which we can for the sake of a synchronic analysis combine under the unifying umbrella term 'ambient culture'.[38] According to Eco, there are several categories of relationship with prior texts: 'in the course of my fictional work critics have

34 See also 'A Response by Eco', in *Illuminating Eco: On the Boundaries of Interpretation*, ed. by Charlotte Ross and Rochelle Sibley (London and New York: Routledge, 2016; first published London: Ashgate, 2004), pp. 193–99 (p. 194).

35 Carey, 'The Location', p. 115.

36 Hypatia dominates chapters 33 and 34 of *Baudolino*.

37 While Eco returns to the issue in various writings, the most concise treatment of the subject is to be found in his 'Borges'. See also 'A Response by Eco'.

38 Eco, 'Borges', pp. 119, 120.

found influences of which I was totally conscious, others that could not possibly have been influences because I had never known the source, and still others that astonished me but that I then found convincing'.[39] In the case of medieval influences on Eco's work, and the multiplicity of layered meanings in his novels, the argument can be – and indeed has been – made that these are 'totally conscious' and informed by Eco's professional identity as medievalist and theoretical-ideological attitudes towards meaning and its conveyance, tied to his professional identity as semiotician.[40]

Coletti points out that 'One major achievement of *The Name of the Rose* is its detailed representation of the congruence between medieval and (post)modern language theory'.[41] This congruence is part of Eco's own experience as an academic working on both subjects. Whilst it would present too much of a digression from the subject at hand to explore the possibility in depth, it is worth making the observation here that because of Eco's influence on the discipline of semiotics, it is conceivable that it was his work on the combination of the two subjects that in fact caused the 'congruence' referred to by Coletti in the first place. One could make a similar argument regarding some of the major themes that have been identified in *Baudolino* by previous scholarship.[42] One (to which we shall return in 3.3 below) is the lie or fictionalised reality.[43] Irony is a crucial component therein, and this will therefore be addressed first.

---

39 Eco, 'Borges', p. 120.

40 There are too many discussions of this issue to reproduce a comprehensive bibliography here. See, for example, Theresa Coletti, *Naming the Rose*; Peter Bondanella, *Umberto Eco and the Open Text: Semiotics, Fiction, Popular Culture* (Cambridge: Cambridge University Press, 1997), ch. 1; Christina Farronato, *Eco's Chaosmos: From the Middle Ages to Postmodernity* (Toronto, Buffalo and London: University of Toronto Press, 2003); studies in Erik Schilling, ed., *Umberto Eco Handbuch. Leben – Werk – Wirkung* (Stuttgart and Berlin: J. B. Metzler and Springer, 2021). There is a parallel between Eco and Lewis here, since there is a similar influence of Lewis's medievalist profession and his theological interests on his literary output discussed in Chapter 2.

41 Coletti, 'Eco's Middle Ages and the Historical Novel', p. 73.

42 Indeed, as Coletti points out, in *Baudolino*, 'Once again, representation of medieval history and culture enables Eco to articulate in fiction his theoretical and philosophical interests'; 'Eco's Middle Ages and the Historical Novel', p. 74. For a recent overview, see Susanne Friede, 'Baudolino' in *Umberto Eco Handbuch. Leben – Werk – Wirkung*, ed. by Erik Schilling (Stuttgart and Berlin: J. B. Metzler and Springer, 2021), pp. 189–95.

43 See, for example, Mercer, 'Truth and Lies'; Mohamed Bernoussi, 'Baudolino, une fascination sémiotique pour le mensonge', *Cahiers de Narratologie*, 22 (2018) <https://doi.org/10.4000/narratologie.8216>.

Reading Eco's *Baudolino* as a medievalist, one of the most striking features one encounters is what Eco himself terms 'intertextual irony', defined as 'a way to make a second verbal text visible, or detectable, through a first one'.[44] Since this plays such a major role in that particular aspect of *Baudolino* that interests us here, it is worth quoting Eco in full on the subject of this technique:

> 'Intertextual irony is a strategy by which an author makes non-explicit allusions to other works, and in doing so creates a double effect: (i) naive readers, who do not understand the reference, enjoy the text as if they were receiving its message for the first time [...]; (ii) competent readers catch the quotation, and they sense that it is ironic, especially if the quoted situation or sentence changes its sense and implies a sort of debasement. This procedure has been defined as *double coding*'.[45]

Important to this post-modern strategy is the distinction that Eco emphasizes should be drawn between 'a naive reading as an accident (due to lack of information on the part of the reader) from a naive reading programmed as legitimate by the author, even though a cultivated reading is equally admitted'.[46] Eco both theorises here and practises (in his novels) this technique of double coding and intertextual irony, but it is important to take him in context of other modern authors who do this also and who provide a cultural context and backdrop for both Eco's understanding and his practice of the technique. This playful engagement with and of the reader at multiple levels is a feature highly reminiscent also of Jorge Louis Borges.[47] Indeed,

---

44 Eco, 'To See Things and Texts', p. 114.

45 Eco, 'To See Things and Texts', p. 114. The italics are Eco's.

46 Eco, 'To See Things and Texts', p. 115. The brackets are Eco's.

47 Ireland and the Irish also feature in Borges. The subject deserves a separate study in its own right. See, for example, Jorge Luis Borges, 'La forma de la espada', where an Irishman states that for him and his companions in 1922, 'Irlanda no solo era [...] el porvenir utópico y el intolerable presente; era una amarga y cariñosa mitología' (Ireland was not only [...] the utopian future and the intolerable present; it was a bitter and beloved mythology), Borges, *Ficciones* (Madrid: Alianza Editorial, 1999), p. 139 (my translation). See also Borges's discussion of Swift in Borges, 'Jonathan Swift: Viajes de Gulliver', in Borges, *Biblioteca personal* (Madrid: Alianza Editorial, 2000), pp. 134–35. For references to Borges's fascination with the Irish, see also the interview published as Seamus Heaney and Richard Kerney, 'Borges and the World of Fiction: An Interview with Jorge Luis Borges', *The Crane Bag*, 6 (1982), 71–78 (pp. 75–76).

Eco mentions Borges's discussion of the imaginary translation of *Don Quixote* by Pierre Menard in the eponymous story.[48]

In the same essay Eco refers to James Joyce, who practiced the same technique – much to the frustration of many a reader. According to Eco:

> In Joyce's *Ulysses* there are two levels of sense (the story of Bloom as an allegory of the story of Ulysses), but Joyce wanted his readers to discover the double reading in some way, and the title itself is the clue. It is a waste of time to read *Finnegan's Wake* and to miss its patchwork of ultraviolet allusion to the whole of human culture. The readers who read or listen to it as though they were enjoying pure music can undoubtedly be charmed by the sounds and rhythms but are not really reading what Joyce wrote.[49]

Eco reads Joyce as a medievalist, used to the philological and hermeneutic analysis of medieval text. In the preceding paragraph he mentions Dante and the four senses of interpretation, including the allegorical, which is a crucial way of reading the *Divine Comedy* (unless maybe, Eco suggests, one is a 'surrealist poet').[50] Although Eco emphasizes the difference between allegorical reading and intertextual irony or double coding, the habit of the former inevitably colours his appreciation for the latter. Interestingly, the double-coding in *Ulysses* may include also a nod towards the *immram* tradition.[51]

To appreciate just how much this awareness of the coexistence of multiple levels of reading coming from his identity as medievalist influences Eco as literary theoretician and practician of postmodern literature, it suffices to

48 Eco, 'To See Things and Texts', p. 116. For a more general, and deeper engagement of Eco with Borges, see Eco, 'Borges'. For the story in question, see Jorge Luis Borges, 'Pierre Menard, autor del Quijote', in Borges, *Ficciones*, pp. 41–55. The story was first published in 1939. For reference to Borges's influence on Eco, see also Coletti, *Naming the Rose*, p. 15; Capozzi, 'Knowledge', pp. 169–70; Wladimir Krysinski, 'Borges, Calvino, Eco: The Philosophies of Metafiction', in *Literary Philosophers. Borges, Calvino, Eco*, ed. by Jorge J. E. Garcia, Carolyn Korsmeyer and Rudolphe Gasché (New York and London: Routledge, 2002), pp. 185–204, and other essays in the same volume.

49 Eco, 'To See Things and Texts', p. 115. The brackets are Eco's. The connection between *Ulysses* and the *immram* traditionis a topic worth exploring, but its complexity and extent makes it unmanageable for the scope of the present study. See, however, also Robert Tracy, 'All Them Rocks'.

50 Eco, 'To See Things and Texts', p. 115; see above, p. 54.

51 See discussion in Tracy, 'All Them Rocks'.

compare his view of Joyce's readers, to the radically different approach offered by Vladimir Nabokov in his lectures on literature. Nabokov seems to be on the side of what Eco calls 'pure music', as he feels the need to:

> especially warn against seeing in Leopold Bloom's humdrum wanderings and minor adventures on a summer day in Dublin a close parody of the *Odyssey*, with the adman Bloom acting the part of Odysseus, otherwise Ulysses, man of many devices, and Bloom's adulterous wife representing chaste Penelope while Stephen Dedalus is given the part of Telemachus. That there is a very vague and very general Homeric echo of the theme of wanderings in Bloom's case is obvious, as the title of the novel suggests, and there are a number of classical allusions among the many other allusions in the course of the book; but it would be a complete waste of time to look for close parallels in every character and every scene of the book. There is nothing more tedious than a protracted and sustained allegory based on a well-worn myth; and after the work had appeared in parts, Joyce promptly deleted the pseudo-Homeric titles of his chapters when he saw what scholarly and pseudoscholarly bores were up to.'[52]

I have quoted Nabokov at length here, because in my capacity as the scholarly type of bore, I propose to engage with various elements in this quotation in the following discussion. It is not difficult to demonstrate that Nabokov represents here a way of reading – and reading Joyce in particular – diametrically opposed to both Eco's method of reading and his method of composition. Nabokov, in the final sentence of the above, seems to be much in favour of Joyce's elision of 'pseudo-Homeric titles'. This offers a striking contrast to Eco's explicitly articulated pride in having 'found for every chapter [of *The Island of the Day Before*] the title of a seventeenth-century book.'[53] More than that, one suspects that Nabokov's 'scholarly and pseodoscholarly bores' are precisely the readers who feature prominently (and to my mind positively, almost as the ideal reader) in Eco's following sentence (continuing his discussion of his chapter titles for the same novel): 'It was a *tour de force*, but a poorly paying one, since my

52 Vladimir Nabokov, 'James Joyce (1882–1941). *Ulysses* (1922)' in Vladimir Nabokov, *Lectures on Literature*, ed. by Fredson Bowers, with introduction by John Updike (San Diego, New York, and London: Harcourt Brace & Co, 1980), pp. 285–370 (p. 288).

53 Eco, 'To See Things and Texts', p. 118.

play was understood only by a few specialists of that period and mainly by rare-book dealers and bibliophiles.'[54]

Nabokov and Eco thus show two diametrically opposed attitudes to reading and to literature. Nabokov – as literary critic who also practiced the writing of literature and academic who practiced its analysis – belongs to the point in the development of literature which sits uncomfortably alongside Joyce's modernist experiment and precedes Eco's postmodern ones. Nabokov belongs to the Henry James school of 'realism' steeped in psychology, and I would argue is deeply allergic to allegory in general, as his consistently negative attitude to Dostoyevski demonstrates.[55] Nabokov's instruction for the reader pushes the student to the position of what Eco would describe as a 'naive reader'. Conversely, where Nabokov rejects the search for allusions as a 'complete waste of time', Eco delights in it, and gives it such a central place in his work, that to make sure the 'undetectable quotations' make it into the translations, he would provide his translators with 'pages and pages of notes'.[56] It will be noted in the discussion of allegorical readings of Gulliver's adventures in Chapter 4 below, that reading texts allegorically does have a tendency to promote the production of enormous amounts of commentary tracing individual allusions, often retreating into minutia.[57]

My point here is not to attempt to promote one method of reading over another, but to suggest that these alternative attitudes to literature are largely conditioned by the disciplinary origins of the academics proposing them. Nabokov comes from a background in literary criticism (not only of the academic but of the public discourse type), while Eco is a medievalist and semiotician. They draw on different toolboxes. This shows how important it is to take into account the writer's 'day job' so to speak, in the analysis of his work. Because Eco has left so much self-reflective and theoretical writing it is less of an issue in the analysis of his work, as can be seen from the emphases in the secondary literature cited throughout this discussion, but it is an issue that is important in discussing the role of their academic discipline in the creative output of some of the other medievalist writers (e.g. Lewis).

54 Eco, 'To See Things and Texts', p. 118.

55 See Vladimir Nabokov, *Lectures on Russian Literature*, ed. by Fredson Bowers (New York: Harcourt Inc., 1981), pp. 97–136 (pp. 98, 103, 105).

56 Eco, 'To See Things and Texts', p. 117.

57 See below, pp. 114–16.

At the same time as playing with intertextual irony, Eco also warns us of the dangers of reading too much into a text, and the possibility that the reasons for a particular feature of a novel might exist not in the world of intertextual relations but in its connections with reality.[58] He also warns about seeking 'precise allusions' in his works, since sometimes the process of creation was such that meanings would become attached to names later in the creative process, as characters and events would develop, sometimes in unexpected directions.[59] This chapter, therefore, focuses on a reading of *Baudolino* as an *echtra* narrative, with elements of *immram*, but with this caveat in mind.

3.2 Umberto Eco's Construction of Space

Section 3.1 focused on Eco's use of double coding and intertextuality in the creation of a new fictional world tightly connected both to the real world (or at least to the historian's understanding of it) and to previous fictional worlds. I will try now to explain what exactly Eco creates in *Baudolino*. My focus, defined by the intertextual matrix of the present book, is on Eco's geography and the characters' movement through it. The novel constructs a different type of space, which as we shall see in the following discussion, not only engages the readers in a cat-and-mouse game chasing Eco's elusive reality, but also makes the readers question their own reality.[60]

My use of the term 'construction of space' both echoes and avoids Henri Lefebvre's influential concept of 'production of space'.[61] Lefebvre's idea of

58 Eco, 'On Some Functions of Literature', in Eco, *On Literature*, pp. 1–15 (pp. 4, 7–9); and for the specific example of the burning abbey library in *The Name of the Rose*, Eco, 'Borges', p. 121.

59 Eco, 'Borges', p. 124.

60 'Construction of space' has been used in the context of an analysis of Eco's novels previously, by Kamal Hayani El Mechkouri, who focuses on isolating two types of spatial representation in Eco's work, which he terms *espaces clos et les espaces ouverts* 'closed spaces and open spaces'; 'La construction de l'espace chez Umberto Eco', *Cahiers de narratologie*, 33: *L'art du roman chez Umberto Eco* (2018) <https://doi.org/10.4000/narratologie.8071>.

61 Henri Lefebvre, *The Production of Space*, trans. by Donald Nicholson-Smith (Oxford: Blackwell, 1991); originally published as *La production de l'espace* (Paris: Anthropos, 1974). For more on Lefebvre, his theories and their modern implications, see, for instance, Michael E. Leary-Owhin and John P. McCarthy, ed., *The Routledge Handbook of Henri Lefebvre, The City and Urban Society* (London and New York: Routledge, 2020).

space existing not independently of humans but rather as object of experience and the product of social and political processes, carries a heavy Marxist burden of connotations ('production' in the capitalist labour sense).[62] In my reading of *Baudolino*, Eco does not produce the space of Prester John's land but rather presents it to the reader as an artificial construct.[63] It is up to the reader (and us) to decide whether this constructed space is the creation of Eco or Baudolino, ourselves as readers, or of the medieval mind, merely borrowed by Eco for us and represented through the prism of Baudolino's fantasy and/or experience. If the construct is medieval, Eco positions himself (and Baudolino) as means of transmission, but he also conditions the legend's reception.[64] The medieval setting of *Baudolino*, like that of *The Name of the Rose*, is about much more than an 'appeal to the audience attracted to this exotic medieval past' to borrow Coletti's description of the books' covers.[65]

Space, and the representation of space, is an important concern for Eco.[66] In *Baudolino* space is perceived through a medieval prism. An important aspect of Eco's work, in light both of his function as novelist and identity as a medievalist, is the ability to introduce the reader to and indeed *into* the Middle Ages and make the era, with all of its cultural and temporal specifics, fantastic included, seem familiar to the reader. Eco himself qualifies this as a reversal of the technique of defamiliarisation, which we have already seen used by Lewis.[67]

In Eco's technique, 'the (culturally ignorant) character often describes with astonishment something he sees and about which he does not understand very much, whereby the reader is led to understand it'.[68] This is his

---

62 See discussion in Andy Merrifield, 'Henri Lefebvre. A Socialist in Space', in *Thinking Space*, ed. by Mike Crang and Nigel Thrift, Critical Geographies, 9 (London and New York: Routledge, 2000), pp. 167–82 (pp. 169, 171–72, 175–76); Łukasz Stanek, *Henri Lefebvre on Space: Architecture, Urban Research, and the Production of Theory* (Minneapolis and London: University of Minnesota Press, 2001), pp. 1, 25, 128–29.

63 Most significantly in Chapter 12, 'Baudolino writes the letter of Prester John'; Eco, *Baudolino*, pp. 132–44.

64 In the most extensive discussion of the composition of the letter present in the narrative, Eco explicitly refers to a number of genuine texts, primarily medieval ones (a notable exception is Pliny's natural history), which belong to the intertextual matrix of the Prester John letter; Eco, *Baudolino*, pp. 141–42. See also discussion below.

65 Coletti, *Naming the Rose*, p. 3.

66 Eco, 'To See Things and Texts'.

67 See above, pp. 62–63.

68 Eco, 'Borges', p. 127; brackets Eco's; see also his example on pp. 127–28.

technique in introducing the marvellous creatures of Prester John's kingdom in *Baudolino* and more generally in describing the journey itself – the reader learns about Eco's models by reading the text. Eco explicitly drew on the 'Marvels of the East' tradition and specifically the so-called *Letter of Prester John*.[69] As Coletti explains, 'By invoking the Letter of Prester John and the journey to the East, *Baudolino* aligns past and present intellectual structures and conceptions of textuality and truth. At the same time, *Baudolino* frames its idea of the Middle Ages in terms of the writing of history itself, a process that it depicts as rendering suspect all representations of the past'.[70] *Baudolino* often explicitly echoes both medieval texts and medieval modes of expression and narration.[71] A case in point is the illustration depicting a *mappa mundi* (world map) accompanying the heroes' discussion of geography.[72] Eco also frequently quotes medieval sources verbatim. Some selections are purposefully ambiguous, since, for instance, the four lines Baudolino recites to Niketas to illustrate his poetic talent come from the *Carmina Burana*, a text made famous in Carl Orff's 1937 version.[73]

69 For discussions of the medieval legend of Prester John, see, for example, Vsevolod Slessarev, ed., *Prester John. The Letter and the Legend* (Minneapolis: University of Minnesota Press and London: Oxford University Press, 1959); Anne-Dorothee von den Brincken, 'Presbyter Iohannes, Dominus Dominantium: Ein Wunsch-Weltbild des 12. Jahrhunderts', in *Ornamenta Ecclesiae. Kunst und Künstler der Romanik. Katalog zur Ausstellung des Schnützgen-Museums in der Josef-Haubrich-Kunsthalle*, I, ed. by A. Legner (Cologne: Schnütgen-Museum, 1985) pp. 83–90; essays in *Prester John, the Mongols, and the Ten Lost Tribes*, ed. by C. F. Beckingham and B. Hamilton (Aldershot: Ashgate, 1996); B. Wagner, *Die "Epistola Presbiteri Johannis" lateinisch und deutsch. Überlieferung, Textgeschichte, Rezeption und Übertragungen im Mittelalter. Mit bisher unedierten Texten* (Tübingen: Max Niemeyer, 2000); Marco Giardini, *Figure del regno nascosto. Le leggende del Prete Gianni e delle dieci tribù perdute d'Israele fra Medioevo e prima età moderna* (Florence: Olschki, 2016), pp. 9–13 for a brief overview of the Latin letter tradition. Keagan Brewer, *Prester John: The Legend and its Sources* (London: Routledge, 2019), presents a selection of the primary sources in one volume with contextualising introductions.

70 Theresa Coletti, 'Eco's Middle Ages and the Historical Novel', p. 74.

71 Coletti, 'Eco's Middle Ages and the Historical Novel', p. 74. Note, however, that Coletti argues that this applies to *Baudolino* to a much lesser extent than to *The Name of the Rose*, ibid. 75.

72 Eco, *Baudolino*, p. 81; trans. Weaver, p. 76.

73 Carl Orff, *Carmina Burana. Cantiones Profanae* (Wauconda: Bolchazy-Carducci, 1996), 'In Taverna. 11. Estuans Interius', ll. 17–20, 29–32, p. 55. Orff's text is based on a real medieval manuscript, but is also an instance of medievalism in itself; see discussion in Kirsten Yri, 'Medievalism and Antiromanticism in Carl Orff's *Carmina Burana*', in *The Oxford Handbook of Music and Medievalism*, ed. by Stephen C. Meyer and Kirsten Yri

The various elements of the letters of Prester John and descriptions of his kingdom scattered throughout *Baudolino* draw on surviving medieval sources. For instance, even Kyot's suggested list of the inhabitants of the kingdom is a verbatim quotation from the medieval *Letter of Prester John*: *Sagittari, uomini cornuti, fauni, satiri, pigmei, cinocefali, giganti alti quaranta cubiti, uomini monocoli* in Eco's text is almost identical to the Latin tradition of the Prester John legend: *sagittarii, homines argestes,* [*homines cornuti*], *fauni, satiri et mulieres eiusdem generis, pigmei, cenocephali, gygantes, quorum altitude est quadraginta cubitorum,* [*monoculi*], *ciclopes*.[74] The differences between Eco's rendition and the Latin text are crucial to the novel: he conflates the giants and cyclopes, and his introduction of Hypatia, in order to maintain the element of surprise for the reader with the revelation of her goat-like legs, leads to the omission of the note about *mulieres eiusdem generis* (women of the same type) after the mention of satyrs in the list. The entire Chapter 12, where Baudolino and his friends compose the first fake letter of Prester John, is saturated with quotations and intertextual references to the 'real' surviving letter to the Byzantine emperor. These include the addition of the ten lost tribes of Israel to John's kingdom, the references to the riches of the kingdom, the palace of the priest, the lack of lies and thievery in the kingdom, and the description of a magical and impossibly positioned mirror.[75] In characteristic fashion, Eco

(Oxford: Oxford University Press, 2020), pp. 269–300. See also J. A. Schmeller, ed., *Carmina Burana. Lateinische und deutsche Lieder und Gedichte einer Handschrift des* XIII. *Jahrhunderts aus Benedistbeuern auf der K. Bibliothek zu Munchen* (Breslau: Wilhelm Koebner, 1894), poem CLXXII, stanzas 3 and 4, pp. 67–68. For a recent discussion of the medieval collection, see Albrecht Classen, 'The *Carmina Burana*: A Mirror of Latin and Vernacular Literary Traditions from a Cultural-Historical Perspective: Transgression is the Name of the Game', *Neophilologus*, 94 (2010), 477–97.

74 Eco, *Baudolino*, p. 147, trans. Weaver p. 141; Latin text from Friedrich Zarncke, ed., 'Der Brief des Priesters Johannes an den byzantischen Kaiser Emanuel', *Abhandlungn der köninglich sächsischen Gesellschaft der Wissenschaften*, 17 (1879), pp. 873–934 (p. 911); reprinted in *Prester John. The Mongols and the Ten Lost Tribes*, ed. by Beckingham and Hamilton, pp. 40–102 (p. 79).

75 The descriptions range across two chapters in Eco's novel; see Eco, *Baudolino*, pp. 134–50; trans. Weaver, pp. 127–43. Compare Zarncke, ed., 'Der Brief des Priesters Johannes an den byzantischen Kaiser Emanuel'. For description of utopia through absence of things negative is also a feature of the Irish otherworld tradition; see discussion below, pp. 124–25.

interweaves this with passages echoing texts of the Grail tradition.[76] This is what Eco describes as 'playing creatively with hypertexts'.[77]

The voyage to the land of Prester John is central to *Baudolino*. The reader, unbeknownst in the first encounter with the novel, is introduced to this wonderous goal early on, and then incrementally. In the beginning of Chapter 2 as Niketas is turning over Baudolino's manuscript in his hands, Baudolino explains that he had lost the rest of his story 'in the escape from the kingdom of Prester John ...'[78] He is interrupted by Niketas, the Watson figure of the novel, who serves as the reader's voice interacting with the story, asking the reader's questions. In this instance, Niketas says: 'Prete Giovanni? Mai sentito nominare' ('Prester John? Never heard of him'), eliciting from Baudolino/Eco the promise to Niketas/reader: 'Te ne parlerò, forse anche troppo' ('I will tell you more about him – maybe even too much').[79]

I take Niketas as the Watson figure because, like Watson, he fulfils the function of mirroring (and conditioning) the reader's response to the main protagonist, and to the events in the narrative. In the first place, as will be seen in the discussion below, he continuously functions as a means for the reader's doubts and questions to be voiced within the narrative. He is the recipient of explanations about those aspects of medieval Western culture which might be unfamiliar to *Baudolino*'s readers, such as medieval political structures, social and cultural phenomena which are not widely known.[80] This is the reversed defamiliarization technique referred to above.[81] In the second place, Niketas is presented as thoroughly human and earthly, as his ability to carry on with his daily habits while the city burns around them demonstrates (which in turn astonishes Baudolino).[82]

---

76 A good starting point for the study of the medieval Grail tradition is Richard Barber, *The Holy Grail. Imagination and Belief* (London: Allen Lane, 2004). This massive medieval mega-franchise (if one may be permitted an anachronistic term) has also been argued to draw deeply from the Old Irish narrative tradition. See John Carey, *Ireland and the Grail* (Aberystwyth: Celtic Studies Publications, 2007).

77 Eco, 'On Some Functions of Literature', in Umberto Eco, *On Literature*, pp. 1–15 (p. 13).

78 Eco, *Baudolino*, p. 17; trans. Weaver, p. 11.

79 Eco, *Baudolino*, p. 17; trans. Weaver, p. 11.

80 Eco, *Baudolino*, p. 38 (political structures); pp. 44–45 (Otto's *Chronicle*); p. 47 (sinecure and absentee bishops); trans. Weaver, pp. 32–33; p. 39; p. 42. Niketas also gives voice to the (expected) surprise of the reader at Baudolino's account of a bishop acting as patron to a poet who composes love poetry (*Baudolino*, p. 88; trans Weaver, p. 83).

81 See pp. 89–90.

82 This is usually represented by reference to food, though not exclusively; Eco, *Baudolino*, pp. 56–57, 66, 233–34, 462; trans. Weaver, pp. 51–52, 61, 226–27, 457. For Watson's similar positioning in relation to Conan Doyle's readers, see for example, Ron

The second reference to the Kingdom of Prester John and the upcoming journey narrative is more obscure, a nod to the knowing: 'Io ho viaggiato molto, signor Niceta, forse sino all'India Maggiore' ('I have done much traveling, Master Niketas, maybe even as far as Greater India'), but it is marked again for the reader by Niketas's interjection 'Non sei sicuro?' ('Are you sure').[83] This forms part of a gradual build-up composed of oblique references to the mythical Christian kingdom, which are also overtly interconnected by mention of India, marvels of the East, and travel generally. The lengthiest discussion is of Baudolino's extensive reading at the Saint Victoire library, which culminates with speculation on the reality of Prester John.[84] This passage also introduces the modern reader – studying the subject alongside Baudolino – to the medieval worldview. It explains, including an illustration, the *mappae mundi* 'world maps' of the T-O type, including their division of the world into three regions (Asia, Europe and Africa), and their relationship with the knowledge, inherited by the Middle Ages from Antiquity, that the world was not flat but a sphere.[85] One of Eco's targets here is the illusion, shared by many modern readers, that the medievals thought the world was flat.[86] This is not the case, and the

Buchanan, '"Side by Side": The Role of the Sidekick', *Studies in Popular Culture*, 26 (2003), 15–26 (pp. 18, 21–22, 24).

83 Eco, *Baudolino*, p. 34; trans. Weaver, p. 28. Note that the nuance of the interjection in the original Italian is slightly different from that conveyed in the translation. Niketas actually asks Baudolino 'Aren't you sure?'

84 Eco, *Baudolino*, pp. 77–82 (Prester John reference, p. 78); trans. Weaver, pp. 72–77, 74.

85 Eco, *Baudolino*, pp. 80–81; trans. Weaver, pp. 76–77. Both the maps and the references to the material read in the library return throughout the narrative, e.g. *Baudolino*, pp. 340–41; trans. Weaver, pp. 333–34. For discussions of the medieval ideas concerning the sphericity of the world, see, for example, David Woodward, 'Reality, Symbolism, Time and Space in Medieval World Maps', *Annals of the Association of American Geographers*, 75 (1985), 510–21 (esp. pp. 517–19); Naomi Reed Kline, *Maps of Medieval Thought. The Hereford Paradigm* (Woodbridge: Boydell Press, 2001), pp. 30–34. The origins and extent of the modern misconception are discussed in Jeffrey Burton Russell, 'The Flat Error: The Modern Distortion of Medieval Geography', *Mediaevalia*, 15 (1989), 337–53.

86 Later in the novel, Eco presents a clash between the two views, represented by the Westerner Baudolino and the Byzantine Zosimos, as the latter espouses the flat earth theory; Eco, *Baudolino*, pp. 221–22, 261–63; trans. Weaver, pp. 214–15, 256–58. Zosimos explicitly refers to Cosmas Indicopleustes, a sixth-century thinker who postulated a rectangular Earth; Eco, *Baudolino*, pp. 222–23, 264; trans. Weaver, pp. 215–16, 257. As David Woodward points out, Cosmas appears to have been little known in the medieval period; Woodward, 'Reality', p. 517. Umberto Eco's inclusion of the flat earth theory in the book, therefore, is a nod more towards contemporary expectations of medieval views, than an accurate representation of the dominant medieval views themselves.

issue has been discussed *in extenso* by medievalists and historians of geography over the past half century and more, including in books aimed at the general public. Yet somehow the perception persists.

Again and again Prester John resurfaces in the narrative, sometimes in connection to Baudolino's reading, sometimes to his lies, sometimes to his early teacher Otto of Friesing, sometimes in the context of potential political implications of the legend, and usually acknowledging the apocryphal nature of the legendary individual and his kingdom.[87] These references can be interpreted as part of the a conceptual journey towards the magical eastern kingdom. As in all *immrama*, the journey itself, its process, its stages, is more important to *Baudolino* than the goal itself. The stay of Baudolino and his companions in the land that lay at the doors of the priest's kingdom is described in detail, but it is the build-up towards that stay, and the return home, that form the novel's core.[88] Baudolino only ever reaches the land of Prester John's appointed son, Deacon Johannes. The Kingdom itself, like Lewis's Land of the far East to which the Dawn Treader voyages, remains tantalizingly out of reach.

In this the contrast with Swift's Gulliver is at its most apparent, because Gulliver, as will be seen in the discussion in Chapter 4 below, does not set out to reach his fantastic islands, but ends up there through sheer accident. The unintentionality of Gulliver's journey is thus more similar to the *echtra* genre. With typical intertextual humour, Eco places a reference to Swift in his own fantastic land, as the word for a 'horse' in the language of the blemmye is *houyhmhnm*, rendered in the English translation of the novel as *houymhmm*.[89] This is an unambiguous reference to Swift's houyhnhnms. Similarly, the pygmy greeting is, with also but a slight alteration to the spelling, that of the Lilliputians.[90] This is again part of Eco's creative play with hypertexts. It is also another indication that the interconnections within the

We are back to the parallel with Marco Polo in the conflict of reality with audience expectations. See above, p. 39; also below, p. 100.

87 The references are too frequent in the book to cite them all. See, for instance, Eco, *Baudolino*, pp. 77, 93, 118, 123, 126, 285–86; trans. Weaver, pp. 73, 88, 111, 116, 131, 279. For the connections between the historical tradition of the *Letter* with Barbarossa and bishop Otto, see Giardini, *Figure*, pp. 6–7.

88 This is not to say that Baudolino's stay at, or the description of, the marvellous land occupies a small space in the text; it is the focus of seven of the book's 40 chapters; Chapters 29–35, *Baudolino*, pp. 369–461; trans. Weaver, pp. 362–456.

89 Eco, *Baudolino*, p. 400; trans. Weaver, p. 394.

90 Eco, *Baudolino*, p. 400; trans. Weaver, p. 394; Swift, *Gulliver's Travels*, p. 334, in *The Essential Writings of Jonathan Swift*, ed. by Rawson and Higgins. Both references to Swift are noted in Mullan, 'Catching the Prester John Bug'.

textual corpus descending from Old Irish voyage narratives discussed in this book are manifold.

Baudolino's journey, however, takes place on multiple levels in the narrative as the kingdom of Prester John morphs from an undefined idea to Baudolino's and his friends' drug-induced fantasy, to their physical journey, to Baudolino's memory and account to Niketas. In the meantime, the reader is also on a journey of exploration – introduced by Eco to both the hero's fantasy (of questionable believability) and to genuine medieval sources, including texts variously positioned on the truth-claim spectrum, including for example encyclopedic texts (Isidore).[91]

Kamal Hayani El Mechkouri reads the kingdom of Prester John in *Baudolino* as what he terms a static 'closed space', which gives the characters, author, and reader an opportunity for pause and reflection.[92] In this, the space of the legendary kingdom plays, according to Hayani El Mechkouri, the same narrative function as the chamber constructed by Arzdrouni for Barbarossa earlier in the text.[93] He also acknowledges the importance of travel and displacement in the novel (as in other Eco novels): 'les personnages principaux se déplacent beaucoup, et ce, en parfaite osmose avec les transformations narratives ou les séries d'actions et de réactions qui sont déterminantes dans l'avancement de l'intrigue. Ce voyage acquiert tantôt une fonction informative, tantôt une fonction cathartique.'[94] In Hayani El Mechkouri's reading of Baudolino's journey to the kingdom of Prester John, the fantastic is a function of the imprecision which reflects and emulates the spatial imprecision and symbolic focus of medieval *mappae mundi*.[95] In his reading, informed by Lotman's spatial semiotics, the journey is less a physical movement along defined spatial coordinates than it is a progression along a route of moral and religious self-actualisation.[96] In this respect,

91 The sources are discussed in greater detail below, pp. 96–100.

92 'La construction de l'espace chez Umberto Eco', §13.

93 Hayani El Mechkouri, 'La construction de l'espace', §14. See Eco, *Baudolino*, pp. 294–304 for the section of the novel under discussion.

94 Hayani El Mechkouri, 'La construction de l'espace', §24; see also his discussion of the novel in §§29–31, 40–42.

95 Hayani El Mechkouri, 'La construction de l'espace', §31.

96 Hayani El Mechkouri, 'La construction de l'espace', §31; quoting Lotman, *La sémiosphère*, trans. by Anka Lodenko (Limoges, Presses Universitaires de Limoges, 1999), p. 87. For an English translation of Lotman's discussion of the concept of *semiosphere*, see Lotman, 'On the Semiosphere', trans. by Wilma Clark, *Sign System Studies*, 33.1 (2005), 205–29. See also Lotman, *Universe of The Mind*. It is telling that the introduction to the latter translation was written by Eco.

the journey of Baudolino and his companions shares the tropological aspect of the *immram*-type narrative.[97]

As Capozzi points out, Eco also engages the reader in dialogue about reality that is also fundamentally anchored in Lotmanian theory generally, as well as in the Bakhtinian interpretation of intertextuality.[98] Before turning to the question of how Eco manages to convince the modern reader to suspend disbelief while reading an *immram/echtra*-type narrative, without labelling it as fantasy in modern genre definitions, it is worth dwelling a little longer on the manner in which Eco represents the land of Pdnapetzim and thus translates the medieval Irish otherworld and the medieval European Land of Prester John to a new audience.

The land of Pdnapetzim where Baudolino and his companions arrive (with Eco and the reader) in search of the Kingdom of Prester John is inhabited by marvellous beings usually associated with India in medieval encyclopedic and cartographic discourses: Blemmyes, sciapods, cyclopes (referred to by Eco as simply giants, but described as one-eyed), pygmies who fight with cranes.[99] The battle concluding the stay in this land explores the potential implications of these characteristics in tragicomic ways. The journey thence is described in style similar to travel accounts to the east (one thinks in particular of Marco Polo's real journey but also of Mandeville's imagined one).[100] However, when they arrive they are told that this is merely a province attached to the kingdom of the priest, which lies beyond a natural barrier, the passage through which is difficult to find and traverse. The fact that there is no contact with this kingdom, except through the eunuchs who serve the ruler of the province, Deacon John, Prester John's heir apparent, leads ultimately to doubts regarding whether the kingdom is real at all, ultimately changing for some of the characters into a sense of certainty that it did not exist.[101] It is also, within the world of the novel, impossible to establish, because the

97 See also above, p. 80–81.

98 Capozzi, 'Knowledge', p. 167, and above, pp. 49–50.

99 See quotation above, p. 91; see also Rudolf Wittkower, 'Marvels of the East: A Study in the History of Monsters', *Journal of the Warburg and Courtauld Institutes*, 5 (1942), 159–97; David Williams, *Deformed Discourse. The Function of the Monster in Medieval Thought and Literature* (Montreal and Kingston: McGill-Queen's University Press, 1999); Peter Dendle, 'Cryptozoology in the Medieval and Modern Worlds', *Folklore*, 117 (2006), 190–206.

100 See above, p. 39 n. 150.

101 Eco, *Baudolino*, pp. 391, 466, 484; trans. Weaver, pp. 384–85, 461, 479.

eunuchs claim that after the destruction of the province at the hands of the White Huns the only route to the Kingdom of Prester John will be destroyed after they retreat there.[102] Ironically, however, it is the land they did arrive in (if we believe Baudolino's narrative) that matches reasonably closely, the medieval descriptions of the Kingdom of Prester John, a 'real' medieval otherworld.

Thus, crucially, there are ambiguities built into the novel regarding not only the existence of the land of Prester John, but whether the travellers had reached it, whether Pdnapetzim/land of the Deacon John is the same as the land of Prester John, and whether any of Baudolino's story about the journey is true at all. The supernatural nature of the land that Baudolino and his companions do reach is underlined not only by the presence of the marvellous beings who in our real world inhabit the margins of medieval *mappae mundi*, but also hinted at by the odd sense of the passage of time, reminiscent of the *immram/echtra* otherworlds.[103] As with the travellers who had visited the otherworld in Irish narratives, Baudolino and his remaining companions only notice that time had passed after they had left the legendary land, when they realise that their horses had aged without their noticing (and so had they themselves), and reinforced by Baudolino's confessed inability to keep track of time on the return journey.[104] The different rate of the passage of time is reminiscent of Narnia (discussed above) and in both cases is a reflection of the Irish otherworld voyage tradition.[105]

In Eco's case both time and space are subjective. The reader experiences both only through Baudolino's unreliable account. A crucial element in terms of Eco's use of space in *Baudolino* is thus the overlay of different worlds that have been analysed in previous scholarship primarily in

102 Eco, *Baudolino*, pp. 391, 459; trans. Weaver, pp. 384–85, 454.

103 For discussions of the iconography of monsters in medieval world maps see, for instance, Kline, *Maps of Medieval Thought*; Asa Simon Mittman, *Maps and Monsters in Medieval England* (London and New York: Routledge, 2006); Chet Van Duzer, '*Hic sunt dracones:* The Geography and Cartography of Monsters', in *The Ashgate Research Companion to Monsters and the Monstrous*, ed. by Asa Simon Mittman and Peter J. Dendle (London and New York: Routledge, 2016), pp. 387–435 and references to earlier discussions therein.

104 Eco, *Baudolino*, pp. 463, 464; trans. Weaver, pp. 458, 459.

105 See above, pp. 52–53; see also Liuzza's discussion of time-travel and related themes in *Star Trek*, and science fiction in general; Liuzza, 'The Future'. Similar tropes are also found in *Stargate*, specifically in episodes with Irish otherworld narrative characteristics; see below, pp. 166–67.

truth-value terms: the world Baudolino lives in versus the world he imagines.[106] Mercer sees Pndapetzim, Eco's (or Baudolino's) version of the land of Prester John, as a 'second textual plane' in the novel, 'a society of alterity, which Baudolino projects into the space of *terra incognita*, thought to be inhabited, although not by humans'.[107] For Cristina Farronato, Eco's novel also serves as an illustration of his earlier observations about the importance of forgeries to the formation of history, where he had pointed out 'how certain historical fakes succeeded in diverting human history, and [...] asserted the power of the false. *Baudolino* appears as a collection of such fakes ...'[108] The repercussions of the overlay of the different realities in the novel are thus both external and internal. To quote Mercer again:

> The use of fiction in order to reinforce another fiction violates textual boundaries, a violation further exemplified by Baudolino's metaphorical forcing of Prester John to cross over from the epistemological world of Bishop Otto's *Chronica* [...] into the reality of this textual subworld, which Baudolino furnishes with histories and mythologies from old background books'.[109]

The double challenge for the author is how to help the reader navigate through the morass of truth, lies, half-truths, fantastic realities, imaginary worlds, worlds of imagination, otherworlds, books, vanished manuscripts, and everything in between. This is the issue to which we now turn.

3.3 Making the Incredulous Reader Believe in the Fantastic

In order to tell Baudolino's *echtra* to the land of Prester John, Eco the master of multi-layered narratives engages the reader's disposition to (dis)believe the fantastic journey on three fronts. For the purposes of the following

106 See, for example, Mercer, 'Truth and Lies', p. 20.

107 Mercer, 'Truth and Lies', p. 20.

108 Farronato, 'Umberto Eco's *Baudolino*', p. 319.

109 Mercer, 'Truth and Lies', p. 20. We will encounter the same layering of textual worlds in the overlay between the real world shared by readers, author and narrator, onto the fictional world of the narrator – where the crossing from one plane to the other is effected by sleight of hand in the textual map drawn in the storm passage – of *Gulliver's Travels*; see below, pp. 110, 118–20.

discussion I will label these as: truth, reality, and meaning. 'Reality' stands here primarily for narrative-internal reality, but it will be shown that on a number occasions Eco's masterful authorial slight-of-hand manages to introduce doubt and ambiguity into the reader's own reality.

This is in contrast with Lewis's absolute realities, where Narnia is anchored as real to the reader's own real world.[110] In the fictional world of the *Voyage*, it is Eustace, who 'thought of course that they were making it all up' who is 'stupid' and in error.[111] Indeed, the issue of what is real and what is imagined is addressed in each of the texts in our corpus. In *Stargate*, for instance, this issue is centre-stage in Season 8 Episode 15 'Citizen Joe'.[112] In this episode, which does not focus on the main characters of the show, an everyman, a barber called Joe, is found to have forged a connection through an alien artefact with one of the protagonists of the series, Jack O'Neill. Since O'Neill as the leader of the exploratory team known as SG-1 goes to other planets, Joe witnesses some of his adventures. Joe does not realise that what he is seeing is real and takes it as inspiration, attempting to write fiction on the basis of these experiences.[113] Thus, Joe, who experiences the adventures by proxy, tries to create another proxy, a book, for others to experience the same adventures also. Books, as we have seen, have an important function in Lewis's novel – Eustance had not read the 'right' ones.[114] Books also play a major role in Eco's text: Baudolino (and the readers), encounter the land of Prester John with minds conditioned by book

110 Evidenced by the repetition of the term 'real' in the description of Edmund and Lucy's 'secret country'; Lewis, *Voyage*, p. 15.

111 Lewis, *Voyage*, p. 17.

112 Discussed in Beeler, '*Stargate SG-1*', p. 278.

113 A similar episode is found in *Star Trek, Deep Space* 9 (Season 6 Episode 13 'Far Beyond the Stars'). The episode re-casts a main character of the series – Captain Benjamin Sisko – in the role of a writer, Benny Russell, as part of a spiritual experience and challenge, in which he is faced with a twentieth-century 'reality' in which his real life as twenty-fourth-century captain becomes the subject of a science fiction work that he is trying to publish. Sisko is forced to come to terms with his real-life challenges but also finds himself doubting not only the in-vision 'reality' during the experience but also the original reality he returns to after the experience. The episode serves also, perhaps inadvertently, as an apologetic aside for those aspects of the Original Series which appear to contradict the ideals it espouses – aspects without which it perhaps might not have made it to the screen at all. These aspects are named and critiqued in, for example, Booker, 'The Politics', p. 206. See also Johnson-Smith, *American Science Fiction TV*, pp. 83–84.

114 See above, p. 62.

knowledge.[115] Book knowledge as basis for the experience of the 'real' world is a major concern in Eco's work, as it is in the work of some of his predecessors, including Calvino (and in a more critical tone, Lewis).[116]

As has already been mentioned, the kingdom of Prester John, as the goal of the narrative's central journey, is incrementally introduced to Baudolino through reading and to the reader (also through reading!). Baudolino, taking his companions with him, immerses himself in the textual sources relating to the legend, and by extension through the prism of the characters, so does the reader. This creates the basis of a tension between reality and book knowledge (real travel and armchair travel). The tension between preconception and real experience, which is removed in the novel by making real experience in Prester John's land outstrip the preconception in the degree of the fantastic, is very present in real medieval accounts of encounters with the Orient. For the medieval situation, Marco Polo is a case in point – his account ran the risk of being met with disbelief for the lack of such marvels as Baudolino's sciapods.[117] Eco, characteristically, plays with belief and disbelief on several levels. Baudolino, for instance, is incredulous at Zosimos's story of silk-worms: 'Di un uomo che vuole farti credere che la seta la si fa coi vermi, non c'era proprio da fidarsi' ('There's no trusting a man who wants to make you believe silk comes from worms').[118] Eco and his intended readers share a knowing smile here since silk does indeed come

115 Mercer, 'Truth and Lies', pp. 20, 24. For example, when first encountering a blemmye in the land of Prester John, the travellers already know what they are about to see; Eco, *Baudolino*, p. 373; trans. Weaver, p. 365. Baudolino's reading is referred to explicitly later on in the novel as context for his and his companions experiences; Eco, *Baudolino*, pp. 379–80, trans. Weaver, pp. 372–73.

116 See comments in Capozzi, 'Knowledge', pp. 166, 171–72; Peter Bondanella, 'Italo Calvino and Umberto Eco: Postmodern Masters', in *The Cambridge Companion to the Italian Novel*, ed. by Peter Bondanella and Andrea Ciccarelli (Cambridge: Cambridge University Press, 2003), pp. 168–81 (p. 179); and above, p. 61.

117 For discussions, see, for instance, Mary B. Campbell, *The Witness and the Other World. Exotic European Travel Writing, 400–1600* (Ithaca and London: Cornell University Press, 1988), pp. 94–112; Yeager, 'The World Translated', pp. 156, 167–70; Surekha Davies, 'The Wondrous East in the Renaissance Geographical Imagination: Marco Polo, Fra Mauro and Giovanni Battista Ramusio', *History and Anthropology*, 23 (2012), 215–34 (pp. 220–23, 226–29); and Petrovskaia, *Transforming Europe*, p. 84. The sciapods first appear in Eco's novel in Chapter 29 (*Baudolino*, p. 370; trans. Weaver, p. 363). The representation of sciapods in *The Voyage of the Dawn Treader* and in *Baudolino* has been addressed recently by Hannah Priest, who argues that both works use the medieval 'monstrous races' as not merely curiosities to decorate their worlds of the fantastic but also, in true medieval tradition, as commentary on the modern, and representations capable or allegorical reading; Priest, '"Oh, the funnies, the funnies"'.

118 Eco, *Baudolino*, p. 224; trans. Weaver, p. 217.

from worms. In turn, the mundanity of reality in contrast with perception is also present in *Baudolino*, as Mercer observes, in relation to the representation of Rome.[119] Here, unlike the medieval authors he relies on, Eco negotiates two sets of readers: the in-book medieval audience who – through intertextual exposure to other marvel narratives – are prepared to see and believe the marvels of Rome and India, and the modern audience whose expectations, reading a historical novel set in the middle ages, exclude – initially at least – the overtly supernatural and fantastic.

The topos of distant marvels is later reversed again in typical Ecoean fashion when Baudolino recounts the marvels of the West to Deacon John in the far East.[120] For the Deacon it is Baudolino who comes from the otherworld. Here real things familiar to the reader are made marvellous through defamiliarisation, the major technique which keeps returning again and again in this discussion. This takes place in a kingdom inhabited according to Baudolino by Blemmyes, pygmies, and sciapods, among other marvellous beings familiar to us through medieval narratives of the wondrous East. This is the *echtra*-like otherworld of riches and wonders, where time flows differently. The external reader is conditioned by Eco to accept the narrative on its own terms through a number of techniques, one of which is the reverse of the medieval technique of establishing veracity. Whereas medieval authors might claim veracity by positing a particularly reliable point of view character or narrator – saints fulfil this function particularly well – Eco bombards the reader with multiple references, primarily by other characters, to Baudolino's unreliability.

In the very first chapters of the novel, Baudolino is referred to as a liar by multiple characters on multiple occasions, including within his own account to Niketas.[121] Eco introduces several wrinkles here to this seemingly straightforward canvas. The first is that Baudolino the liar is one of those who calls Baudolino a liar.[122] Niketas, the reader's voice, points this out in an internal monologue in Chapter 3:

119 Mercer, 'Truth and Lies', p. 23; the passage in question is Eco, *Baudolino*, pp. 41–42; trans. Weaver, pp. 35–36.

120 Eco, *Baudolino*, pp. 411–14, trans. Weaver, pp. 405–06.

121 By Otto of Freising, for instance: 'tu sei un mentitore nato' ('you are a born liar'), 'il ragazzo è mendace di natura' ('the boy's a liar by nature'), Eco, *Baudolino*, pp. 48, 52; trans. Weaver, pp. 43, 47. The reference to Baudolino as liar also closes the novel as a whole; Eco, *Baudolino*, p. 526; trans. Weaver, p. 521.

122 In his account of his initial meeting with Frederick Barbarossa, Baudolino says 'io ci avevo racontato bale tuta la sera' ('I had been telling him made up stories all night'),

"Tu," si diceva Niceta, "sei come il cretese mentitore, mi dici di essere un buggiardo matricolato e pretendi che ti creda. Vuoi farmi credere che hai raccontato bugie a tutti meno che a me."

("You," Niketas said to himself, "are like the liar of Crete: you tell me you're a confirmed liar and insist I believe you. You want me to believe you've told lies to everybody but me".)[123]

This is the voice of the reader's suspicion, and perhaps confusion as to how this story should be taken, since its reality seems to be slippery and uncertain. Niketas's next statement relates to an important aspect of Eco's destabilising technique: meaning. We will return to this after having addressed 'truth' (or rather the issue of lying) concerning reality. It is worth pointing out that part of Eco's destabilising technique is to use the term 'truth' for what might otherwise be called 'reality'. This enables his characters to affect and subvert their reality (because it can be done to 'truth') in ways which would not have been possible with use of the more stable term.

The second wrinkle in the narrative canvas is that there is a tendency for what Baudolino intended to be lies to turn out true, almost as if he were moulding the surrounding reality.[124] In the very first instance when this happens, the citizens of Terdona witness Baudolino's performance of ecstatic prophecy about their defeat and decide to surrender to Frederick, told first in Baudolino's hesitant youthful voice in Chapter 1 (which serves as a prologue to the novel) and then repeated by the sixty-year-old Baudolino to Niketas in Chapter 2.[125] Baudolino is almost painfully aware of this ability to change his reality, as he confesses to Niketas: 'Sai, signor Niceta, quando tu dici una cosa che hai immaginato, e gli altri ti dicono che è proprio così,

Eco, *Baudolino*, p. 15; trans. Weaver, p. 9. The passage is in Baudolino's eclectic spelling.

123 Eco, *Baudolino*, p. 45; trans. Weaver, pp. 39–40. Niketas' suspicions resurface at multiple points in the narrative, and particularly in relation to the believability of the kingdom of Prester John and Baudolino's experiences there; Eco, *Baudolino*, p. 331; trans. Weaver, up. 324.

124 This is one of the most striking and immediately apparent features of the novel, and is commented on, for instance, in Mullan, 'Catching the Prester John Bug'. In the novel, the feature is articulated by Baudolino himself on a number of occasions. One of the most illustrative examples being: 'Il Sambatyon lo abbiamo citato anche noi nella lettera del Prete, [...] e dunque è evidente che da qualche parte chi sia' ('We mentioned the Sambatyon also in the Priest's letter, [...] and so obviously it must exist somewhere'); Eco, *Baudolino*, p. 335; trans. Weaver, p. 328.

125 Eco, *Baudolino*, pp. 15, 36; trans. Weaver, pp. 10, 30.

finisci per crederci anche tu' ('You know, Master Niketas, when you say something you've imagined, and others then say that's exactly how it is, you end up believing it yourself').[126] The reader may chuckle at this, and fall into the trap. Since the surrounding reality is Eco's narrative about Baudolino, it is of course really being moulded to Baudolino's stories, and thus those stories shape this reality and cease to be lies. An example of this is Baudolino's invention of fictive works he claims were housed in the library of Saint Victoire, including *De optimitate triparum* which he ascribed to the Venerable Bede, in his letters to Rahewin, which lead the latter to request them from the library, leading in turn to accusations that the librarian misplaced them.[127] Baudolino finishes the story by supposing that perhaps someone had, 'to put matters right', finally composed these works after all.[128] This represents another pattern within the novel – the tendency of characters to support and play along with fabrications.

The idea is explained by Baudolino himself as he tells Niketas why there would be no problem if Frederick 'returned' to Prester John the fake Grasal (grail), a cup made from Baudolino's father's cup, which of course the eastern king would have never seen before, let alone owned.[129] Baudolino's explanation attributes to Prester John the motivations displayed by most characters in the novel – the temptation to benefit from the fabrication, whereas denial of the lie would have none to negative effect. In the world of *Baudolino*, the characters do not so much consciously lie but rather come to believe fervently in fabricated 'truths'. Baudolino himself, true to his reputation as the ultimate lie-creator established in the novel's beginning, draws a parallel between his transformation of his father's cup into a grail, with the transformation of the Holy Host during mass.[130]

In terms of the Prester John legend, this build-up of lie-to-truth is also incremental. Baudolino researches what is known of the legend, then writes the letter himself, then becomes obsessed with finding the kingdom as though it were real, is faced with evidence of its existence that looks like that created by him and his friends but seemingly independent of their

126 Eco, *Baudolino*, pp. 35–6; trans. Weaver, p. 30.
127 Eco, *Baudolino*, pp. 90–1; trans. Weaver, pp. 85–86.
128 Eco, *Baudolino*, p. 91; trans. Weaver, p. 86.
129 Eco, *Baudolino*, p. 286; trans. Weaver, p. 279–80.
130 Eco, *Baudolino*, p. 287; trans. Weaver, p. 280. Baudolino is undeterred by Niketas's just observation that he is not a priest. One might also draw a parallel here with the description of the proliferation of relics earlier in the novel; Eco, *Baudolino*, p. 274; trans. Weaver, p. 267.

efforts, encounters others who claim knowledge of the kingdom and the route thence, journeys to the kingdom himself and finally apparently finds it.[131] The fabricated letter creates a reality independent of its author as, for instance, when Zosimos, who had just told Baudolino he had never heard of Prester John, upon reading the letter remarks that he had read eyewitness accounts of his kingdom before. Baudolino suspects that Zosimos is also lying, but this only exacerbates the situation for the reader.[132] A little further in the narrative, Frederick receives the letter of Prester John, but not the one written by Baudolino (it is addressed to Manuel Comnenus, but is otherwise identical to Baudolino's letter), and the fabrication acquires an independent existence of its own.[133]

Baudolino's reaction to the arrival of the new letter is astonishment, because it is too close to his fabrication to have been written by the real Prester John, had he existed, but it was also not the same letter that Baudolino had composed.[134] In this instance, the mystery is soon solved as Baudolino realizes this letter had been fabricated on the basis of his own by Zosimos, but this is merely one layer in a multitude of confusions.[135] The upshot within the narrative is that Baudolino himself becomes unsure of 'truth': 'il problema della mia vita è che io ho sempre confuso quello che vedevo e quello che desideravo vedere' ('the problem of my life is that I've always confused what I saw with what I wanted to see') he says towards the opening of the narrative.[136] The upshot for the reader is the destabilising of the narrative reality. That moment of 'hesitation' that defines the fantastic for Todorov is introduced in the novel as the reader's hesitation when faced with reality (and, as shall be suggested below, this does not stop at the novel).[137] This hesitation is present throughout the novel, as what the characters believe to be real is often juxtaposed with what they know to be fake. A case in point is when the companions agree to pretend to be the twelve Magi en route to the kingdom of Prester John; another is the reference to

131 Eco, *Baudolino*, pp. 77–80, 93, 100, 135, 139–51, 178–79, 227–28, 258, 362–461; trans. Weaver, pp. 72–4, 88, 94, 129, 132–44, 172, 220–21, 253, 355–456.
132 Eco, *Baudolino*, pp. 218–19; trans. Weaver, p. 212.
133 Eco, *Baudolino*, p. 226; trans. Weaver, p. 219.
134 Eco, *Baudolino*, pp 226–27; trans. Weaver, p. 220.
135 Eco, *Baudolino*, p. 228; trans. Weaver, p. 222; Zosimos later confesses (Eco, *Baudolino*, p. 258; trans. Weaver, p. 252).
136 Eco, *Baudolino*, p. 35; trans. Weaver, p. 30.
137 Todorov, *Introduction*, p. 29; see above, p. 40.

fake relics in the discussion of the direction to take in their real journey to the (fake/real) kingdom of Prester John.[138]

The reader, with Niketas, may initially be suspicious of Baudolino's claims: 'il signor Baudolino mi vuole suggerire che [...] come lui proferiva una frase qualsiasi – tale era il suo potere che essa diveniva verità' ('Master Baudolino wants to suggest to me [...] that if he simply uttered an ordinary sentence, such was his power that it became truth.).[139] Note that here, as in most instances discussed below where the word *verità* 'truth' is used, the subject of the statement is usually 'reality'. The coincidences leading to Baudolino's words becoming reality, as in the siege of Terdona, may amuse the reader, and appear initially to be merely convenient narrative devices, but Eco expertly intertwines these, and Baudolino's self-proclaimed unreliability, with a re-definition of what the reader might take to be the novel's reality or 'truth'. This truth/reality becomes real through the process of narration, just as the letter of Prester John written by Baudolino and his friends made the kingdom real to them, and ultimately partially so in the world of the novel. The kingdom they find is not, purportedly, that of Prester John, but rather a province ruled by his heir, who himself voices doubts about the existence of the kingdom of his 'father'.[140] The marvellous land Baudolino tells Niketas he finds, however, matches the descriptions of the medieval Prester John legend, also as they are recounted in the novel's early chapters. If we can take Baudolino's word for it, that is. We are thus back to Niketas's function as the Watson of the novel. He is not the narrator, but he is the cause of the narration, bringing the narrative about, as Eco points out to the reader – through Baudolino:

> Tu sei diventato la mia pergamena, signor Niceta, su cui scrivo tante cose che avevo persino dimenticato [...]. Penso che chi racconta storie debba sempre avere qualcuno a cui le racconta, e solo così può raccontarle anche a se stesso.[141]
>
> ('You have become my parchment, Master Niketas, on which I write many things that I had forgotten [...]. I think that one who tells stories

138 Eco, *Baudolino*, pp. 323–24, 328, 342–44, 371, 385, 387, 406, 408; trans. Weaver, pp. 316–17, 321, 335–37, 364, 378, 380, 400, 402. For the connection between the legends of the Magi and of Prester John, see Giardini, *Figure*, pp. 8–9.

139 Eco, *Baudolino*, p. 66; trans. Weaver, p. 61.

140 Eco, *Baudolino*, pp. 408–09, trans. Weaver, p. 403.

141 Eco, *Baudolino*, p. 214.

> must always have another to whom he tells them, and only thus can he tell them to himself').[142]

Ultimately, in the final chapter of the book, Niketas, too, feels he has become his parchment.[143] He is troubled by the question of what, as a historian of Byzantium, he is to do with Baudolino's story.

The upshot of this combination of techniques is that the novel forces the reader to accept not only the fantastic, but the possibility of multiple layers of truth, or rather multiple co-existing truths (=realities). Thus, the otherworldly journey of the *echtra* narrative is adapted to the sensibilities of modern readers. The method used is an alternative to Lewis's fairy-tale approach. Eco's intended adult readership is more sceptical (one imagines, perhaps somewhat unfairly and unflatteringly, Eustace's parents as the type) and this reader has to be coaxed and cajoled, even tricked, into going along with the lie.

The multiplicity of truths is suggested initially in the background, in the reference to Otto of Freising's contradictory historical accounts and his rewriting of history in his *Chronicle*'s second version (the first was appropriately scratched out from the parchment by Baudolino).[144] Then, it is re-stated more forcefully and explicitly for the reader as the final words of Chapter 4 by the to-be-chronicler of Baudolino's words, Niketas:

> Avrà un'anima, si domandava, questo personaggio che sa piegare il proprio racconto a esprimere anime diverse? E se ha anime diverse, per bocca di quale, parlando, mi dirà mai la verità?[145]
>
> ('Can he have a soul, Niketas wondered, this character who can bend his narrative to express different souls? And if he has different souls, through which mouth, as he speaks, will he tell the truth?')[146]

I would argue that the implication here is not *which Baudolino tells the truth?*, but *which truth tells which Baudolino?*[147] From this point onwards,

142 Eco, *Baudolino*, trans. Weaver, p. 207.
143 Eco, *Baudolino*, chapter 40.
144 Eco, *Baudolino*, p. 45; trans. Weaver, p. 39.
145 Eco, *Baudolino*, p. 55.
146 Eco, *Baudolino*, trans. Weaver, p. 50.
147 Note, however, that Eco seems to imply also the changeability of Baudolino himself, as Niketas compares him to a chameleon; Eco, *Baudolino*, p. 363; trans. Weaver, pp. 356–57.

the reader is exposed to multiple truths, including in repeated references to the history of Otto, a 'maestro [...] che non sa più distinguere tra due verità' ('teacher who can no longer distinguish between two truths').[148] Note that here it is explicitly not a question of two alternative interpretations of history, or truth and lie, or multiple lies, or alternative narratives: it is explicitly a question of two alternative truths and thus two realities.

The novel's references to alternative truths are not always explicit. For example, in the account of books on love, the truth-value (or perhaps truism-value, given the subject matter) of books is implied, but the contradiction is explicit: 'aveva letto da qualche parte che talora la lontananza può guarire dalla malattia d'amore (e non aveva ancora letto altri libri dove al contrario si diceva che è proprio la lontananza a soffiare sul fuoco della passione)' ('he had read somewhere that distance can cure the love illness (and he had not yet read other books where, on the contrary, it is said that distance is precisely that which fans the flames of passion)').[149] What is truly destabilising for the reader's sense of truth/reality is that these books, and the truisms they express, exist not only in Baudolino's world but that of the reader. Eco thus deftly pulls the rug from under the reader's sense of the real not only in relation to the world of the novel but beyond and outside it, in the 'real' world.

Having taken both 'truth' and 'reality' away from the reader, replacing these with potential (probably) lies which shape the multiple truths (standing for reality), Eco does not stop and does the same to 'meaning'.[150] Towards the beginning of the novel, Niketas, the reader's reliable Watson, voices the reassuring opinion that 'Non ci sono storie senza senso' ('There are no stories without meaning'), comforting the reader that he himself is 'uno di quegli uomini che sanno trovarlo anche là dove gli altri non lo vedono' ('one of those men who can find it even where others fail to see it').[151] This a reassuring (both for his companion and the reader) response to Baudolino's suggestion that his story might not have *senso* 'meaning'.[152] This reassurance is Eco's way of lulling the reader into a false sense of security. Meaning, like truth, is thereafter conflated with a number of other concepts. Illustrative is Baudolino's early complaint to Niketas that when he

148 Eco, *Baudolino*, p. 60; trans. Weaver, p. 55.

149 Eco, *Baudolino*, p. 63; trans. Weaver, p. 58. Brackets Eco's.

150 As Johnson-Smith points out, the 'reliance upon potential rather than reality' is a feature of science fiction; *American Science Fiction TV*, p. 66.

151 Eco, *Baudolino*, p. 17; trans. Weaver, p. 12.

152 Eco, *Baudolino*, p. 17; trans. Weaver, p. 12.

tries to remember what had happened to him he becomes confused ('mi si confondono le idee') and he finds he cannot 'give them a meaning' ('dare loro un senso').[153] Confusion implies the inability to put the 'facts' into their proper order in terms of either chronological sequence or causal relations. Thus, 'meaning' as the end-result of interpretation, is conflated with plot and narration. Since Baudolino is the one telling this story, the reader is thus warned that it may become confusing and 'meaning' might not be obviously presented. *Baudolino*, thus, as narrative, takes the reader on the same type of postmodern voyage as Calvino's *Se una notte d'inverno un viaggiatore*, but – and this I see as a characteristic of Eco – pretends that it does not by introducing Niketas, the Watson who translates the meandering and confused narrative into plot.[154]

The narration itself slips from first-person into third-person on multiple occasions, but most strikingly in the description of the wonders of the physical journey to the Orient, the gymnosophists, the three-headed serpents, the basilisk, the manticore. In these chapters there is no interaction with Niketas and Baudolino's voice seems to merge with Eco's as the travellers are referred to as *they* rather than *we*.[155] This, too, has a destabilising effect on the canvas of narrative reality.

The whirlwind experience that is reading *Baudolino* can thus be interpreted as a postmodern take on an *immram* or *echtra* voyage tale. Eco takes full advantage of the fascination of the wonderous journey, and the pull of the magical wished-for land, both on the characters and on the readers, to create a narrative where truth and invention mingle in kaleidoscopic confusion.[156] The simplest moral is that drawn by Baudolino himself in the narrative when faced with the magically raging-then-silent river Sambatyon, but without the famed flames: 'Dove si vede che non bisogna sempre dare ascolto a quello che ci dicono [...] Viviamo in un mondo dove la gente s'inventa le storie più incredibili' ('So you see you mustn't always believe what

153 Eco, *Baudolino*, p. 28; trans. Weaver, p. 22.

154 Italo Calvino, *Se una notte d'inverno un viaggiatore* (Turin: Einaudi, 1979). For a discussion of the two writers, and further references, see Bondanella, 'Italo Calvino and Umberto Eco'; see also essays in *Literary Philosophers. Borges, Calvino, Eco*, ed. by Jorge J. E. Garcia, Carolyn Korsmeyer and Rudolphe Gasché (New York and London: Routledge, 2002).

155 Eco, *Baudolino*, pp. 328–54; trans. Weaver, pp. 335–61. The return of Niketas and Baudolino's 'present' is marked by the beginning of the next chapter, Chapter 28, p. 362 (trans. Weaver, p. 355).

156 Giardini, *Figure*, p. 9.

they tell you. [...] We live in a world where people invent the most incredible stories').[157] Some of these stories are invented from shards of other stories, as in the case of *Baudolino*.[158] Like Borges, about whom he wrote the following words, Eco himself is remarkable for 'his ability to use the most varied debris of the encyclopedia to make the music of ideas'.[159] His novel belongs to the line of reception of the *immram/echtra* type tales partly, as we have seen, as the result of direct influence, and partly because the kaleidoscopic picture of the fragments he used fell that way. In this his work is different from that of Lewis, the other great medievalist-novelist, discussed in the previous chapter. Lewis's novel is not a kaleidoscopic picture made of 'debris' but a concentrated effort to rewrite an *immram* narrative within a new story-world framework. The following chapter examines an illustrious predecessor of Lewis and Eco in the tradition of Irish voyage tales who stands (unintentionally, one would argue) between the two approaches, at the fork on the interpretative road. The subject of Chapter 4, Jonathan Swift, thus arrives, like his hero Gulliver, at a destination he had not, perhaps, entirely intend to visit.

---

157 Eco, *Baudolino*, p. 368, trans. Weaver, p. 361.

158 The original Prester John legend itself contains traces of other traditions; see discussion in Giardini, *Figure*. Sambatyon is an example of this (pp. 14–18).

159 Eco, 'Borges', p. 134.

CHAPTER 4

Jonathan Swift, the *Echtra* and the *Immram* Tradition

As Alain Bony points out, Swift's hero 'n'a pas son pareil pour arriver là où il n'allait pas' ('has no equal in arriving where he was not going').[1] In this Eustace (Lucy and Edmund less so) is very much Gulliver's heir. Baudolino, perhaps, arguably less so, since he was actively seeking the magical kingdom of Prester John, but he, too, arrives somewhere else (the Deacon's kingdom). Eustace in particular is reminiscent of Gulliver, since an obsession with minute detail is a feature of Swift's text. As Alff observes, the letters prefacing the text set up Gulliver as narrator as 'not as a fanciful creator of worlds, but the opposite, a diligent compiler of facts'.[2] Such obsession with recording facts was regarded by Lewis as a medieval characteristic: 'distinction, definition, and tabulation were his delight' but also, in its modern incarnation in Eustace and his kind, as potentially dangerous.[3] The passage at the beginning of the 'Voyage to *Brobdingnag*' on managing the ship in a storm, providing a whirl of nautical terms and details, plagiarized by Swift from *The Mariners Magazine* (1669), exemplifies this obsession with detail, and we will return to this in the context of real-life anchoring of the narrative.[4] Eustace's diary entry with its reference to modern steamships, discussed in Chapter 2, is very much in the same tone.[5]

There are multiple direct links not only between the texts discussed in the previous chapters and *Gulliver's Travels* but also between the authors. Lewis enjoyed Swift's writing and *Gulliver's Travels* in particular, the latter

1 Alain Bony, *Discours et vérité dans* Les Voyages de Gulliver *de Jonathan Swift* (Lyon: Presses Universitaires de Lyon, 2002), p. 21. My translation.

2 David Alff, 'Swift's World of *Gulliver's Travels*', in *Routledge Companion to Imaginary Worlds*, ed. by Mark Wolf (London: Routledge, 2017), pp. 332–38 (p. 333).

3 Lewis, *The Discarded Image*, p. 10. For further discussion in the context of Eustace's obsession with 'facts' in Lewis's *Voyage of the Dawn Treader*, see above, pp. 61–62, 67.

4 *The Mariners Magazine; or, Sturmy's Mathematical and Practical Arts … By Capt. Samuel Sturmy* (London, 1669); see *The Essential Writings of Jonathan Swift*, ed. by Claude Rawson and Ian Higgins, pp. 366–67 and p. 367 n. 3, with reference to William A. Eddy, *Gulliver's Travels: A Critical Study* (Princeton: Princeton University Press, London: Humphrey Milford, 1923), pp. 143–44.

5 See p. 65 above.

 | DOI:10.1163/9789004734548_005

for its imaginative aspect specifically as fantasy voyage literature.[6] Indeed, he cites Swift as his example of fantastical writing done right:

> I feel that in art there shd. be strangeness in one direction and ordinariness in another, never strangeness in both.
> In *Gulliver* you get strange adventures in a studiously ordinary way.[7]

According to Schakel, pride is seen by Lewis as the central theme of *Gulliver's Travels*, with that work serving as, 'a primary model for Lewis's *Out of the Silent Planet*' with the 'imaginary voyage as a means of social criticism'.[8] This is an *immram*-like quality, and indeed, it can be argued that that *Gulliver's Travels* also contributes, alongside the more obvious model of the *Navigatio*, to the design of Lewis's *Voyage*.

Lewis's description of Gulliver's strange adventures delivered 'in a studiously ordinary way' draws attention to the way that the mysterious islands in Swift's text are anchored in real-world navigation and real-world geography. This notion of anchoring the fantastic in the mundane is also cited by Amis, who discusses *Gulliver's Travels* as a precursor to science fiction, drawing parallels between the representation of imaginary islands in this narrative and of imaginary planets in later ones.[9] He makes the point that Swift's text 'is clearly an ancestor of science fiction' because of 'the notorious pains taken by Swift to counterfeit verisimilitude in the details of his story'.[10] This aligns the narrative with Amis's definition of science fiction, as narratives of what could be (or what could be imagined) as possible given current scientific knowledge at the time of composition.[11] Amis's other argument is that in Swift's narrative the islands are 'satirical utopias' and 'this

6 Peter J. Schakel, 'Restoration and Eighteenth Century', in *Reading the Classics with C. S. Lewis*, ed. by Thomas L. Martin (Grand Rapids, MI: Baker Academic, and Carlisle: Paternoster Press, 2000), pp. 187–202 (p. 191). For Lewis on Swift and Gulliver, see C. S. Lewis, 'On Science Fiction' in Lewis, *Of Other Worlds: Essays and Stories*, ed. by W. Hooper (New York and London: Harcourt, 1966), pp. 55–86.

7 Letter to Cecil Harwood, 26 December 1945; in *The Collected Letters of C. S. Lewis. Volume II. Books, Broadcasts, and the War, 1931–1949*, ed. by Walter Hooper (New York, Harper Collins, 2004) p. 689.

8 Schakel, 'Restoration and Eighteenth Century', p. 192. The only connection Schakel draws with the *Voyage of the Dawn Treader*, however, is that he considers its 'critique of "progress"' (in chapter 4) to be 'in the spirit of Swift and Pope' (p. 195).

9 *New Maps*, pp. 30–31. See also above, pp. 7, 26 and below, pp. 140–43.

10 *New Maps*, p. 30.

11 Amis, *New Maps*, pp. 18, 22.

point, where invention and social criticism meet, is the point of departure for a great deal of contemporary science fiction'.[12] We will return to the issue of social criticism and utopia, both crucial elements of *immrama*, in relation to *Star Trek* below.[13]

Like the heroes of *immrama*, Gulliver navigates a predominantly fictional islanded world set firmly within real-world geography, and even incorporating a real-world island, in Swift's case Japan. The notion that Swift's text is political obscures its use of *Navigatio* and *immrama* for inspiration. The latter were also not to be taken literally. It is also worth pointing out that Amis also reverses the comparison by presenting the adventure narratives located in imaginary lost worlds on Earth as 'located somewhere on the borders of science fiction'.[14] This brings us to another twentieth-century echo of Swift's narrative that deserves mention in this context as a narrative of a journey to an otherworld, conventionally positioned at the edges of science fiction and located on the rim of the possible within the geographical and scientific knowledge of the time. This is Conan Doyle's description of an imaginary land where dinosaurs had survived in his *Lost World* (1912).[15]

Like Swift's Gulliver, Conan Doyle's heroes remain within the real world, and arrive at their fantastic destination by conventional travel means, and not through any magic or dream-state.[16] Like Swift's Gulliver, they bring mementos from their very real journey back to Britain.[17] Like Swift, Conan Doyle engages in slight-of-hand exercises to anchor his imaginary lands in the real-world travel logistics and real-world technologies for the illustration of the edition, using photographs to achieve an unsettling effect on the reader.[18] The first edition used a combination of paintings (labelled

12 Amis, *New Maps*, p. 31.

13 See Chapter 5, pp. 134–36, 144, 149.

14 Amis, *New Maps*, pp. 45–46, note. An example of the genre that springs to mind but is not mentioned by Amis is Conan Doyle's *The Lost World* (1912). The publication of this narrative falls well within the period outlined for the popularity of the genre by Amis: 1870–1935.

15 For a discussion of the *Lost World* as a member of the 'lost world' genre of adventure stories and as part of the history of science fiction, see Conor Reid, 'The Lost Worlds of Arthur Conan Doyle's Professor Challenger Series', *Journal of the Fantastic in the Arts*, 28 (2017), 271–89.

16 For Gulliver, see Alff, 'Swift's World', p. 334.

17 For Gulliver, see Alff, 'Swift's World', p. 334.

18 See discussion in Richard Fallon, 'Arthur Conan Doyle's *The Lost World:* Illustrating the Romance of Science', *English Literature in Translation, 1880–1920*, 63 (2020), 162–92.

as reconstructions based on one of the character's drawings) and composite photographs.[19] This is characterised by Richard Fallon as a 'mock-photo-journalistic apparatus'.[20] In this, Doyle can be seen as a precursor of Eco, and Swift in turn as a precursor of Doyle. While Alff is correct in identifying the immediate context of *Gulliver's Travels* as the genre of seventeenth- and early-eighteenth-century travel narratives with 'Travel' or 'Voyage' in the title, I propose to argue in the present chapter that as a member of the intertextual matrix outlined here, the roots of Swift's text go deeper into the Irish tradition.[21] This is not to argue that there was no external, classical influence on Swift. As Beatrice M. Bodart-Bailey observes, Swift in general 'showed himself as traditionalist arguing that modern theories and discoveries were overvalued when compared to the body of ancient wisdom contained in the classics'.[22] He had also written a journey diary within the contemporary tradition, for the Chester-Dublin trajectory, now known as the *Holyhead Journal*, but this was written after Gulliver was published (and was never published itself).[23]

Crucially, Gulliver's story differs from examples provided by Alff in its fictionality – the lands described are obviously imaginary, a feature shared, on the other hand, with *immrama*. Read in this context, the conventional interpretation of *Gulliver's Travels* as also a satire on the genre, might need to be qualified.[24] While the work might respond to contemporary travel narratives

19 Fallon, 'Arthur Conan Doyle's *The Lost World*', pp. 164–65.

20 Fallon, 'Arthur Conan Doyle's *The Lost World*', p. 165.

21 Alff, 'Swift's World', pp. 332–33, lists the following works: Charles Patin, *Travels thro' Germany, Bohemia, Swisserland, and Holland* (1701); Johannes Nieuhof, *Voyages and Travels into Brasil and the East Indies* (1703); James Brome, *Travels Over England, Scotland, and Wales* (1707). For comments on the popularity of the travel narrative genre in the seventeenth century, see also Frederick Bracher, 'The Maps in "Gulliver's Travels"', *Huntington Library Quarterly*, 8 (1944), 59–74 (p. 59). For a more recent discussion of Swift, travel, and travel literature, see Shef Rogers, 'Travel and Exploration', in *Jonathan Swift in Context*, ed. by Joseph Hone and Pat Rogers (Cambridge: Cambridge University Press, 2024), pp. 93–99.

22 Beatrice M. Bodart-Bailey, '*Gulliver's Travels*, Japan and Engelbert Kaempfer', *Otsuma Journal of Comparative Culture*, 22 (2021), 75–100.

23 Clive Probyn, *Jonathan Swift and the Anglo-Irish Road* (Leiden: Brill and William Fink, 2020), p. 1. Considerations of space make it impossible to engage with Swift's attitude to Dublin and to Ireland fully here; for a recent discussion of Swift's Dublin, see David Dickson, 'Dublin', in *Jonathan Swift in Context*, ed. by Joseph Hone and Pat Rogers (Cambridge: Cambridge University Press, 2024), pp. 270–76.

24 As expressed, for instance, by Alff: '"Travels" signifies an attempt at satirizing the truth-making stratagems of a literary genre while also evoking the travails of Gulliver,

(and their less believable aspects, or tendencies towards exaggeration), its fictionality, exaggeration, and truth-claims might be a combination of a reaction to these and a building on an older and established tradition of allegorical tales of journeys to imaginary lands.

4.1 Swift and Allegorical Reading

As Michael Sinding points out, there has been some debate as to the degree to which *Gulliver's Travels* is allegorical.[25] As mentioned below, 'allegory' is subject to many possible definitions.[26] In simple terms it is, as Jason J. Gulya puts it, 'a form for speaking otherwise'.[27] That Swift's text yields itself well to allegorical reading is evidenced by its presence as an example in such contexts as the opening of Jeremy Tambling's discussion of allegory, where it features, alongside Daniel Defoe's *Robinson Crusoe*, between the references to medieval texts and Orwell's *Animal Farm*.[28] It is the purpose of this section to argue that the text's openness to allegorical reading (and thus the scholarly debate itself) is a function of its belonging to the *immram* genre tradition. By formulating the issue in this way, postulating the capacity of the text to inspire an allegorical interpretation, rather than describing it as inherently by nature an allegory, I aim to centre the question of reception in this discussion.[29] As Phillip Harth observes, reading *Gulliver's Travels* as an allegory 'is a recently acquired habit', and not the way that eighteenth- and nineteenth-century readers experienced the narrative, as they will have seen allusions in the text to contemporary politics, but would not have read it as a consistent allegorical narrative.[30]

---

his labors of survival, ceaseless hardships, and vocational ascent from ship doctor to captain' ('Swift's World', p. 333).

25 Michael Sinding, 'Metaphor, Allegory, Irony, Satire and Supposition in Factual and Fictional Narrative', in *Narrative Factuality: A Handbook*, ed. by Monika Fludenik and Marie-Laure Ryan (Berlin: De Gruyter, 2020), pp. 165–84 (pp. 173–74).

26 See p. 115 n. 31.

27 Jason J. Gulya, *Allegory in Enlightenment Britain. Literary Abominations* (Cham: Palgrave Macmillan, 2022), p. 6.

28 Tambling, *Allegory*, p. 1.

29 Clare Bucknell describes the text as one that 'seems to invite and then refuse political interpretation'; 'Satire' in *Jonathan Swift in Context*, ed. by Joseph Hone and Pat Rogers (Cambridge: Cambridge University Press, 2024), pp. 125–31 (p. 126).

30 Phillip Harth, 'The Problem of Political Allegory in *Gulliver's Travels*', *Modern Philology*, 73 (1976), 40–47 (p. 40).

Another reason for taking the allegorical reading as potential rather than inherent quality of the narrative lies in the definition of allegory I employ.[31] In his discussion of allegory in *Gulliver's Travels*, Sinding describes the concept, in its origins, 'as a form of interpretation (*allegoresis*), [which] developed into a form of composition' and 'uses a narrative fiction to refer in some indirect but systematic way to another domain of reference, typically conceptual and/or historical, religious, moral, or political'.[32] It is significant that the first reference in his discussion, in context of how allegory had been seen by 'literary scholars', is to C. S. Lewis.[33]

One of the issues in the case of *Gulliver's Travels* is whether the reference is systematic or whether, as argued by Harth, the gaps in the allusions are filled by historians and literary scholars desperate to read a consistent allegory into it.[34] Harth discusses specifically the journey to Lilliput, but the same argument can be extended to Gulliver's other journeys. Swift's references to the dangers of printing the text might be interpreted as supporting evidence for reading the whole as an extended allegory, but might equally well have been prompted by the presence of specific allusions satirizing the government.[35] Harth's argument against an allegorical reading of Swift's text rests on the definition of allegory as a consistent political allusion built into the narrative as a whole. Conversely, Robert P. Fitzgerald's reading of Gulliver's third voyage (to Luggnagg) as not only a commentary on the idea of eternal life but as satire on Louis XIV and the Académie Française – both aspects that he terms allegorical – also is weighted heavily towards political satire.[36] Allegory, however, particularly in its medieval tradition, is not necessarily (or exclusively) political. Indeed, there is a strong scholarly tradition of opposition between the two types.[37] Swift's engagement with the political type of allegory in his other works is well-known, but there has been a tension between the two also in scholars' readings of *A Tale of a Tub* – as an

31 As Tambling points out, there are many possible definitions, Tambling, *Allegory*, p. 1.

32 Sinding, 'Metaphor', p. 173.

33 Sinding, 'Metaphor', p. 173 n. 7. The reference is to Lewis, *The Allegory of Love*.

34 Harth, 'The Problem', p. 42.

35 See, for instance, discussion in Harth, 'The Problem', p. 43, though Harth argues that Swift cannot have been so afraid as to encode his text so completely as scholars who seek to read it as an allegory seem to suggest (p. 44).

36 Robert P. Fitzgerald, 'The Allegory of Luggnagg and the Struldbruggs in "Gulliver's Travels"', *Studies in Philology*, 65 (1968), 657–76 (p. 658).

37 See Ann W. Astell's discussion of Lewis's separation of the two, *Political Allegory in Late Medieval England* (Ithaca and London: Cornell University Press, 1999), p. 2.

allegory on the one hand and as a commentary on the Reformation on the other.[38] The case of this text is particularly informative for our purposes. As Gulya argues, Swift both constructs this text as an allegory and uses it to problematize and question the processes and principles of allegorical reading, pushing his readers both to read allegorically and to be sensitive to over-interpretation which may twist the text's actual intended meaning.[39] In Gulya's reading, *Gulliver's Travels* then takes this further by mixing allegory with other generic ingredients.[40]

The brief discussion of the allegorical potential of Swift's text in this section makes no claims to bibliographical completeness – much ink has been spilt in a quest 'to look for close parallels in every character and every scene of the book', to reprise Nabokov's phrasing, quoted earlier.[41] My goal here was not to establish whether Swift has a predominantly political (as political satire) or moral allegory in mind for Gulliver's various journeys, but rather to highlight the text's openness – intentional, I would argue – to allegorical interpretation. This function of the narrative is created and conditioned by Swift's indirect use of the *immram* generic model, combined with *echtra* elements. To pick up on a point made by Gulya, Swift is typical of Enlightenment writers who 'broke that now distinct genre of allegory into its parts and experimented with combining those parts with those of other genres'.[42] This generic re-mixing centres the travel narrative but brings with it the allegoric potential inherent in the medieval text almost as a side-effect (although perhaps with more intentionality).[43] Ultimately, as Sinding suggests, Swift 'both prompts and frustrates mappings of the actual world, to multiple spaces of time and place, at several levels of abstraction'.[44] The spatial aspect of Gulliver's voyages is, of course, an *immram* frame, and crucially, like the *immrama*, it plays with the audience's own world and its geography and spatial dynamics. It is to this aspect of the text that we must now turn.

38 Gulya, *Allegory*, pp. 55–62; see also Bucknell, 'Satire', pp. 126, 130; David Manning, 'The Church of England', in *Jonathan Swift in Context*, ed. by Joseph Hone and Pat Rogers (Cambridge: Cambridge University Press, 2024), pp. 232–39 (p. 238).

39 Gulya, *Allegory*, pp. 61–62.

40 Gulya, *Allegory*, pp. 62–63. Gulya terms this 'mode-ification of allegory' (p. 62), a situation where a texts use 'allegorical connections without themselves being classified as allegories' (p. 9).

41 Nabokov, 'James Joyce', p. 288.

42 Gulya, *Allegory*, p. 8.

43 See above, p. 4.

44 Sinding, 'Metaphor', p. 175.

4.2 Swift's Real-World Framework

While, as Ruth Menzies observes, it is common for the 'imaginary voyage' to be 'characterised by a certain ambiguity which originates to a considerable extent in the deliberate blurring of boundaries between reality and fiction', the 'the opening and closing sequences, describing the outward and return journeys, are almost invariably realistic in nature, and the countries visited by the traveller are usually located on the fringes of the known world'.[45] Thus, the real world geography provides the start and end point in such narratives, and we see this indeed in terms of our corpus in the beginning and end of *immrama* and *echtrai* journeys in Ireland, in the start and end points of Gulliver's journeys in England, in the start and end points of Lewis's *Voyage* (and indeed all Narnia adventures, except the final) as well as the *Stargate SG-1* expeditions on present-day Earth. However, Gulliver's journey keeps to the real-world geography (messy though the representation is) for quite a while, in describing the journey, and, crucially, in the description of one of the islands he visits, Japan.

As we will see in this section, *Gulliver's Travels* combine classical inspiration and echoes with a grounding in seventeenth- and eighteenth-century travel practicalities and experiences, travel literature of the period, and also influences of Old Irish voyage narratives (belonging to both the *immram* and the *echtra* types). There are in particular echoes of the *echtra* 'otherworld' return in Gulliver's complaint that when each time he returned home from a voyage he found that the dialect spoken at home had changed almost beyond his understanding.[46] This is reminiscent of the variations in the flow of time in the otherworld.[47]

Bodart-Bailey's argument that the 'real-life journey' pretence in *Gulliver's Travels* was necessary because it would enable Swift to avoid being 'accused of what he had set out to do, namely brazenly mock the government and the society he lived in' is only convincing insofar as the pretence provided an excuse – presumably the public was not so gullible as to actually believe

---

45 Ruth Menzies, 'Re-writing *Gulliver's Travels*: the Demise of a Genre?' *e-Rea. Revue électronique d'études sur le monde anglophone*, 3 (2005) <https://doi.org/10.4000/erea.613>, §1.

46 Christine Rees, *Utopian Imagination and Eighteenth-Century Fiction* (London and New York: Longman, 1996), p. 126, citing H. Davis, ed., H. Williams introduction to Jonathan Swift, *Gulliver's Travels* revised edition of 1926 (republished in Blackwell: Swift, *The Prose Works*, vol. 11, 1965), p. 7.

47 See above, pp. 52–53, 97 and below, pp. 152–53, 164, 166–67.

the truth of Gulliver's claims.[48] The ambiguity in relation to truth and truth-claims treads the same narrow line, particularly in respect to the inclusion of the non-fictional exotic (Japan) alongside the downright imagined (Lilliput, Brobdingnag, Laputa and Houyhnhnm-land) as the medieval European voyage narratives (Mandeville and Marco Polo) echoed also in Eco's *Baudolino*. In each case there is an anchoring in real-world geography. In Swift's text, this is emphasized by lengthy passages describing navigation with tantalising imitation of accuracy and precision, making the fantasy worlds of his islands seem almost locatable, just out of reach, as illustrated by this passage form the opening of 'A Voyage to *Brobdingnag*', describing the adventures of Gulliver's ship, originally 'bound for *Surat*':

> We had a very prosperous Gale till we arrived at the *Cape of Good-hope* [...] we could not leave the *Cape* till the End of *March*. We then set sail, and had a good Voyage till we passed the *Streights* of *Madagascar*; but having got Northward of that Island, and to about five Degrees South Latitude, the Winds [...] began to blow with much greater Violence, and more Westerly than usual; continuing so for twenty Days together, during which time we were driven a little to the East of the *Molucca* Islands, and about three Degrees Northward of the Line, as our Captain found by an Observation he took the 2d of *May* ...[49]

The detail, which makes it possible to trace part of the route on a map, though it may result in cartographic impossibilities, works alongside Swift's use of real maps (adjusted slightly to include his fictional lands) to illustrate his work.[50] In this instance, the framework for the fictional journey is set up in relation to the reader's real world. Swift also seems to be engaged in a reverse movement. The fictional geography of Gulliver's later voyages is open to mapping onto a real-world framework. Fitzgerald, for instance, has argued that the geography of the voyage to Luggnagg can be mapped easily onto the real-world geographical framework provided by Britain and France, and has used this point to support his argument for an allegorical reading to the voyage.[51] In the case of Gulliver, as David Alff observes, this proximity is

48 *'Gulliver's Travels,'*, p. 81.

49 Swift, *Gulliver's Travels*, p. 366, in Rawson and Higgins, ed., *The Essential Writings of Jonathan Swift*.

50 To give but one example highlighted by Bracher, Swift's directions for Liliput put the island somewhere in the middle of Australia; 'The Maps', p. 67.

51 Fitzgerald, 'The Allegory', pp. 658–59.

emphasised by the presence of maps illustrating the text from the first edition onwards:

> Swift places his imaginary lands in proximity to real places through map plates that appear at the beginning of each volume. One map sticks Lilliput southwest of Sumatra. Brobdingnag occupies a peninsula jutting out of central California. Laputa hovers over the pacific ocean east of Japan. The Country of Houyhnhnms lies southwest of Australia. These lands appear to occupy real space in the world, and yet reaching them is harder than their cartography would suggest.[52]

Gulliver's Travels carry, from the first edition onwards, an unauthorized copy of a map by Herman Moll. The map was identified by Frederick Bracher as that originally published in 1719 under the title 'A New & Correct Map of the Whole World Shewing ye Situation of its Principal Parts. Viz the Oceans, Kingdoms, River Capes, Ports, Mountains, Woods, Trade-Winds, Monsoons, Variation of ye Compass, Climats, &c.'[53] As Bracher observes, 'Three of the maps (Lilliput, Brobdingnag, and Houyhnhnmland) were obviously traced directly from Moll's map; they correspond exactly in size, in outline, and, with a few exceptions [...], in place names and spelling'.[54] Swift's mapmaker positioned the fictional lands within the framework of the copied maps, sometimes shifting the location of the representation of real landmasses slightly to accommodate the intrusion.[55] Bracher suggests that Swift may not have been made party to the plan of using the maps to

52 Alff, 'Swift's World of *Gulliver's Travels*', in *Routledge Companion to Imaginary Worlds*, ed. by Mark Wolf (London: Routledge, 2017), pp. 332–38 (p. 333). For the maps, see the digital images on the British Library website <https://www.bl.uk/collection-items/first-edition-of-gullivers-travels-1726> [accessed 4 October, 2023].

53 Bracher, 'The Maps', p. 61–62. A digital facsimile of the copy of this map held by the Library of Congress Geography and Map Division Washington, D.C, under the callmark G3200 1719.M6 TIL is available at <http://hdl.loc.gov/loc.gmd/g3200.ct007070> [accessed 12 October 2023]. For a discussion of the narrative capacity of Moll's maps, and an up-to-date bibliography, see Alex Zukas, 'Cartography and Narrative in the Maps of Herman Moll's The World Described', *XVII–XVIII*, 78 (2021). Special issue: *Cartes et cartographies dans le monde anglophone aux XVIIe et XVIIIe siècles / Maps and Mapping in the English-Speaking World in the 17th and 18th Centuries* <http://journals.openedition.org/1718/8764> [accessed 12 October 2023].

54 Bracher, 'The Maps', p. 62.

55 Bracher, 'The Maps', pp. 63–64, 67–69.

illustrate his works.[56] However, the maps and Swift's geographical passages work in concert to anchor the text in the tradition of real-life voyage accounts rather than in the tradition of imagined, fantastic, or otherworld voyages to which it belongs. The full title of Swift's text, which no one uses, is *Travels into the Several Remote Nations of the World. In Four Parts* (see Figure 4.1). This title implies factual description and thus complements the function of the maps. Without the maps to link it to 'modern' geographical exploration, and without the modern title, Gulliver's travels would be too much like an *immram*.

4.3 Gulliver's Islands and the Problems of Utopia

Despite the attempts, primarily by means of form and external appearance, to distance the book from the Irish fantastic voyage tradition, it is replete with *immram* characteristics. One of the main *immram* characteristics of *Gulliver's Travels* is in the nature of the travel involved. Another is the agglomeration of *topoi* in the depiction of the island realms.[57]

As David Alff points out, while 'readers tend to isolate [the places Gulliver travels] from one another, partitioning Gulliver's four-part exploration into a string of episodic jaunts', 'despite their dissimilarities, Lilliput, Brobdingnag, Laputa, and Houyhnhnm Land belong to a single fictional world with a traceable literary heritage and cohesive political agenda'.[58] (Alff's list omits Japan from the list of Gulliver's visit locations). Crucial to this sense of unity, as Alff further observes, is the actual title of the work: *Travels into Several Remote Nations of the World. In Four Parts. By Lemuel Gulliver, First a Surgeon, and then a Captain of Several Ships*.[59] (See Figure 4.1)

Travel literature developed into a distinct genre in the seventeenth century, and its emergence marked a distinct stage in the history of the reception of earlier travel narratives. For example, it is in the seventeenth century that the title of Marco Polo's famous travelogue finally became established as the *Travels*.[60] Marco Polo's *Travels*, before being assimilated into the naming practices of the newly established genre, had been known by a

56 Bracher, 'The Maps', pp. 64–65, 70, 73.

57 Rees, *Utopian Imagination*, p. 126: 'Almost every topos known to the genre is in there somewhere'.

58 Alff, 'Swift's World', p. 332.

59 Alff, 'Swift's World', p. 332.

60 Akbari, 'Introduction', p. 9.

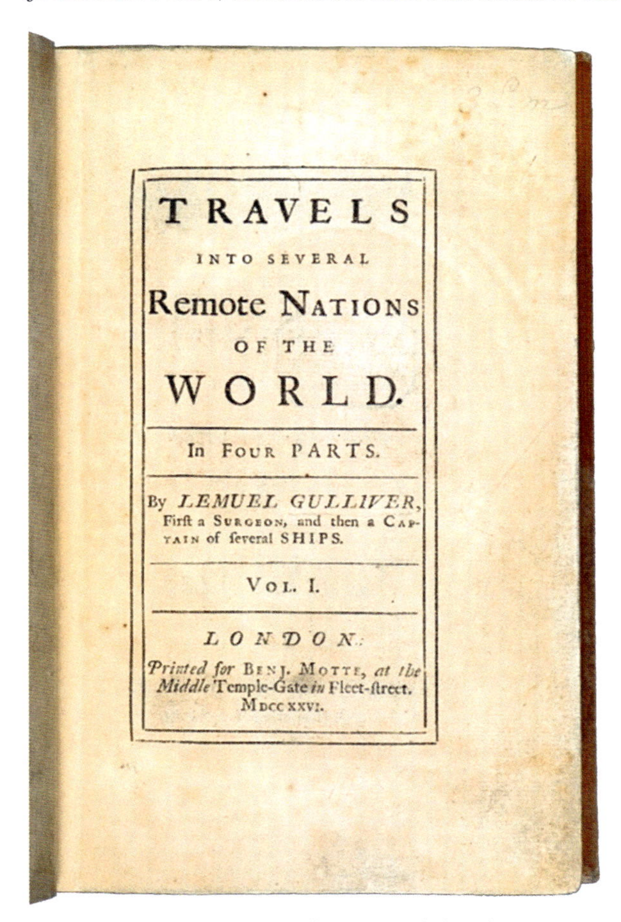

TRAVELS

INTO SEVERAL

Remote NATIONS

OF THE

WORLD.

In FOUR PARTS.

By *LEMUEL GULLIVER*,
Firſt a SURGEON, and then a CAPTAIN of ſeveral SHIPS.

VOL. I.

LONDON:

Printed for BENJ. MOTTE, *at the Middle* Temple-Gate *in* Fleet-ſtreet.
MDCCXXVI.

FIGURE 4.1 Title page of *Gulliver's Travels* (1726), BL C.59.e.11. Public Domain (SOURCE: https://www.bl.uk/collection-items/first-edition-of-gullivers-travels-1726)

variety of appellations: *Il Milione, Le Devisement dou Monde, Le livre des merveilles du monde, De mirabilibus mundi,* and even *Li Livres du Graunt Caam.*[61] The emergence of the travel literature genre also coincided with the emergence (*avant la lettre*) of the practice of tourism.[62] Fictional travel allowed to blur the line between the real and the fantastic, and thereby to

61 Akbari, 'Introduction', p. 9.

62 Bohls, 'Introduction', in *Travel Writing, 1700–1830. An Anthology*, ed. by Elizabeth A. Bohls and Ian Duncan (Oxford: Oxford University Press, 2005), pp. xix–xx.

extend the range of the possible, as arm-chair travel. As Bohls observes, 'Fictional voyages were certainly among the bestsellers of the eighteenth century. *Robinson Crusoe* (1719) and *Gulliver's Travels* (1726) both piggybacked on the popularity of non-fiction travel accounts'.[63] These fictional travel accounts allowed the reader to experience the impossible, and the author to explore human condition, and in *Gulliver's* case, comment on and satirize contemporary society and politics.

Swift's narrative engages in particular with the utopian imagination, constructing imaginary (other)worlds in a tradition most famously exemplified by Thomas More's *Utopia* (1516).[64] As Houston points out, 'ambiguity and irony have always been a feature of the utopian mode of discourse'.[65] This is certainly shared by Swift's text, but its relationship with the genre of utopian writing is significantly more complex, as Houston shows, and contingent on definitions of 'utopia' and 'utopian'. 'Broadly speaking there is a distinction between those critics who take *utopian* to mean idealistic or perfectionist about human society and perfectibility, and those for whom the deciding factor is the nature of its engagement with the utopian tradition with a particular utopian text, usually (indeed, almost exclusively) More's *Utopia*'.[66] Utopia is not exclusively associated, however, either with political manifestos of with contemporary science fiction. Aspects of the utopian imagery have been traced also in the Irish tradition, including the medieval tradition.[67] Moylan positions the *Navigatio* in particular as a 'text that stands as an early high point in the imaginative stream that draws on the creation of inspirational otherworlds, and does so especially with the figure of the island'.[68]

Houston argues that Swift's composition does not itself belong to the utopia genre but rather engages with concepts of utopia and with the genre from the outside.[69] The genre includes one of the works that are identified

---

63 Bohls, 'Introduction', p. xxi.

64 Chlöe Houston, 'Utopia, Dystopia or Anti-utopia? Gulliver's Travels and the Utopian Mode of Discourse', *Utopian Studies*, 18 (2007), 425–42. For the text, see Susan Bruce, ed., *Three Early Modern Utopias. Thomas More: Utopia / Francis Bacon: New Atlantis / Henry Neville: The Isle of Pines*, Oxford World's Classics (Oxford: Oxford University Press, 1999) or G. M. Logan and R. M. Adams, ed., *Thomas More. Utopia*, Cambridge Texts in the History of Political Thought, 2 (Cambridge: Cambridge University Press, 1989).

65 Houston, 'Utopia, Dystopia or Anti-utopia?', p. 425.

66 Houston, 'Utopia, Dystopia or Anti-utopia?', p. 246.

67 Moylan, 'Irish Voyages'.

68 Moylan, 'Irish Voyages', p. 301.

69 Houston, 'Utopia, Dystopia or Anti-utopia?, p. 247.

as particularly strong influences on *Gulliver's Travels* – Lucian's *Vera Historia* (*True History*). The similarities between Swift's narrative and Lucian's are too striking to be ignored and have been much discussed.[70] One is tempted to wonder, in this connection, whether the reading of Swift's text through a classicising prism, with emphasis on Lucian rather than *immrama*, and on classical writers rather than the traditions of the country where he lived, might not have obscured other Irish influences in his text. Christine Rees, for instance, describes the Lilliputian system of child-reading as 'Spartan in the exact sense of the term', because it presupposes separating the young from their parents at an early age, noting that in making the parents pay for their children's education the 'Lilliputians run counter to most utopians, who regard education as the financial as well as moral responsibility of the state'.[71] Yet the system is in that regard strikingly similar to the medieval Irish institution of fosterage – placing young infants (sometimes babies) – in the care of a family who is not biologically related, with the biological parents bearing the financial costs of the upbringing.[72] One might speculate that Swift was not aware that a system strikingly similar to that which he proposed for the Lilliputians had existed in Ireland for centuries, but it seems something of a stretch. According to Andrew Carpenter, Swift was 'only tangentially involved' in Irish-language culture.[73] Just how much Swift drew on Irish (not necessarily Irish-language) history and culture is a matter that requires a separate investigation.[74] It was suggested by H. D. Kelling that Swift used Irish alongside French, Latin and Greek to create the languages spoken in the lands visited by Gulliver.[75] In terms of the *immram*

70 William A. Eddy, 'A Source for *Gulliver's Travels*' *Modern Language Notes*, 36 (1921), 419–22, p. 419; Compean, 'Swift and the Lucianic Tradition'; Menzies, 'Re-writing *Gulliver's Travels*'.

71 Rees, *Utopian Imagination*, p. 129.

72 For a recent in-depth discussion of the subject, see Thomas C. O'Donnell, *Fosterage in Medieval Ireland. An Emotional History* (Amsterdam: Amsterdam University Press, 2020).

73 Andrew Carpenter, 'Literary Scene. Ireland', in *Jonathan Swift in Context*, ed. by Joseph Hone and Pat Rogers (Cambridge: Cambridge University Press, 2024), pp. 255–62 (p. 261 n.9).

74 See Alan Harrison, *The Dean's Friend: Anthony Raymond 1675–1726: Jonathan Swift and the Irish Language* (Dublin: de Burca, 1999), chapter 5; originally published in Irish as *Ag Cruinniú Meala: Anthony Raymond (1675–1726), Ministéir Protastúnach, agus Léann na Gaeilge i mBaile Átha Cliath* (Dublin: An Clóchomhar, 1988).

75 H. D. Kelling, 'Some Significant Names in Gulliver's Travels', *Studies in Philology*, 48 (1951), 761–78, (pp. 764, 768, 773, 776).

influence on *Gulliver's Travels*, including the utopian elements, this would have in any case, as with Lewis, be mediated most likely by the Latin tradition of the *Navigatio*.

Some of the utopian aspects of Swift's writing are echoed later in *Star Trek*. The emphasis on the rational (logic, in *Star Trek*) as the foundation of an ideal society, is present in particular in Swift's depiction of Houyhnhnmland.[76] This emphasis on rationality, 'Reason', is very similar in *Star Trek*'s idealised depiction of Vulcans.[77] If *Star Trek* draws on Swift, the earlier author, in turn, is indebted partly to the classics but partly also to the Irish otherworld. A most striking echo of the descriptions of the idealised otherworld, land of life and plenty, found in *Gulliver*, is quoted by Houston to emphasise the similarities with More.[78] This is a passage describing the ideal society of the Houyhnhnms entirely through absence of negatives (rather than presence of positives).[79] This is strongly reminiscent of the description of the otherworld in, for example, *Immram Brain*, a curious Old Irish tale dating from about the seventh century, that as has already been mentioned defies genre divisions between *immram* and *echtra*.[80] In this text, an otherworldly woman invites Bran to her land, which she describes as follows:[81]

> cen brón, cen duba, cen bás,
> cen nach n-galar cen indgás,
> is ed etargne n-Emne,
> ní comtig a comamre.
>
> (Without grief, without sorrow, without death,
> Without any sickness, without debility,
> That is the sign of Emain –
> Uncommon is an equal marvel.)

---

76 Houston, 'Utopia, Dystopia or Anti-utopia?, p. 432.

77 Swift, 'A Voyage to the Country of the Houyhnhms', in *The Essential Writings of Jonathan Swift*, p. 483. A crucial distinction is that while Swift appears to be critical of the scientific discourses of the time; *Star Trek* is a technological utopia. See, for instance, discussion in Douglas Lane Patey, 'Swift's Satire on "Science" and the Structure of *Gulliver's Travels*', ELH, 58 (1991), 809–39.

78 Houston, 'Utopia, Dystopia or Anti-utopia?, pp. 432–33.

79 Swift, 'A Voyage to the Country of the Houyhnhhms', p. 489.

80 Meyer, ed. and trans. *The Voyage of Bran*; see also above, pp. 25, 33, 36–37.

81 Text and translation from Meyer, ed. and trans. *The Voyage of Bran*, stanza 10, pp. 6, 7.

She also describes the land in a sequence of further stanzas in terms of the presence of wealth, not only, as in the stanza quoted above, in terms of the absence of negative features and experiences. The otherworld as source of wealth is also a stable tradition in medieval Irish (but also Welsh texts) and resurfaces in our corpus in the wealth of the land of Deacon John (visited by Baudolino) and of Prester John (imagined by Baudolino), as well as, in its science-fiction iteration, as the technologically advanced otherworlds of *Stargate*, discussed in Chapter 6 below.[82] The similarities between the utopian descriptions in *Immram Brain* and in *Gulliver's Travels* invite a discussion of the concept of the utopian otherworld space.[83] Since the definition of utopia has for a long time been subject of discussion and debate, it is worth revisiting in light of our specific textual matrix.

The clearest definition of the usual use of the term 'utopia' is provided by Sotirios Triantafyllos, writing that it 'refers to literary works that followed the model set by More and described fictional better societies set in faraway lands'.[84] The term is also frequently used for the 'fictional better societies' themselves, although as Hutchinson points out, these should properly be termed 'eutopia'.[85] Utopia, as the shorthand for an idealised otherworld is useful for the discussion of Swift's text and also will be used in the following chapters for the discussion of the human and alien civilisations of *Star Trek* and the alien societies in *Stargate*. The 'no space' term *utopia* to describe the fantastic otherworlds linkable to the Old Irish tradition is particularly appropriate given their general localizability in the real world. Even when real-world anchorage is seemingly provided in the misleadingly realistic-sounding description of the voyage, as in Swift's text, or by such insistence as has Brendan's Island added to pre-modern maps, the idealized aspect of the place makes it by definition unreachable.[86] The paradox is perfectly articulated by Stephen Hutchinson:

---

82 See pp. 26, 91, 101 above and pp. 168–69 below.

83 For a discussion of utopias and the utopian genre from a spatial perspective, see Sotirios Triantafyllos, *Topos in Utopia. A Peregrination to Early Modern Utopianism's Space* (Wilmington: Vernon Press, 2021).

84 Triantafyllos, *Topos in Utopia*, p. xv n. 1.

85 See also discussion in Steven Hutchinson, 'Mapping Utopias', *Modern Philology*, 85 (1987), 170–85 (p. 170). In any case, utopia as a term thus generally appears to have positive connotations, and is invariably tied to More's text as either origin of influence or model for comparison, and almost invariably is used for the ideal society as shorthand.

86 Hutchinson, 'Mapping Utopias', pp. 172, 176.

> "Utopia" as a name attaches itself to a given somewhere and affirms the existence of that place while negating this positive onomastic function through its meaning. Into the nonspace of nowhere a fully inhabited world is projected by the imagination. The name thus signals both the negative ontological status of the island and the fictive nature of the text that self-mockingly describes a nonexistent world.[87]

To the utopian genre Hutchinson ascribes Gulliver's islands, the Land of Prester John (and medieval ideas of India more generally), the Promised Land of Saints of Saint Brendan (as 'Staint Brendan's isle'), amongst other imaginary lands of wonder, as literary utopias that were considered real by (at least some of) the texts' audiences.[88] The paradox inherent in the term utopia is also inherent in the tension between reality and fantasy in each of the texts discussed in this book, though in each instance this paradox is dealt with differently. Thanks to the grounding of the intertextual matrix in the Old Irish narrative tradition, we can use the term 'otherworlds' to designate the entire collection of these worlds.[89] Utopia, the idealised non-space, thus provides a framework and starting point for the discussion of the various otherworlds involved. Importantly, Swift's otherworlds are not all as eutopian as the land of the Houyhnhnms. Lilliput and Brobdignang are hardly ideal lands, and the destination of Gulliver's fourth voyage, Japan, is hardly an imagined land, since it, in fact, exists in the real world of the reader.

A set of different terms is therefore required to complement the term 'utopia', for the discussion of those alien environments which are not depicted as idyllic, or that are not imaginary.[90] I will thus supplement the term with Margaret Atwood's coinage 'ustopia' for the non-idealised otherworlds, and Michel Foucault's 'heterotopia' for the other(real)worlds.[91] Dystopia would not serve my purpose as it represents the other – uniformly

87 Hutchinson, 'Mapping Utopias', p. 171.

88 Hutchinson, 'Mapping Utopias', p. 176.

89 Hutchinson refers to these as 'worlds' but does not use the term 'otherworld'.

90 Hutchinson convincingly argues that taking the *eutopian* otherworlds exclusively, without paying attention to their non-eutopian counterpars, is problematic, yielding to selective reading of isolated sections of texts; Hutchinson, 'Mapping Utopias', p. 178. For a brief discussion of the non-utopian recurring aliens of *Star Trek*, see for example Johnson-Smith, *American Science Fiction TV*, pp. 86–89.

91 Atwood, 'The Road to Ustopia'; Michel Foucault, 'Of Other Spaces', trans. by Jay Miskowiec, *Diacritics*, 16 (1986), 22–27 (pp. 24–25). Foucault's concept of heterotopias is sufficiently flexible to have already found application in discussions of medieval literature; Megan G. Leitch and K. S. Whetter, 'Introduction', in *Arthurian Literature XXXVI:*

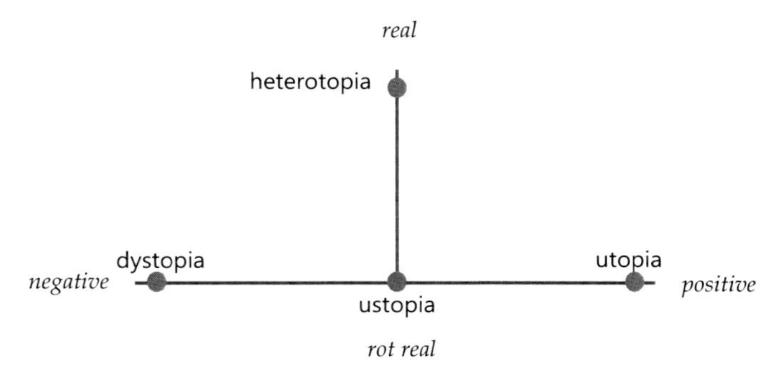

FIGURE 4.2 Literary otherworlds. A coordinate system for utopia, dystopia, ustopia and heterotopia

negative but still imagined – extreme. I also resist using the alternative and less positive concept of heterotopia as 'place that is other' for the use of imagined lands, since in Foucault's original definition, it described real places.[92] It will thus be reserved for places that exist but that are described as 'other', as foil for the author's and audience(s)' homeland reality. Heterotopia thus in principle opposed to utopia not on the **positive-negative** axis (as dystopia is) but rather opposed to both of those concepts on the axis **real-not real.** An unreal/imaginary land equivalent of heterotopia that occupies an equally intermediate position between utopia and dystopia is most adequately covered by Atwood's coinage 'ustopia'.[93] (Figure 4.2.)

Crucially for our purposes, the so-called 'Celtic otherworld' is also a not real counterpoint for heterotopias. Like the islands of the *immrama*, various otherworlds depicted in the Old Irish *echtrai* can, but do not have to be idyllic utopias.[94] They also occupy a liminal space between the real and the imagined in the texts.

Triantafyllos sees much of the classical and medieval literature that deals with utopias as a combination of genres, including travel writing and the utopia.[95] In his reading, the Promised Land of Saints of the *Navigatio* becomes the debated utopian space, somewhere between fantasy and reality, 'with its exact location frequently debated by sailors and scholars, and a

Sacred Space in Arthurian Romance, ed. by Megan G. Leitch and K. S. Whetter (Woodbridge: Boydell and Brewer, 2021), p. 3.

92 Foucault, '*Of Other Spaces*', pp. 24–25.

93 Atwood, 'The Road to Ustopia'.

94 For the *immrama*, see Hillers, 'Voyages', p. 66.

95 Triantafyllos, *Topos in Utopia*, p. 4.

permanent place on the medieval *mappae mundi* reserved for it'.[96] Utopia, therefore oscillates between reality and fantasy, under the influence of human yearning for the ideal.

The unreachable nature of the ideal, when it is positioned in the real world (even if only as a literary device) yields impermanence – otherwise what would stop the audience from trying to find it? The exile from the utopian otherworld, thus an unwilling return to his own world, distinguishes Gulliver from most of the *echtra* travellers, who either remain in the otherworld or choose to return.[97] This he has in common with the *immram* tradition of the *Navigatio*, as echoed in the conclusion of Lewis's *Voyage*, both of which conclude with a scene where those who had been granted a glimpse of the paradisical utopian otherworld are told to return to their world to live out their lives first.[98] The two texts in our collection which constitute a combination or *echtra* and *immram*, Swift's *Gulliver's Travels* and Eco's *Baudolino*, allow their heroes to dwell in the utopian otherworld for a brief moment, but force them to return to their own land ultimately.[99] We will see that the same pattern can be observed in the television series discussed in Chapters 5 and 6 below. While the rowing-about narrative of *Star Trek* presents the human homeland of the United Federation of Planets as utopia in itself, and thus lifts the need for yearning for utopia (in all but the return narrative of *Voyager*), the *echtra*-based *Stargate* presents a number of utopian encounters, cut short by expulsion or requirement to return home.[100] It is noteworthy that all the planetary worlds in *Stargate* are 'other', frequently designated in the series not only by the term 'planet' or by its designated alpha-numeric code, but also by the term 'off-world'. Not all otherworlds in *Stargate* are planetary, however. A case in point is Daniel Jackson's brief stint as an ascended being (one who acquires infinitely more knowledge and power through having upgraded to an energy-only existence, having shed physical form, but in exchange unable to use his powers to help his friends) in Season 6. As with *echtra*-type narratives, Jackson is

96 Triantafyllos, *Topos in Utopia*, p. 5.

97 This also, as Houston points out, distinguishes Gulliver from some of his predecessors in the utopian genre; 'Utopia, Dystopia or Anti-utopia?', pp. 433–34.

98 O'Donoghue, *Brendaniana*, p. 174; Lewis, *Voyage*, p. 255. See also Mulligan, *A Landscape of Words*, p. 48; Moylan, 'Irish Voyages', pp. 308, 314–15; and Chapter 2 above, pp. 54, 70.

99 See discussion above, p. 94.

100 For *Star Trek*'s utopian features, see, for example, Johnson-Smith, *American Science Fiction TV*, pp. 93, 96; see also discussion and further references below, pp. 144, 149.

ultimately expulsed from this otherworld (although the indication is that he chose to leave, in order to assist his friends in the mortal realm). A similar expulsion motif – where the otherworld is in planetary mode – is found at the conclusion of the episode 'The Nox', when the extremely advanced and friendly Nox permanently close their stargate to any interplanetary visits at the conclusion of the SG team's encounter with them.[101]

Gulliver's utopian experience with the Houyhnhnms thus provides a key node in the network of texts belonging to the *immram* and *echtra* genres transforming the religious tropological aspect of *immrama* into social commentary, in Gulliver's expulsion from the secular paradise of the horse-like creatures with a choice of joining the humanoid dystopia of the Yahoos or the human dystopia of his own homeland. Only centuries later does the utopian imaginary of the *immram* type arrive at a view of the ideal world as the future real world of human civilization. It is in the 1960s *Star Trek* that we first catch a glimpse of what a rowing-about narrative might look like when the travellers are natives of the earthly paradise. This reading of *Star Trek* as a member of the *immram* genre is the subject of the following chapter.

---

101 The Nox re-appear, and are also mentioned on a number of occasions later in the series; see discussion in Gil, 'Remember the Nox', p. 186.

CHAPTER 5

Star Trek as *Immram*, and 'Space, the Final Frontier…'

In his 1625 essay 'On Travel', the great early modern philosopher Francis Bacon made the following observation:

> It is a strange thing that in sea voyages, where there is nothing to be seen but sky and sea, men should make diaries; but in land-travel, wherein so much is to be observed, for the most part they omit it; as if chance were fitter to be registered than observation.[1]

We have seen that, indeed, Lewis's Eustace keeps a diary on the *Dawn Treader*.[2] Baudolino's overland travel story may have resulted in a written text, but as he told Niketas in the passage cited above, he had lost it. By contrast, Gulliver's seafaring narrative *is* the story we read in *Gulliver's Travels*. Following our multidimensional route in this book out into space we find that this aspect of sea-travel translates well into the spacefaring narrative of *Star Trek* in the form of the voice-over 'captain's log' (sometimes first officer's log, sometimes personal log, but always a diary-like narrative). Thus, Bacon's comment could be extended to include (fictional) space travel. This and the following chapters take as their premise that the sea voyages translate into twentieth- and twenty-first-century science fiction, with its addition of extra dimensions to the world as it is experienced by the readers and viewers, as space travel, and that space-faring science fiction can also be read in light of the *immram* and *echtra* genres.

Following the spatial framework for the journey within this book, having (practically) circumnavigated the globe with Gulliver we take off to explore the three-dimensional worlds of other planets with *Star Trek's* fantastic voyages into outer space. That the voyages to other planets would replace the earlier voyage literature describing sea-travel of earlier periods was also a view held by Lewis.[3] With the blank spaces on the map being exhausted, in

1 Francis Bacon, *The Essays*, ed. by John Pritcher (London: Penguin, 1985), p. 113.
2 See Chapter 1 above, pp. 65–66.
3 Schakel, 'Restoration and Eighteenth Century', p. 191.

 | DOI:10.1163/9789004734548_006

the twentieth and twenty-first centuries, the *immram* genre takes off into space. Indeed, narratives of supernatural or marvellous voyages such as the *immrama* or the travels of Gulliver, are frequently referred to as a precursor to the modern science fiction, but almost always with a diachronic sense of relative chronology: voyage narratives come first, and partly morph into and are partly replaced by, science fiction.[4] Academic narratives thus often treat change in genre systems as a natural development (and to some degree it is, insofar as any socio-cultural phenomenon can be described as 'natural').[5] However, genre, as a taxonomic system, is also an analytical tool, which analysis can choose to employ, much as one might choose alternative mathematical approaches to prove the same theorem.[6] *Star Trek* can be categorised as science fiction, but it can also be grouped with other types of narrative. Andrew S. Fazekas writes of the franchise: 'Like any good tale of the fantastic, *Star Trek* has always focused on discovering and showcasing places beyond the audience's immediate environment – in other words, exploring strange new worlds'.[7] This focus on the 'strange new worlds', which are in essence, as I will argue, the space-based equivalents of Old Irish 'otherworlds' is the first suggestion that we may be dealing with yet another heir of the *immram* tradition. The anonymous author of the *Navigatio* and Lewis both used the structure provided by a voyage from island to island to explore religious themes. Swift used islands visited by Gulliver as vehicle for political and social commentary, and *Star Trek: The Original Series* and its later spin-off heirs used planets visited by the Starship Enterprise for the same purpose.[8]

This chapter examines *Star Trek* from the perspective of genre expectations of an *immram* text. By aligning *Star Trek* with these texts we allow ourselves to read the journeys of the three Enterprises (Kirk's NCC-1701, Picard's NCC-1701D and Archer's NX-01) in new ways, opening up new possibilities to understanding their appeal to generations of viewers and the

4 Rieder, *Science Fiction*, p. 2. Amis, for example, dates the origins of science fiction as 1920s–30s, regarding developments before 1914 as its 'prehistory' (*New Maps*, pp. 16, 17 n.).

5 Rieder, *Science Fiction*, p. 2.

6 See Philip Ording, *99 Variations on a Proof* (Princeton: Princeton University Press, 2019). For the idea of re-assigning the same work to different genres in different cultural contexts, see Tony Bennett, *Outside Literature* (London: Routledge, 1990), p. 101; quoted and discussed in Rieder, *Science Fiction*, p. 3.

7 Fazekas, *Star Trek*, p. 8.

8 Chris Gregory, *Star Trek: Parallel Narratives* (Basingstoke and London: Macmillan, 2000), p. 2.

unprecedented faithfulness of their fan-base. While I do not mean to argue with M. Keith Booker's statement that '*TNG* joined *TOS* in boldly going where no television series had gone before', I would add to it the caveat that both went *exactly* where the medieval Irish had gone before, and with much success. This chapter will address the idea that the *Star Trek* series, and in particular the *Original Series* (1966–1969), *The Next Generation* (1987–1994), *Star Trek: Voyager* (1995–2001) and *Enterprise* (2001–2005) all constitute new additions, in a new medium, to the genre of the *immram*. *Voyager* is something of an outlier in the group because, as Booker points out, the series' 'main arc is inward, toward home, rather than outward, toward the unknown'.[9] As I already mentioned, however, since in the *Star Trek* universe it is Voyager's home, Earth, that is the utopia, the crew's homeward journey both inverts and replicates Brendan's search for the utopian Promised Land of Saints.[10]

The *Star Trek* series I have selected for discussion share an episodic structure, building on the model set by the *Original Series*. Although story-arcs spanning multiple episodes were gradually introduced in subsequent iterations of *Star Trek*, continuous plots spanning an entire season did not become the standard storytelling mode until the advent of the third generation of *Star Trek* with the release of *Discovery* in 2017.[11] I will argue that this loose and episodic narrative structure of the first two generations of *Star Trek* series corresponds to the definition of 'sailings about'. Van Riper describes the narrative structure of *The Next Generation* (TNG), with reference to its model, the *Original Series* (TOS) as follows:

> … the dramatic structure of TNG mirrored that of TOS, with the *Enterprise* on a mission to "boldly go where no one has gone before". Each new episode brought the crew to a different world and a fresh challenge – scientific, ethnographic, diplomatic, or military – that was typically resolved by the closing credits.[12]

It is the different challenges associated with different 'worlds', in practice planets, and therefore space islands, that invokes the image of the sailing-about in space, or *immram*. Indeed, the *immrama* have a staccato episodic

9 Booker, *Star Trek: A Cultural History* (Lanham: Rowan and Littlefield, 2018), p. 29.
10 See above, p. 128.
11 Van Riper, 'Star Trek: The Next Generation', p. 28; see also above, p. 12.
12 Van Riper, 'Star Trek: The Next Generation', p. 28.

structure similar to that of the television series discussed here. The list of contents of the *Immram Curaig Maíle Dúin* in Whitley Stokes's edition and translation of the text could as easily have been a list of *Star Trek Original Series* episodes, with titles such as 'The Island of the enormous Ants', 'The feats of the Island Beast', and 'The Island of the Laughers'.[13]

Various inspirations have been posited for the series. When pitching it to the studios, for instance, its creator Gene Roddenberry likened it to the long-running *Wagon Train*, a TV series that combined the journey theme with a Western.[14] Rather than running contrary to the accepted generic genealogy of *Star Trek* in the Western, the present chapter provides a complimentary reading, supplementing the insights of previous research.[15] In this it builds partly on the equally well-known and much cited nautical inspiration for the *Original Series:* C. S. Forester's series of novels about Horatio Hornblower.[16] Starfleet, particularly in 'Old Trek' (*Original Series* and *The Next Generation*) has a distinctly navy-like aura, including much of the jargon, sense of peril and remoteness at the mercy of the elements, human frailty in the face of the unknown (more pronounced in the *Original Series* than in its heirs). However, despite its notorious reliance on a heavily idealised British navy as a model for the ship and crew conceptualisation, the *Original Series* departs from that model in the captain's constant and consistent participation in away missions, leaving his ship at each island/planet encountered (this is reversed in *The Next Generation*). This seems surprising only if the text is regarded exclusively in the light of navy narratives such as the Hornblower series of novels. By contrast, if read as an *immram*, the captain's behaviour follows exactly that of the Old Irish narrative tradition. In the *Immram Curaig Maíle Dúin*, 'Máel Dúin is the first to disembark and

---

13 Stokes, ed. and trans., 'The Voyage of Mael Duin (Part 1)', p. 451. I am grateful to Nike Stam to pointing out the importance of the similarity between the episodic structure of *immrama* and that of the early *Star Trek* series.

14 Booker, *Star Trek*, p. xiii; although Booker observes that in its essence *Star Trek* was unprecedented – unlike anything else on television up to that time.

15 For the roots of *Star Trek* in the Frontier-exploring genre of the Western, see for instance, Johnson-Smith, *American Science Fiction TV*, p. 48; Michèle Barrett and Duncan Barrett, *Star Trek: The Human Frontier* (New York: Routledge, 2017), pp. xxi, 9, 51 n. 2.

16 Lane and Bowles, *Star Trek. The Adventure*, p. 38; Stefan Rabitsch, '"And Yet, Everything We Do Is Usually Based On The English": Sailing The *mare incognitum* of Star Trek's Transatlantic Double Consciousness with Horatio Hornblower', *Science Fiction Film and Television*, 9 (2016), 439–72; Stefan Rabitsch, *Star Trek and the British Age of Sail: The Maritime Influence Throughout the Series and Films* (Jefferson: McFarland, 2019).

explore (*dofoichlenn*, from *do-foichell*, "traverses, moves across, travels") an island', as Mulligan points out.[17] *Star Trek*'s Captain Kirk thus goes where Máel Dúin has been before.

The tropological aspect of the *immrama* is also a heavy feature in *Star Trek*, where this tropological aspect goes hand in hand with the utopian imagination.[18] The moral lessons of Saint Brendan, the influence of which is traceable in Lewis's work (and even, to some extent, echoed in Eco's) are on hand in *Star Trek*'s moralistic storytelling. *Star Trek* is famous for its function as utopian critique of the social, economic and political present.[19] Booker, for instance, like many critics, focuses on *Star Trek*'s presentation of the future, its focus on using this representation of the future for discussing societal problems of the present, and its focus on characters.[20] The famed utopianism of *Star Trek* should also be seen in a wider context within the modern genre it is conventionally ascribed to – science fiction.[21] This chapter will thus also address the issue of *Star Trek* as utopian narrative.

At the outset, however, it must be noted that as Simon Spiegel points out, while the term 'utopia' is used much in discussions of the franchise (and particularly of its first two series), *Star Trek* does not quite fit the utopia genre strictly defined.[22] It will be seen that the difficulty can be solved

17 Mulligan, *A Landscape of Words*, p. 52.

18 See above, pp. 29–32 for discussion of the tropological aspect of the *immrama*.

19 Garcia-Siino, Mittermeier and Rabitsch, 'Introduction', p. 3; Lisa Doris Alexander, 'Star Trek: Deep Space Nine', in *The Routledge Handbook of Star Trek*, ed. by Leimar Garcia-Siino, Sabrina Mittermeier, and Stefan Rabitsch (New York and London: Routledge, 2022), pp. 37–45 (p. 39); Johnson-Smith, *American Science Fiction TV*, p. 59; Booker, 'The Politics'.

20 Booker, *Star Trek*, pp. xiv–xvi.

21 For a treatment of the utopia in science fiction, see, for instance, Amis, *New Maps*, pp. 86–133. As Amis observes, tolerance of alien cultures appears to be a staple in the genre (it is thus not unique to *Star Trek*): 'The right of the explorers naturally they will be American or British explorers to go round setting up their trading stations wherever they please is similarly taken for granted in science fiction, as such things are in many other circles. However: the concept of dealing kindly with the intelligent […] is reassuringly widespread, carrying as it does the rider that if their way is not our way (a pretty safe assumption), it must nonetheless be respected' (*New Maps of Hell*, p. 93). See also Phillip E. Wegner, *Imaginary Communities: Utopia, the Nation, and the Spatial Histories of Modernity* (Berkeley: University of California Press, 2002).

22 Spiegel, 'Utopia', pp. 467, 470. Spiegel's narrow definition of utopia sees it as a predominantly descriptive genre which focuses on the detailed depiction of the idealized society, following the tradition established in More's original *Utopia* (p. 468). See also F. S. Braine, 'Technological Utopias: The Future of the Next Generation', *Film & History: An Interdisciplinary Journal of Film and Television*, 24 (1994), 1–18.

if *Star Trek* is read not as a member of the utopia genre, but of the *immram*, and its social and political commentary/criticism therefore follows not the explicit plan-like descriptive patterns modelled on More's *Utopia*, but rather continues the tropological message tradition of medieval voyage narratives.[23] Interestingly, it has been suggested that even More's text can be tentatively charted as a branch in the *Navigatio*'s reception history, thus creating yet another overlap between the intertextual connections radiating from our matrix.[24]

Star Trek has been characterised by Booker as 'a cultural phenomenon whose significance would resonate through the decades', and it is partly the utopian aspect and partly the technological that accounts for that appeal.[25] Like the *immrama*, these series have a tropological significance. Roddenbery, *Star Trek*'s creator, defined the *Original Series* as 'morality tales'.[26] This tropological aspect of the text is described by Van Riper in relation to *The Next Generation* and *Original Series* as a 'use of science fiction allegory to comment on present-day concerns'.[27] This is similar to that encountered in both Swift and Lewis, and distinctly *immram*-like. Indeed, as we have seen in the discussion in the previous chapter, the engagement with imaginary lands, idealised as utopia, disparaged as dystopia, othered as ustopia, is not an exclusive remit of science fiction and is a feature shared by most fantastic journey narratives, including those that draw on the Irish tradition.

For example, *Star Trek Voyager*, like the *immrama*, 'probes issues of identity, moral development and locating an appropriate home, themes mediated through the beings and landscapes encountered', to borrow the words

23 Spiegel, 'Utopia', p. 468 on the utopian model; see also Patricia Clare Ingham, with Karma Lochrie, eds. *Journal of Medieval and Early Modern Studies*, Special Issue *Medieval and Early Modern Utopias* (2006).

24 Moylan, 'Irish Voyages', p. 304.

25 Part of its appeal is also, of course, that it is entertaining storytelling. Booker, *Star Trek*, p. xii. See also Masse, 'On Second Thought', p. 95 on *Star Trek*'s influence on modern technology.

26 Garcia-Siino, Mittermeier and Rabitsch, 'Introduction', p. 2, quoting J. M. Dillard, *Where No One Has Gone Before: A History in Pictures* (New York: Pocket Books, 1994), p. 42. Cf. also Gene Roddenberry in Roger Fulton, *The Encyclopaedia of TV Science Fiction*, 2nd edn (London: Boxtree, 2000), p. 542; quoted in Johnson-Smith, *American Science Fiction TV*, p. 59.

27 Van Riper, 'Star Trek: The Next Generation', p. 28; see his pp. 30–33 for a discussion of the historical, cultural, social and political context in with the *Original Series* and *The Next Generation* were created, and with which they engaged.

used by Mulligan to describe the *Immram Curaig Maíle Dúin*.[28] Indeed, like the coracle (curragh) of Máel Dúin and his companions, Voyager is propelled into outer reaches of the galaxy by a great wave, interrupting its mission, which was to capture a rebel ship, and not so far removed from concepts of revenge and retribution to make the parallel with Máel Dúin's situation specious. Máel Dúin's journey was initially spurred on by motives of revenge for his father. Voyager's journey, like Máel Dúin's, is 'transformative' and constitutes a return to the place of origin (less precise) and reconciliation (in the first instance with the crew of the ship that was pursued as they are integrated with *Voyager*'s own crew).[29] Like Máel Dúin and his companions, Janeway and her crew are at the mercy of the vast reaches of space when it comes to means of sustenance, with threat of provisions running low never too far away.[30]

The famous opening of the two earliest *Star Trek* series, setting out the voyage of exploration as one leading to undiscovered regions of space 'where no man has gone before' (in the 1960s) and 'where no one has gone before' (in the 1990s), echoes the open-ended geography of the medieval *immram*, heading out into the West beyond the reaches of the known world, and of Lewis's Dawn Treader making the same journey eastwards. As Byrne rightly observed, the closed nature of the medieval Western European geography, delineating the inhabited world into a clear bounded area of Asia, Africa and Europe, with the Mediterranean as the tamed region of sea enclosed by these lands, meant that Britain and Ireland were located outside the comforting compass of these lands, opening up into the unknown on the western edge of the inhabited world.[31]

Although medieval world maps (*mappae mundi*) are still often believed to display the complete flat world, they are rather the medieval equivalent of a modern projection of a hemisphere on a flat plane. They also imply the existence of the rest of the Earth beyond the tamed, known, and mapped area. Thus, the Irish *immram* or rowing-about in the western direction, was

28 Mulligan, *A Landscape of Words*, p. 49. For a brief introduction to the medieval text, which Carey qualifies as 'the most flamboyant specimen' of the *immram* genre ('Voyage Literature', p. 1745).

29 Cf. Mulligan's discussion of the *Immram Curaig Maíle Dúin*; *A Landscape of Words*, p. 50.

30 When Máel Dúin and his companions run out of the apples they had picked up on a previous island, *bá mór a ngorta 7 a n-ítu* ('their hunger and thirst were great'); Stokes, ed. and trans., 'The Voyage of Mael Duin (Part 1)', pp. 476, 477.

31 Byrne, *Otherworlds*, p. 143. See also above, pp. 44, 45, 93.

quite literally a move into the unknown and the uncharted. At the beginning of the seven-year run of *The Next Generation*, Captain Jean-Luc Picard's first monologue includes the explanation, for the benefit of the audience, that his ship is headed to a new space station on a distant planet, 'beyond which lies the great unexplored mass of the galaxy'.[32] The crucial difference, of course, to practically all the other texts explored in this book, is the unique lack of sense of precarity in the boat used for this particular rowing-about. Picard's spaceship is closer in design to the liners fondly remembered by Eustace in the *Voyage*, and is certainly a far cry from a curragh.[33] Kirk's Enterprise, and particularly Archer's twenty-second-century vessel, designed as it was to function as an early precursor to the others, are less extravagant. For Archer's *Enterprise* in particular the audience is invited to experience the concern and worry of the ship's maiden voyage into the reaches of outer space, as the anxious Ensign Hoshi Sato comments on the vibrations caused by the engine in the pilot episode.

5.1 Planets as Islands

As I stated in explaining the structure of this book in the introduction, the relative spaces of the travel and exploration narratives appear to progress from two-dimensional travel on the surface of the topographic map, to three-dimensional travel through space, but the major characteristics of the narratives themselves are retained. 'Flat' islands become round planets, but their function remains the same. Thus, Moylan's observations regarding the aptitude of islands as spaces of utopia can be extended to the planets of the space-based narratives of both *Star Trek* and *Stargate*.[34] Moylan's words, including quotations from Rod Edmond and Vanessa Smith's discussion of island narratives, deserve to be reproduced in full in order to engage with the implications of the detail:

32 'Encounter at Farpoint, Part 1', *The Next Generation*, 1.1 (1987).

33 See above, p. 65.

34 For previous applications of the concept of 'islandness' to *Stargate*, see, e.g. MacKinnon, '*Stargate Atlantis*'. MacKinnon reads the television series generally within the framework of island studies and specifically as an iteration of the Atlantis myth. There is an extensive field termed 'island studies'. For an exploration of islands in poetry, see, for example, Rajeev S. Patke, *Poetry and Islands. Materiality and the Creative Imagination* (London: Rowan and Littlefield, 2018), p. 7 for an overview of secondary literature.

> To be sure, the island, in particular, is a powerful form of this spatial figuration, with its dynamic quality of "at once microcosm and excess": thus, a methodological articulation that works from a "bounded and therefore manageable space," on the one hand, and a fragmentary surplus ("the original supplement of continents") of fantastic possibility and open contingency, on the other.[35]

If we replace 'island' with 'planet' as the equivalent in travel narratives for the space-age audience, the statement remains valid. The planets visited by the viewer together with the *Stargate* teams retain the 'dynamic quality' highlighted by Moylan as 'manageable spaces' (Edmond and Smith's term) for explorations of 'fantastic possibility and open contingency'.

If *Star Trek* is the space-faring equivalent of sea voyages, then planets function in its narrative the way islands had in stories of the sea. Indeed, the observation made by Rajeev S. Patke about islands can be extended to include *Star Trek*'s planets: 'Islands fascinate us: we travel to them, read about them, dream about them; some of us live on them, and a small number of us write about them'.[36] We can also compare the conventionality of *Star Trek*, and its reliance on audience expectations to the same phenomena in *Navigatio*.[37] As Chris Gregory writes:

> In the case of *Star Trek*, the audience is perfectly aware that the main characters will survive at the end of each week's episode, and that there must be some kind of "adventure" to motivate the drama. Audiences implicitly understand that this framework is merely a conventional structure and take much pleasure in their own ironic recognition of this fact. In this way, *Star Trek's* audience has learned to "read" the psychological, social or political themes which are coded into its fictional scenario.[38]

One of the elements that the texts examined in this book share is the land-centric background of their primary audience cultures.[39] While sea-travel

35 Moylan, 'Irish Voyages', p. 300; quoting Rod Edmond, and Vanessa Smith, 'Editors' Introduction', in *Islands in History and Representation*, ed. by Rod Edmond and Vanessa Smith (London: Routledge, 2003), pp. 1–19 (p. 5).

36 Patke, *Poetry and Islands*, p. 3.

37 Compare the role of audience expectations in *Stargate*, discussed by Beeler, '*Stargate SG-1*', p. 267.

38 Gregory, *Star Trek*, p. 6.

39 John R. Stilgoe, *What Is Landscape?* (Cambridge, MA, and London: MIT Press, 2015), p. 8.

was familiar to the Irish, living on the sea was far from the daily experience of the audience of the *Navigatio* or the *immrama*.[40] While travel to other parts of the world was established as part of the colonial and trade reality in Swift's time, it was not part of his entire readership's own personal experience.[41] While space-travel is a reality in the twentieth and twenty-first centuries, only a very small number of human beings have so far experienced it, and proportionally infinitesimal in comparison to the audience numbers for the *Star Trek* and *Stargate* franchises.

Both science fiction series, and *Star Trek* in particular (due to heavier reliance on ship travel) reproduce the sense of awe in relation to the vastness of space that accompanied the description of sea-faring in earlier cultures. As Barbara Hillers observes, in the *immram* narratives, '[t]he entire voyage takes place at sea, which is in itself already a liminal, and certainly a perilous place'.[42] The void of interstellar space is by the same reasoning even more liminal, and certainly no less perilous. Spatial phenomena, such as that which pulls Starship *Voyager* off-course in the opening scenes of *Star Trek: Voyager* episode 'The Void' (season 7 episode 14), are reminiscent of the dangers of the sea threatening the safety of the ships in the *immram* narratives.[43] One is reminded of the *gaeth mor* 'great wind' that blows the boat of Máel Dúin and his companions off course at the beginning of their journey.[44]

The conception of space 'weather' as a fictional parallel to sea weather phenomena is made explicit on a number of occasions. Most marked is the double emphasis on this parallel at the conclusion of the pilot episode for *Enterprise*, 'Broken Bow'. Ensign Mayweather (whose also name seems significant in this context) points out to the captain that there is an 'ion storm' in their path, and Archer responds 'we can't be afraid of the wind, Ensign'.[45]

---

40 See, for example, Mulligan's comments in *A Landscape of Words*, pp. 28, 34, 37.

41 For the presence of colonial reality in literary discourse in the preceding period see, for instance, Kristina Bross, *Future History: Global Fantasies in Seventeenth-Century American and British Writings* (Oxford: Oxford University Press, 2017).

42 Hillers, 'Voyages', p. 66.

43 See discussion in Mulligan, *A Landscape of Words*, pp. 33–34, 36–37. The association of sea with dangers, and islands with shipwreck, is engaged with in Brigitte le Juez and Olga Springer, ed., *Shipwreck and Island Motifs in Literature and the Arts* (Leiden and Boston: Brill and Rodopi, 2015).

44 Stokes, ed. and trans., 'The Voyage of Mael Duin (Part 1)', pp. 462, 463. The giant swarm of ants that tries to eat the crew on their next stop would hardly be out of place in a *Star Trek* episode (and the entomophobia it represents is echoed strongly in the replicator episodes of *Stargate SG-1*, with their masses of crawling bug-like robots bent on consuming and assimilating all in their path (462–65).

45 *Enterprise*, Season 1 Episode 1, 'Broken Bow'.

Archer's response is a direct reference to the flashback sequences shown throughout the episode to his father teaching him to fly a toy ship, and a direct quotation of his father's words. I would argue that the flying ship is already an extension of the seafaring allusion, emphasised by the fact that the flashback sequences show the young Archer and his father on the beach, with the sea in the background. The continuity of sea to starship is also emphasised for the viewer in this episode by the presence of a sequence of images of ships: sail ship, steamship, space shuttle, starship, on the wall in Archer's ready room.[46]

The continuity between islands and planets in fantastic voyage literature and science fiction has been remarked on by Amis, working back from space-travel narratives: 'if we want to find early forms of [this kind of writing] in days when the Earth was still incompletely explored and space was utterly inaccessible, the obvious place to look is not on other planets but in remote regions of our own, in particular, of course, undiscovered islands'.[47] It is worth noting that this remark comes just before Amis embarks on his discussion of *Gulliver's Travels* as a precursor to science fiction.[48]

Cosmic objects, isolated as they are in the vastness of space, have often been associated with the image of the islands, solitary in the wide expanse of the sea. Immanuel Kant, for instance, thought of galaxies, at that time visible only 'as nebular or diffuse stars' as 'island universes'.[49] The use of planets as a narrative device to provide varied settings for adventures, exotic and fascinating new alien worlds for the audience, and an individual canvas for the social, ethical or moral dilemma and lesson to be learned in each episode, echoes the use of islands in the *Navigatio* and in the vernacular *immrama*. Once again Mulligan's description of the Old Irish *immrama* can be equally well applied to the modern *immram* text under consideration here. 'Drifting through a largely non-navigable ocean, the voyagers land on terrifying and wondrous islands whose topographies and inhabitants are marvelous and monstrous and [...] are meant to *monstrare*, "show", and *monere*, "warn".'[50] The 32 islands encountered by the characters in *Immram Curaig Máile Dúin* prefigure *Star Trek*'s planets by providing a variety of

46 There is an emphasis placed on this by showing it on several occasions in the first episode alone; *Enterprise*, Season 1 Episode 1, 'Broken Bow', around the 15:00, 32:10; 1:05:52; 1:23:30 marks.

47 *New Maps of Hell*, p. 30.

48 *New Maps of Hell*, pp. 30–31.

49 Bülent Atalay, *Math and the Mona Lisa. The Art and Science of Leonardo da Vinci* (New York: Collins and Smithsonian Books, 2006), p. 219.

50 Mulligan, *A Landscape of Words*, pp. 48–49. By contrast, Sobecki sees the 'fear of the sea' as 'only a minor element of the *immrama*', 'dormant' in the Latin *Navigatio*, and

settings 'which include Edenic oases, islands of monstrous beasts and richly decorated fortresses with well-laid tables, enchanting music and beautiful women, as well as the more modest homes of Desert-Father-esque hermits'.[51] The 'Desert-Father-esque hermits' are as such a feature of most *immram*-style narratives, including as we have seen, Eco's *Baudolino* and Lewis's *Voyage*.[52] Enchanting music and beautiful women abound in episodes of the *Original Series* ('Mudd's Women' is an example); monstrous beasts are not lacking, either (one thinks in particular of 'Devil in the Dark' Season 1 Episode 25), and one might find plenty examples from *The Next Generation*. 'Desert-Father-esque hermits' of the galaxy include most notably the 'guardian' left by Tkon, a long-dead ancient empire, who takes a liking to Riker because the latter keeps thinking of quotations from the military strategist Sun Tzu ('Last Outpost'), and the Caretaker (*Voyager*, pilot episodes), among many others.

Like the otherworldly islands of the Irish *immrama*, the planets of the *Star Trek* universe are often locations of the supernatural.[53] Hillers' description of the former is equally applicable to the latter: 'the heroes of the early Irish voyage tales encounter benevolent and malevolent creatures and visit idyllic as well as perilous islands'.[54] Replacing 'Irish voyage tales' with 'Star Trek episodes' and 'islands' with planets we might render this as: 'the heroes of **the *Star Trek* episodes** encounter benevolent and malevolent creatures and visit idyllic as well as perilous **planets**'. In this part of the chapter I propose to explore the implications of *Star Trek* series as *immrama* for reading the planets of *Star Trek* as the equivalent and intellectual and cultural inheritors of the symbolic complex of meaning associated with the islands in *immram* narratives. Indeed, if the Irish sailing about not only involves islands but starts with one, the same can be said of *Star Trek*, taking the planets as equivalents of the medieval narratives' islands: the starting point (and anchor point for the 'home' in the narrative, especially for *Voyager*) is planet Earth, equivalent of the Ireland of the *immrama*.[55] I do not propose to

---

brought forward only in the French *Voyage de Saint Brendan* of Benedeit; Sobecki, 'From the *désert liquide* to the Sea of Romance', p. 201.

51 Mulligan, *A Landscape of Words*, p. 52. See also Egeler, *Islands*, pp. 41–61.

52 For example, there are multiple references in *Baudolino* to hermits, such as the reference to the hermits living on top of columns—a fate awaiting Baudolino himself; in Eco, *Baudolino*, p. 362, trans. Weaver, p. 355. See above, p. 80.

53 Although the supernatural in the case of *Star Trek* is defined as unfamiliar and scientifically complex.

54 Hillers, 'Voyages', p. 66.

55 Kervran makes the point that all lands are islands within the narrative and journey framework of the *Navigatio sancti Brendani*, Kervran, *Brandan*, p. 26.

argue that all aspects of *Star Trek*'s planetary worlds are inherited from the *immrama*. While some of the patterns we see in *Star Trek* do appear to form part of the Irish voyage narratives' modern afterlives, other features reflect a more general human response to islandness. Artificial planets, for instance, play to the feelings evoked by the unsettling and heterotopian nature of artificial islands.[56]

The authors and audiences of *Star Trek* share with the authors and audiences of medieval Irish *immrama* a sense of marginality.[57] The medieval Irish were positioned by the medieval Western geographical discourse on the margins of the *oikumene*, the inhabited world.[58] In the twentieth and twenty-first centuries, astronomical knowledge positions the Earth, third planet of the Solar System, much closer to the margins than to the centre of our Galaxy, the Milky Way.[59] *Star Trek* thus has to contend with the same issue as the *immram* texts – setting out from the edge onto the unknown. This is done in both cases by re-positioning the edge as the centre of a new system of coordinates, though by different means. In the Irish sea-journey narratives, the world's edge is extended outwards, thus pushing Ireland towards the centre. In the case of *Star Trek*, the repositioning is achieved conceptually by placing Earth as the de facto capital of the United Federation of Planets and by imposing an Earth-centred system of coordinates onto the galaxy, separating it into quadrants. The quadrant housing Earth is labelled the Alpha Quadrant. By contrast, the *echtra*-type narrative of *Stargate SG-1* bypasses the issue by using a direct route via a version of the Einstein-Rosen bridge, to traverse the space between Earth and the narrative 'otherworlds' – the other planets.[60] In the case of *Stargate: Atlantis*, the central 'at home' point of the narrative and the starting point of each individual journey, is transposed to the ancient alien city of Atlantis, located in the 'Pegasus Galaxy', a reference to the real-world Pegasus Dwarf

56 See discussion in Klaus Dodds and Veronica della Dora, 'Artificial Islands and Islophilia', in *The Routledge International Handbook of Island Studies*, ed. by Godfrey Baldacchino (London and New York: Routledge, 2018), pp. 392–415 (pp. 403–12).

57 For the significance of the medieval perceptions of Ireland as marginal to medieval Irish identity and literary composition, see Mulligan, *A Landscape of Words*, esp. overview on pp. 1–3, 5.

58 Mulligan, *A Landscape of Words*, pp. 2–3.

59 For the position of our solar system within the Milky Way, in the context of a wider discussion of galaxies and their properties, see, for instance, Peter Schneider, *Extragalactic Astronomy and Cosmology* (Berlin and Heidelberg: Springer, 2015), p. 6, fig. 1.6.

60 For a more in-depth discussion of *Stargate*, see below, pp. 157–73.

Irregular Galaxy, located in the Local Group.[61] Arguably Earth is thus demarginalised as the galaxy in which the action is located is positioned in relation to our Milky Way as the (de facto central) point of reference.

The space-travel solutions in the two television series represent different ways of getting around the problem that in terms of our current understanding of science and the universe, space travel is not so much impossible as impracticable. The conundrum – and solution – were pointed out in the mid-twentieth-century discussion of the science fiction genre by Amis.[62] As Amis, with characteristic panache, puts it: 'most commonly, the author will fabricate a way of getting around Einstein, or even of sailing straight through him: a device known typically as the space-warp or the hyper-drive will make its appearance'.[63] Coincidentally, *Star Trek* opts for the former terminology, with 'warp engines' being the propulsion method of choice, while the *Stargate* franchise initially choses to 'sail right through' Einstein, to use Amis's turn of phrase, by the use of wormholes (based on a popularized version of Einstein's own theories) in the first instance, later supplementing these by hyper-drives.[64]

To return briefly to the issue of the typological aspect of *immrama*, the 'otherworlds' of *Star Trek*, its other planets, carry the function of illustrating the tropological message of the narrative. As pointed out in the introduction to this chapter, a difficulty observed in previous analyses of this complex multi-text is that while it shares some features with the utopia genre, it does not quite fit its requirements and expectations, complicating understanding and creating the illusion of failure. Reading *Star Trek* in the context of the tradition of utopian narratives has led Spiegel, for instance, to refer to the franchise's social critique as 'allegorical platitudes'.[65] According to Spiegel, *Star Trek*'s use of metaphor for its socio-political category

61 For a visual depiction of the Local Group and the position of Pegasus in it, see Linda S. Sparke and John S. Gallagher III, *Galaxies in the Universe. An Introduction* (Cambridge: Cambridge University Press, 2000), p. 136, fig. 4.3.

62 Amis, *New Maps*, pp. 19–20.

63 Amis, *New Maps*, p. 20.

64 Amis, *New Maps*, p. 20. See also Margaret A. Weitekamp, '"Ahead, Warp Factor Three, Mr. Sulu": Imagining Interstellar Faster-Than-Light Travel in Space Science Fiction', *Journal of Popular Culture*, 52 (2019), 1036–57, esp. pp. 1037, 1038, 1046–50; Beeler, '*Stargate SG-1*', pp. 269–70; Johnson-Smith, *American Science Fiction TV*, pp. 155–56.

65 Spiegel, 'Utopia', p. 471.

> indicates the main difference to the utopian mode. There is nothing metaphorical in More's criticism of landlords who push small farmers aside [...]. Most utopias are a reaction to a very specific historical/political situation. It could even be argued that their success does not so much depend on the alternative offered but rather on how accurately they portray the deficits of their respective times.[66]

Star Trek (for the purposes of this argument I refer to the original 1960s series) is indeed much more generalised in its commentary. Its criticisms may be inspired by specific historical, social, economic or political contexts, but it does not dwell on these in extensive detail, with the marginal exception of those episodes which deal with time-travel, and it also does not provide what Spiegel describes as the utopian genre's characteristic 'info dump'.[67] Indeed, the 'allegorical platitudes' remarked on by Spiegel are strikingly similar to the 'longues banalités hagiographiques ou légendaires, remontant à des siècles, voir à l'Ancien Testament' ('long hagiographical and legendary banalities, going back centuries, perhaps as far as the Old Testament') noted for the earliest Brendan material by Louis Kervran.[68] *Star Trek* draws on the same generalising tradition, and may indeed belong to it, if seen as *immram*. It does not make for a much more convincing utopia (when the latter is taken as genre, as by Spiegel) than would any given *immram*, even in the description of the Fortunate Islands of the Brendan legend.

Star Trek may take its cue from particular historical development, but Spiegel is correct in pointing out that it is not concrete nor detailed enough in references to these for the critique to be anything but a generalized moralizing. While Spiegel views this as a shortcoming, it also can be seen as the outcome of a different literary tradition. *Star Trek*'s social criticism can be interpreted more on the lines of a parable. As such it is also translatable to new audiences to a much greater degree than the concretised context-specific criticism of utopias. *Star Trek* shares this timelessness with the *immrama*. Like the *immrama* it also maintains its fascination and watchability despite its age. The voyage of Brendan, for example, still finds its way into

66 Spiegel, 'Utopia', p. 470.

67 Spiegel, 'Utopia', pp. 469–70, also for discussion of time-travel episodes. Amis considers precisely this feature to be a shortcoming of style in the writings of Jules Verne, whom he credits both as progenitor of modern science fiction and of 'technological utopia' (*New Maps*, pp. 34–35, 36, 38).

68 Kervran, *Brandan*, p. 87; my translation.

new publications for the general public.[69] An interesting wrinkle in the utopian world of *Star Trek* appears when the series are considered as part of the *immram* tradition, because they share a key characteristic with core *immrama* that is hardly utopian.

Hillers follows Séamus Mac Mathúna in the view that three texts that begin with a crime comprise the 'core of the *immram* genre': *Immram Curaig Maíle Dúin*, *Immram Curaig Ua Corra*, and *Immram Snedgusa agus Maic Riagla*.[70] The existence of a core implies the existence of a periphery, and I would suggest that the notion of genre as fuzzy set has existed in scholarship on medieval Irish narratives for a while now, without receiving a formal articulation in mathematical terms. *Pace* Rieder, who objects to the idea of genres as fuzzy sets on the ground that it would be too much work to describe and quantify all the details required for a complete mapping of texts onto genres according to this system, I would suggest that a full mapping taking into account the type of typological detail one finds, for instance, in Propp's folktale morphology is not necessary in order to map texts relative to each-other as 'centre' and 'periphery' and to locate cases of intersection.[71] For that purpose of approximative mapping we might use particular elements that have been marked as key by previous scholarship. The beginning of an *immram* narrative with a crime is one such element.[72] Not all *immrama* begin with a crime, but the fact that these 'core' ones do is interesting in the light of the starting points in the pilot episodes of each of the *Star Trek* series which are candidates for the genre and discussed here: *The Original Series*; *The Next Generation*, *Voyager*, and *Enterprise*.

The *Original Series* presents perhaps a unique problem, since its original pilot ('The Cage') was later re-worked into a different episode ('The Menagerie', Season 1 Episodes 11 and 12), as a second pilot was commissioned ('Where No Man Has Gone Before'). The plot of 'The Cage' involved the crew's arrival on a planet whose inhabitants kept a zoo of other sentient

69 The observation regarding the proliferation of books dedicated to Brendan was already made almost half a century ago in Louis Kervran, *Brandan* in 1977, p. 17, who rather conservatively estimated one volume per twenty years in France alone. The publication of Severin's *The Brendan*, an account based on a journey undertaken in 1976 replicating that narrated in the *Navigatio*, boosted interest for the legend in the Anglophone world considerably.

70 Hillers, 'Voyages', p. 68; Mac Mathúna, ed., *Immram Brain*. See also above, p. 25.

71 Rieder, *Science Fiction*, p. 19; Владимир Яковлевич Пропп [Vladimir Yakovlevich Propp], *Морфология сказки* [*Morfologia Skazki*], 2nd edn (Moscow: Наука, 1969 [1928]).

72 See comments also in Swank, 'The Child's Voyage', p. 79.

species, and set their eyes on the ship's captain as a specimen for their collection. The crime is the aliens' abduction of the captain (Captain Pike, replaced after this pilot with Kirk, who lasted the rest of the series), as well as the (female) human captive they had before, and a variety of other denizens of the menagerie. The crime aspect is reinforced through the addition of a different layer when the footage was re-used for 'The Menagerie'. In this episode, Captain Kirk's first officer, Mr Spock, inexplicably commits a crime by going against the law which prohibits visiting a particular planet. He abducts his now-crippled old captain, Pike, and takes him there. This is the planet of the menagerie that had featured in 'The Cage'. The episode is partly a courtroom drama, dealing with Spock's reasons for taking his captain back to this zoo. (His reason turns out to be compassion – the aliens are capable of giving Pike the illusion of still being able-bodied).

The pilot episode of *The Next Generation*, 'Encounter at Farpoint', features both a crime and a trial, albeit the crime does not involve members of the ship's crew. The crime in question is the creation of Farpoint station through the capture of a space-creature which becomes the station, an act committed by the local population with the objective of ingratiating themselves with the powerful political power of the Federation. The trial sets the mood for the whole series, as a cosmic entity of apparently unlimited power, named Q, appoints itself as judge and places the ship's crew on trial as representatives of humanity. At the conclusion of the episode, the trial appears to be adjourned, as the crew sets off on its five-year mission of exploration (and a ten-year television series). The subject returns in the series finale, 'All Good Things' (Season 7, Epsiodes 25 and 26) which re-presents the entire seven seasons of *The Next Generation* as the continuation of the proceedings started at Farpoint.

The pilot episode of *Voyager* does not appear to begin with a crime proper, although the premise of the TV series is that the ship and her crew are abducted against their will by a powerful entity who brings them to the other side of the galaxy, whence they have to find their way home in the course of the series. The episode begins with a space chase with a vessel of resistance fighters called Maquis (after the French resistance of WWII) being pursued by alien authorities. While they manage to escape their pursuers, they are caught by a mysterious spatial phenomenon. The plot of the series is set in motion when the starship USS *Voyager* is sent on a mission to find this missing Maquis ship and is also caught by the same phenomenon, which hurls them also into a distant quadrant of the galaxy.[73]

---

73 See above, p. 136.

Enterprise also begins with what I would argue is a crime, in the sense of infringement of social code or social order, that provides the initial impetus for the journey. The television series begins, as Zaki Hasan aptly puts it, with a 'botched first contact scenario'.[74] An alien (a Klingon) is attacked both by the alien antagonists of the series (Suliban) and by a human farmer on whose farm the aliens fight it out.[75] The farmer shoots him, setting off the events of the episode. The Klingon survives but needs to be taken back to his home world to prevent repercussions for Earth. Despite the insistence of Vulcans – in a guardian role to the 'not yet developed' humans – the brand new Earth ship *Enterprise* is dispatched with the mission, under the command of Captain Jonathan Archer, setting off the adventures in the series ('Broken Bow, Part 1 and 2', Episodes 1.1–2). In this respect the pilot episode of *Enterprise* begins with the intrusion of the space-based 'otherworld' on the world of humans, and with what one might argue is an equivalent of the crime event.

The element which we might call judicial ambiguity – if not outright criminal action – is thus present at the starting point of three of the *Star Trek* series. A farmer's shooting of an alien 'in self-defence' (the viewer knows, however, that the Klingon was not actually attacking) in *Enterprise* is fairly unambiguous but is also set in a pre-Federation era which is allowed, within the *Star Trek* mythos, to be somewhat less utopian. However, the capture of the creature and trial of humanity in *The Next Generation* on the one hand, the kidnapping of the crew by an alien, and the anti-authoritarian and vaguely anarchistic Maquis being pursued by authorities after, one presumes, activity which these authorities consider criminal, in *Voyager* on the other, are striking features if one considers the utopian reputation of *Star Trek*.[76] The idealised society at the heart of the brand is portrayed in these episodes as a fragile construct. Nevertheless, the idealised humanity represented at the core of the series gives it its utopian reputation, and it is this utopian aspect of the series which forms its unique take on the tropological mode of the *immram* genre.

The conclusion of an *immram* voyage with the sought-for otherworld, or Promised Land of Saints (as in the *Navigatio*), the Utter East in Lewis and Land of Prester John in Eco, is not on hand in *Star Trek*, with the exception

74 Hasan, 'Star Trek: Enterprise', p. 58.

75 A similar incursion of the otherworld starts off the *Stargate* series *SG-1*, as the main alien antagonists of the series, the Goa'uld, arrive on Earth through the stargate and kidnap a woman; see discussion below, p. 163.

76 Discussions of *Star Trek* as utopia are numerous. See, for example, Stoppe, *Is* Star Trek *Utopia?* and references in n. 22 above.

of *Voyager*'s reverse trajectory (home becomes the Promised Land). The adventures of the various starships Enterprise are planet-hopping for planet-hopping's sake. However, a number of echoes of *immram*-type features, resembling particularly their C. S. Lewis variations, are on hand in a number of episodes. An example of this is *Star Trek: The Next Generation* Season 1 Episode 5, 'Where No One Has Gone Before'. In this episode, the Enterprise and its crew finds itself propelled to the 'End', or perhaps the 'Beginning' of the universe, a billion light years from our home galaxy. The edge of the world is reminiscent of the goal of Brendan's journey, and the otherworlds of the *immrama*, and the entire episode seems to contain multiple echoes of Lewis's *Voyage*, as the crew of the Enterprise also experience visions, reminiscent of Lewis's island where dreams come true. The *Star Trek* variety of the visions, however, appear to be for the most part comforting rather than otherwise. In this instance, it is not dreams that become reality, but active thought, allowing for a possibility of conscious control. A sense of mystery, though not necessarily or at any rate not overtly religious, pervades the episode, which also runs parallel to Lewis's Narnian design in marking a step in the developmental trajectory of the crew's youngest member – Wesley Crusher – who discovers promise of potential beyond normal human capacities. Ultimately, Crusher embarks on his own journey beyond the remit of the series, leaving the crew ('Journey's End', Season 7 episode 20).[77]

These journeys beyond the realm of the familiar, and into 'other worlds' or otherworlds, however, in *Star Trek* tend to be reassuringly optimistically presented, recalling the optimistic mood of Lewis's Narnians (and Lucy and Edmund, though not perhaps initially Eustace). It is to this pervading optimism that the following section of this chapter is dedicated.

5.2 'Optimism, Captain!' Rowing-about with Cheer

The exclamation in the section title is a quotation from the opening episode of *Enterprise* (Season 1 Episode 1, 'Broken Bow, Part I'). The alien doctor of the earth ship, Phlox, encourages Captain Archer to think positively about the potential outcome of his mission and the prognosis of their passenger (and patient in sickbay), the Klingon Kang, whose injury at the hands of an earth farmer forms the impetus for the ships' maiden voyage. This opening of the last of the 'old Treks' articulates the hopeful attitude to the franchise's particular variety of rowings-about.

77 For the rejection of such opportunities by characters in *Stargate*, who stay in the series, see below, pp. 166–67.

The optimism brings us back to the subject of utopia, and that in turn brings us back to the central text of this book: Swift's *Gulliver's Travels*. As Rees observes in her discussion of Swift's text, utopia and political satire are 'unstable' discourses: 'Just because it professes rationality and order, while being a product of the distrusted imagination, the authority of the utopian discourse is suspect and unstable. The utopian satire is doubly insecure, peculiarly vulnerable to overthrow from within.'[78] Rees does not discuss the *Navigatio*, but that text also constitutes an utopia.[79] According to Rees, however, it is 'not only an imaginary voyage and country that structure these texts, but the utopian imagination itself, that relocated familiar philosophical questions in the *terra incognita* of fiction – and that Swift's work is both a brilliant demonstration and a critique of utopian imagination'.[80] The same argument can be made about *Star Trek* as utopia. It is both an incarnation of and a critique of the genre.[81]

Anti-utopian moments in *Star Trek* sometimes appear to draw on anti-utopian moments in its predecessors. One thinks in particular of the investigations of ethical concerns – respect for the life of others – while almost literally groping in the dark – in the *Voyager* episode 'Night' (Season 5 Episode 1), and in the *Enterprise* episode 'Rogue Planet' (Season 1 Episode 18). In the case of 'Rogue Planet' the suggestion that Archer may be imagining the being he interacts with invokes the dark island where dreams (nightmares) come true in Lewis's *Voyage*.[82] In Archer's case, the dream materialized by the alien inhabitant of the planet was a day-dream (explicitly stated not to be the case in the *Voyage*) originally prompted by listening to W. B. Yeats's 'Song of the Wandering Aengus'.[83] The episode, and Archer's interaction with the alien, with its allusions to an unending quest for an

---

78 Rees, *Utopian Imagination*, p. 123. Rees devotes the entirety of Chapter 5 (pp. 123–77) to Swift's *Gulliver's Travels*.

79 Wollin calls it 'the first utopia of the middle ages' <https://brill.com/display/book/edcoll/9789047410256/B9789047410256_s014.xml> [accessed 6 November 2024]. It is also classified as an utopia by Michael Cronin in his MHRA Centenary Lecture 'Utopia for Modern Languages and How We Can Get There' <https://www.mhra.org.uk/centenary/cronin100> [accessed 12 December 2023].

80 Rees, *Utopian Imagination*, p. 124.

81 See, for instance, Booker, 'The Politics', p. 205.

82 Lewis, *Voyage*, p. 188. It is interesting that it is the lord stranded in the nightmare darkness whose name Caspian keeps forgetting—one wonders if that may not be part of Rhoop's nightmare becoming reality; Lewis, *Voyage*, pp. 30–31, 196.

83 *Enterprise* 1.16, 37:00–38:00. See discussion, in the context of the potentials *Star Trek's* intertextuality and use of literature and allusion in teaching applications, Elizabeth Baird Hardy, '"Where Many Books Have Gone Before": Using Star Trek to Teach Literature', in *Set Phasers to Teach! Star Trek in Research and Teaching*, ed. by Stefan

ideal, can also be read allegorically in light of the overarching mission of exploration that is at the core of the captain's journey, the series, and of *Star Trek* as a whole. In this respect, it connects to medieval traditions rich in allegory, the journey narrative (*immram*) and the dream-vision.[84]

The connection to the specifically Irish branch of the medieval dream-vision tradition is made explicit via the reference to Yeats's poem, which in turn is based on the medieval material provided by the *Aislinge Óenguso* 'Dream of Óengus'.[85] The *Enterprise* episode thus represents a stage in the reception history of another genre of Old Irish literature, the *aisling* 'vision'-tales, already mentioned in connection to Eco's fictional Irishman Abdul.[86] The medieval vision-tales had generated a genre within Irish poetry in the eighteenth century (it is of this genre that Yeats's poem is a late example).[87]

As Nicole Volmering points out, *aisling*, though translated both as 'dream' and 'vision', does not necessitate the connotation of sleep.[88] Archer's encounter with the alien can be thus argued to be the result of an *aisling* as well, as he is wide awake but wandering through a planet without a sun and thus a place of perpetual night-time, also filled with visions and a sense of wonder.[89] Echoes of the same tradition are used, as we have seen, by Eco in *Baudolino* in the Irishman Abdul's love for the distant princess whom he had only seen in a dream, thus providing yet another connection in our matrix.[90]

Rabitsch, Martin Gabriel, Wilfried Elmenreich, and John N. A. Brown (Cham: Springer, 2018), pp. 1–11 (p. 8).

84 See the discussion of allegory above, pp. 54–56. For medieval dream-visions as allegorical texts, see, for instance, Tambling, *Allegory*, pp. 2–3, 7, 35.

85 For the text, see Eduard Müller, ed. and trans., 'Two Irish Tales', *Revue Celtique*, 3 (1876–1878), 342–60; and the more recent translation in Jeffrey Gantz, trans., *Early Irish Myths and Sagas* (Harmondsworth: Penguin, 1981), pp. 107–12. For discussions, see, for instance, Hugh Fogarty, '*Aislinge Óenguso*: a *remscél* Reconsidered', in *Narrative in Celtic Tradition: Essays in Honor of Edgar M. Slotkin*, ed. by Joseph F. Eska (New York: Colgate University Press, 2011), pp. 56–67. For Yeats's use of the material, see Peter McDonald, ed., *The Poems of W. B. Yeats: Volume Two: 1890–1898* (London: Routledge, 2021), pp. 254–55.

86 See above, pp. 74–75, 82.

87 For a brief introduction to the eighteenth-century genre, and further references, see Brian Ó Broin, '*Aisling*', in *Celtic Culture: A Historical Encyclopedia*, ed. by John T. Koch (Santa Barbara: ABC-CLIO, 2006), p. 33; see also above, p. 75 for references to literature concerning the medieval genre.

88 Volmering, 'Medieval Irish Vision Literature:', p. 82.

89 I mean here not the encounter itself but his original imagined vision of the girl in the poem.

90 See above, pp. 74–75, 82.

A similar theme, without an overt reference to the Irish tradition, but borrowing more strongly from the *aisling* genre, was used earlier in *Star Trek* in the *Next Generation* episode 'Haven' (Season 1 Episode 10). In this episode, the fiancé of one of Enterprise's officers is discovered to have dreamed all his life of another woman – literally seeing visions of her face – and falling in love with her.[91] In the course of the episode it is discovered that this woman does exist, and is an alien, travelling on the last ship of a nearly extinct species, the Tarellians. The ambiguous and liminal status of the contagious Tarellians who are thus not allowed close contact with other species and who had until that point been believed to be extinct (thus having a near-legendary status, being the stuff of Starfleet training at the Academy), approximates them to the otherworld.[92] In each case, the *Star Trek* adaptation of the theme adds a note of hope and optimism. I would tentatively venture to suggest that it is this optimism and not the political, social or economic features of the Federation that constitute the real utopian element in *Star Trek* and carry its most important tropological message.

5.3 These are the *Immrama* of the Starship *Echtra*

A small proportion of the readership of this book may experience the sensation of cringing and laughing at the same time when reading the subtitle of this section, sensation no doubt familiar to many from reading the article and conference paper titles of medievalist aficionados of the bad pun. In this case, the bad pun is designed to drive home a point. For the purposes of this argument, I have proposed that *Star Trek* mainly fulfils the requirements of the *immram* genre. Nevertheless, like all of the texts in the corpus examined here, there is at least a whiff of the *echtrai* about it. In this instance, an illustration of that whiff can be found in one of the possible translations for the word *echtra* into English – 'enterprise'.[93] This section

91 For a discussion see, for instance, Harder, '"For As Often As He Slept"', pp. 47–48, 79–84.

92 For a discussion of the love-in-absence topos in medieval Irish literature, specifically in connection to the *Aislinge Óenguso* see Robbie Andrew MacLeod, 'Love and Gender in Medieval Gaelic Saga', unpublished PhD thesis, University of Glasgow, 2024 <https://theses.gla.ac.uk/84302/> (accessed 25 November 2024), pp. 64–65, 93–96, 120–121.

93 Electronic Dictionary of the Irish Language s.v. *echtra*, <dil.ie/19563> [accessed 5 November 2024]; the definition is cited as the 'more specialised definition' of *echtrae* by Duignan, *The Echtrae*, p. 1. I do not suggest that there is necessarily intentional allusion in the name choice for the *Star Trek* flagship, but the connotations of the word are

thus also functions in lieu of a conclusion to the present chapter, emphasizing the fuzzy nature of the genre sets introduced in this book, and providing a link between *Star Trek* and *Stargate*. My aim here is to show that despite assigning them to different 'sub-genres' of the narrative tradition of voyage literature (*immram* and *echtra* respectively), I do not propose to argue that the two texts are completely distinct.

A brief look at the *echtra*-like characteristics of the predominantly *immram*-inspired *Star Trek* will also help bring into sharper relief connections which come to light by putting *Star Trek* and *Stargate* together in terms of the specific intertextual matrix proposed in this book. These connections are different from, and complementary to, those which are obvious from an analysis of these works as members of the contemporary science fiction genre (or of the television science fiction sub-genre). I will not focus on those science-fiction-defined ones. The exceptions to this – those that are typical of the 'science fiction' genre analysis, but may feature in the following discussion only tangentially and from a different perspective, include: space travel, technobabble, alien planets, stellar phenomena, solutions of conflicts between narrative requirement and properties of the physical universe (time travel paradoxes, changes in mass and relative time with close-to-light speed, for example).[94]

Despite lacking a ship of the name, and despite its general *immram*-like island-hopping set-up, a strong *echtrai*-like aspect is present at the conclusion of *Voyager*. I allude here to the time-bending nature of the otherworld.[95] As we have seen, a different rate of the passage of time is a feature characteristic of the Irish (and Welsh) otherworlds.[96] The conclusion to *Immram Brain*, where it turns out that time had passed more slowly with the adventurers than it had at home, is an example.[97] The same phenomenon is encountered on the long journey from Ireland to the White Hill (Tower of London) by the survivors of the conflict in *Branwen ferch Lyr* (also known

---

illuminating in the context of historic development of voyage narratives. This also highlights the openness of associations for the term 'enterprise', which do not have to all be commercial (or political), as Booker would have it; 'The Politics', p. 199.

94 See, for example, Atwood, 'The Road to Ustopia'; see also discussion above, p. 20.

95 See also discussion of Narnian time above, pp. 52–53.

96 See also above, pp. 52, 97, 101, 117, 152–53.

97 Meyer, ed. and trans., *The Voyage of Bran*, §65; I, p. 32. For discussions, see for example, Carey, 'Time, Space and the Otherworld', pp. 7–12; Mackley, *The Legend*, pp. 63, 230 (in relation to the *Voyage of Saint Brendan*).

as the 'Second Branch of the Mabinogi').[98] On the way, the characters stay in Gwales.[99] They had been instructed not to open the door facing Cornwall, and only when they do the memory of their losses floods them, and the journey can continue, but their magical respite had lasted for eighty years. We have already seen an echo of the same phenomenon in Lewis's *Voyage*.[100] The conclusion of *Voyager* does something very similar. For those accustomed to modern science-fiction and space-faring narratives, the notion that time flows slower for the traveller is familiar from those episodes dealing with near-light-speed travel where the time dilation phenomenon is introduced. For the texts examined here, this is more of a feature of *Stargate* than *Star Trek*.[101] *Voyager*'s conclusion, unlike *Immram Brain*, involves no time-dilation or discovery of time having passed differently (as such), but does involve time-travel. The final episode of the series ('Endgame', season 7 Episodes 25 and 26) begins in the future, at a point when *Voyager*'s crew had been back on Earth for a while, having finally arrived home but suffered losses in the process. The plot of the episode is the aged Captain Janeway's final contribution to her ship and crew as she travels back in time and space to the Voyager of her past, to bring it back home earlier. Although in light of the different use of time in *Voyager*'s episode one might regard the parallel as specious, I would argue that in both cases time is used to highlight the contrast between the otherworld journey and the homecoming. The contrast is particularly striking as we have established that *Voyager*'s pilot contains topoi typical of *immrama*. The series thus travels across the fuzzy boundary between two genres in the course of its seven seasons.

The multivalency of allusion in *Star Trek* is similar to what we have seen in *Baudolino*. Like Eco's novels generally, *Star Trek* has a rich tradition of

---

98 See discussion in Carey, 'Time, Space and the Otherworld', p. 7.

99 Derick S. Thomson, ed., *Branwen Uerch Llyr*, Medieval and Modern Welsh Series 2 (Dublin: DIAS, 2003[1961]), p. 17; Sioned Davies, trans., *The Mabinogion* (Oxford: Oxford University Press, 2009), p. 34. For discussions of the otherworldly associations of this episode, see also Proinsias Mac Cana, *Branwen Daughter of Llŷr: A Study of the Irish Affinities and of the Composition of the Second Branch of the Mabinogi* (Cardiff: University of Wales Press, 1958), pp. 84, 108; Sioned Davies, 'Mythology and the Oral Tradition: Wales', in *The Celtic World*, ed. by Miranda Green (New York: Routledge, 1996), pp. 785–94 (p. 789).

100 See above, p. 168.

101 One thinks in particular of the *Stargate: Atlantis* Season 3 Episode 10 'The Return: Part 1', at the opening of which the protagonists encounter a damaged Ancient warship which had been travelling between galaxies at near light speed for thousands of years, with the original crew still very much alive.

intertextual references, also sometimes arcane and a knowing nod to the aficionados, and sometimes obvious. The best-studied are the references to Shakespeare, for instance, particularly in *The Next Generation*.[102] There are also, however, references to *The Three Musketeers, Cyrano de Bergerac, Moby Dick,* the Sherlock Holmes novels, among many other works of literature.[103] There are also references in the series to medieval Ireland, particularly in *Deep Space Nine*, where chief medical officer Lieutenant Bashir and Chief of Operations Miles O'Brien enjoy participating in a holographic re-creation of the eleventh-century Battle of Clontarf and encounter Brian Boru (from whom O'Brien claims to be descended).[104] In terms of medieval references, Robin Hood, the Arthurian legend, and *Beowulf* feature in a number of different episodes.[105] While there is no apparent direct reference to the vernacular *immram* texts in the way that there are to other literary texts, a topos found in the *Navigatio* is used in the opening of the *Voyager* episode 'Darkling' (Season 3 Episode 18). An alien, member of a travelling species, tells Janeway what is recognisably a space version of the story of the whale which Saint Brendan and his companions took for an island.[106] (Baudolino had also re-told this story to Deacon John in Eco's novel).[107] The giant whale started moving, giving away its nature only once the unwitting monks start a fire on its back, thinking that they are on an island.

---

102 Booker, *Star Trek*, p. 16–17. For discussions, see, for example, Mary Buhl Dutta, '"Very Bad Poetry, Captain": Shakespeare in *Star Trek*', *Extrapolation*, 36 (1995), 38–45; Karolina Kazimierczak, 'Adapting Shakespeare for *Star Trek* and *Star Trek* for Shakespeare: *The Klingon Hamlet* and the Spaces of Translation', *Studies in Popular Culture*, 32 (2010), 35–55; Craig Dionne, 'The Shatnerification of Shakespeare', in *Shakespeare after Mass Media*, ed. by Richard Burt (New York: Palgrave Macmillan 2002), pp. 173–91.

103 See, for instance, discussion in Hardy, 'Where Many Books Have Gone Before' and Johnson-Smith, *American Science Fiction TV*, p. 113.

104 *Deep Space Nine* episode 'Bar Association' (Season 4 Episode 16). For more on the battle and Brian Boru, see Seán Duffy, *Brian Boru and the Battle of Clontarf* (Dublin: Gill & Macmillan, 2014).

105 *Star Trek: The Next Generation* episode 'Qpid' (Season 4 Episode 20); *Deep Space Nine* episodes 'The Way of the Warrior', 'The Muse' (Season 4 episodes 1, 2, 21); *Voyager* episode 'Heroes and Demons' (Season 1 episode 11).

106 See O'Meara and Wooding, 'The Latin Version', pp. 34–35; Ludwig Bieler, '*Casconius*, the monster of the *Navigatio Brendani*', *Éigse*, 5 (1945–47), 139–40; Vicki E. Szabo, *Monstrous Fishes and the Mead-Dark Sea* (Leiden and Boston: Brill 2008), p. 51; *The Legend of St Brendan*, pp. 4, 73, 110–14; Natalia I. Petrovskaia, 'Poisson et pêche dans la littérature irlandaise et galloise: le bétail de la mer', *Anthropozoologica*, 53 (2018), 139–46 (pp. 143–44); Mulligan, *A Landscape of Words*, pp. 43–45.

107 See Chapter 3 above, p. 76.

The story in *Voyager* is of a space traveller landing on what he thinks is a planet, only to find that it is a massive creature with its own gravitational pull.

The whale-island as topos is not unique to the *Navigatio*, as it also appears in the legend of Sinbad the Sailor.[108] One might argue that since the legend of Sinbad is better known than the Brendan legend, *Voyager*'s authors are more likely to be drawing on that, and indeed previous discussions have referred to Sinbad and Odysseus as models for the journey home motif.[109] However, the seven-year journey of the *Voyager* crew bears an uncanny similarity to that of Brendan and his companions, and the terms used by Sergio Perosa to describe the latter can also be applied to the former: 'roaming the seas for seven years is a purgatorial experience of toil and anguish, dismay and disorientation'.[110] This is another connection that this series has with the *immram* genre, and of course it has no starship named *Echtra* at the central protagonist of the narrative.

The intertextual reference to the island-fish functions as a tangible echo of the *immram* tradition, for there also characters meet others (from related traditions) who tell them stories connecting narratives in a complex metatextual web. One thinks in particular of the episode in *Immram Curaig Maíle Dúin* in which the protagonist interacts with *senoir clerigh leith* 'an ancient grey cleric', a survivor of the voyage recounted in the *Navigatio*.[111] While Lewis's *Voyage of the Dawn Treader* makes its membership of the *immram* genre explicit by replicating the closure of Brendan's journey, *Voyager* does so through the insertion of intertextual reference to the same in the travelling alien's account.

While intertextual references and cultural allusions are plenty in *Star Trek*, they often function as surface entertainment. Sometimes this is literally entertainment, at the holodeck, the future three-dimensional and tactile

108 Sergio Perosa, *From Islands to Portraits. Four Literary Variations* (Amsterdam and Tokyo: IOS Press and Ohmsha, 2000), p. 3; Cornelia Catlin Coulter, 'The "Great Fish" in Ancient and Medieval Story', *Transactions and Proceedings of the American Philological Association*, 57 (1926), 32–50 <https://www.jstor.org/stable/282763> [accessed 8 April 2024]; Ioannis M. Konstantakos, 'The Island that was a Fish: an Ancient Folktale in the *Alexander Romance* and in Other Texts of Late Antiquity', in *Aspects of Orality and Greek Literature in the Roman Empire*, ed. by Consuelo Ruiz-Montero (Newcastle-upon-Tyne: Cambridge Scholars Publishing, 2019), pp. 281–300.

109 See, for instance, Johnson-Smith, *American Science Fiction TV*, pp. 108, 114–15.

110 Perosa, *From Islands to Portraits*, p. 3.

111 Whitley Stokes, ed. and trans., 'The Voyage of Mael Duin (Part II)', pp. 72–73; discussed in Mulligan, *A Landscape of Words*, pp. 50–51.

equivalent of today's entirely visual tele*vision*. Sometimes, as with the Jasconius/whale-planet story or with the Brian Boru reference it is merely a sidenote in the dialogue, to delight the intertextual literary archaeologist. In *Stargate*, by contrast, such allusions primarily function as part of the worldbuilding of the series. In this it is even more reminiscent of Eco's rich tapestry of intertextuality than *Star Trek* is. It is to the exploration of this tapestry that we now turn.

CHAPTER 6

Stargate as an *Echtra* Narrative

According to Dumville, 'The central theme of an *echtrae* is the entry of the human hero into the supernatural'.[1] If we follow Oskamp's view, cited above in connection to *Baudolino*, that *echtrai* did not have to involve journeys by sea, and translate that into space travel according to the widely accepted notion that *Star Trek*'s *Original Series* had its inspiration in naval stories, then it stands to reason to see *Stargate*, which mostly does not rely on ships and thus does not involve space-sea travel, as the equivalent of *echtrai*.[2] Thus, whereas in the previous chapter I have argued that *Star Trek* fulfils the requirements of an *immram* narrative and that classifying it as such can yield interesting results in our understanding of the 'text', in the following I propose a fresh analysis of the *Stargate* franchise as *echtra*. The mode of travel here is upgraded from the literal rowing-about on boats on the surface of the sea or even the space-faring equivalent thereof in faster-than-light-travelling starships. In *Stargate*, travel across interstellar distances is achieved by means of what is now commonly known as wormhole but which also has the name 'Einstein-Rosen bridge', following its initial description in a paper published by Albert Einstein and Nathan Rosen in 1935.[3] The summary of the paper provides an accessible description of the concept as part of their description of the mathematical solutions which they propose in the paper as involving: 'the mathematical representation of physical space by a space of two identical sheets, a particle being represented by a "bridge" connecting these sheets.'[4] Using this as a fictional mode of transport allows the television storyteller to cut (with some visual effects) from one planet straight to the other, omitting the rowing-about part entirely. The focus is now entirely on the otherworlds.

Any discussion of *Stargate* in connection to pre-modern literary traditions must acknowledge the series' (specifically in the original Emmerich film and in the first spin-off *Stargate SG-1*) reliance on popular knowledge of

1 Dumville, '*Echtrae and Immram*', p. 82.

2 See above, p. 73; reference is to Oskamp, ed., *The Voyage of Máel Dúin*, p. 43.

3 For a brief description and discussion of the narrative effect of this device, see Beeler, '*Stargate SG-1*', pp. 269–70.

4 Einstein and Rosen, 'Particle Problem', p. 73.

 DOI:10.1163/9789004734548_007

mythology and legend, alluded to in the conclusion to the previous chapter.[5] The premise of the film and most of the ten seasons of *Stargate SG-1* is the dominance in the Milky Way of aliens whose culture is essentially that of Ancient Egypt.[6] This is expanded into later seasons to include other world mythologies, with the premise that aliens of the same species had at one point or another in the past posed as supernatural beings or gods here on Earth.[7] Arthurian legend also finds its expression in *Stargate SG-1* in the later seasons (Seasons 9 and 10).[8] It is not my object here to present an analysis of its use, although it presents its own interesting questions on the tensions between requirements of adhering to imagery established in the popular imagination and 'fidelity' to the original sources.[9]

Stargate, once it evolves beyond an exclusive reliance on Egyptian mythology, incorporates a number of elements derived from the Celtic traditions (in addition to its later use of the Arthurian legend). In the episode entitled '2001' (Season 5 episode 10) the team come across a farming culture overseen by advanced aliens, and in the course of the adventure discover that another human civilization had previously existed on the planet, but had been wiped out. The team archaeologist/linguist, Daniel Jackson, discovers this by deciphering a newspaper in a language which he claims is similar to Welsh, as he finds it to be reminiscent of a 'Celtic' text from Wales.[10] The most obvious and thus easy to miss allusion creating (perhaps an accidental) link to the Irish tradition, is in the name of the leader of the Earth team who go on all these adventures to the planetary otherworlds: O'Neill. An echo of the Irish otherworld is found also in the *SG-1* Season 1 episode 'Fire and Water' (Episode 13), where the team is captured by a sea-dwelling alien, who keeps Jackson for questioning and releases the rest to go home with faked memories of the archaeologist's fiery demise. The

---

5 As Beeler points out, Star Trek Original Series also relied on mythology, and audiences' knowledge therof, to provide the plots of a number of episodes; '*Stargate SG-1* and the Quest for the Perfect Science-Fiction Premise', p. 281 n. 10.

6 MacKinnon, '*Stargate Atlantis*', p. 37.

7 Beeler, '*Stargate SG-1*', pp. 272–75. Beeler argues that this is part of the series' success (p. 274).

8 MacKinnon, '*Stargate Atlantis*', p. 37.

9 For a brief discussion of Merlin in *Stargate*, see Natalia I. Petrovskaia, 'The Fool and the Wise Man: The Legacy of the Two Merlins in Modern Culture', in *The Legacy of Courtly Literature. From Medieval to Contemporary Culture*, ed. by Deborah Nelson-Campbell and Ruben Cholakian (Cham: Palgrave Macmillan, 2017), pp. 175–205 (pp. 176, 183, 185–86).

10 See also summary and discussion, in connection to time-travel aspects, in Johnson-Smith, *American Science Fiction TV*, pp. 175–77.

explicit references in the episode are to ancient Babylonian culture, as the alien's mate whom he is searching for had lived on Earth at the time of that civilization. However, the under-water dwelling of the alien echoes also the underwater variety of the medieval Irish otherworld.[11] Explicit allusions, however, are less significant than *Stargate*'s general *echtrai* characteristics.

The *Stargate* otherworlds share with the Old Irish otherworld(s) the reconciliatory and combinatory nature. Put in more mundane terms, both represent a hotchpotch of traditions. In the case of the Old Irish 'otherworlds' a combination of Christian and pagan elements has been observed.[12] In Mac Cana's reading, the Irish otherworld had evolved to become assimilated into the image and conception of Christian (Earthly) Paradise – a trajectory that for us culminates in Narnia, and its 'Utter East' – much like the Arthurian legend had evolved 'from secular heroic-romantic saga to Christian allegory', to borrow his turn of phrase.[13] Something similar can be argued (albeit on a smaller scale) for *Stargate: SG-1* (and to a much lesser extent *Stargate: Atlantis*).[14]

References to literatures and materials other than Celtic – Egyptian, Greek, Minoan, Babylonian – abound in the series and outweigh the meagre references to 'Celtic' legends and texts. One wonders also whether the imaginative background of crystal-based technology of the gate-builders (and those who adopted their technologies for their own use, like the Goa'uld) may be also an echo of what has traditionally been perceived as a characteristic of the 'Celtic' otherworld.[15] Regardless of whether the use of crystal is a coincidence, the framing of the narrative itself opens it, as I argue, to be read in light of the modern reception of Old Irish fantastic voyage narratives, and *echtrai* in particular.

6.1 *Stargate*'s Planetary Otherworlds

The most important, striking, and most visible implication of the alternative genre taxonomy proposed in this book is that as a result *Star Trek* and

11 Carey, 'Otherworlds', p. 31.

12 See, for instance, Proinsias Mac Cana, 'The Sinless Otherworld of *Immram Brain*', *Ériu*, 27 (1976), 95–115 (pp. 95–6).

13 Mac Cana, 'The Sinless Otherworld', p. 99.

14 *Stargate: Universe* is almost entirely devoid of such intertextual aspects, another reason for its exclusion from the present analysis.

15 For this classic view, see, for instance, Patch, 'Some Elements', p. 609 and n. 30 for source references.

Stargate are seen as entirely different types of narrative, belonging to different genres. This is in sharp contrast to the conventional genre divisions which identify both sets of television series as 'science fiction'.

The distinction between the two, which aligns *Star Trek* with the *Navigatio*, and *Stargate* with texts such as *Echtrae Chonnlai*, helps bring into focus also and to some degree explain some fundamental differences. Not only is *Star Trek* as case of island-hopping (where islands are planets), where the journey is, as Dumville points out for the *immram*, indispensable to the narrative, but it also employs each 'island' to illustrate a moral (political, ethical or social) point. Meanwhile, *Stargate*, while it also explores the human condition through metaphorical encounters with alien cultures, is much more explicitly composed of otherworldly visits. After each trip, the teams return to Earth (or, in the case of *Stargate: Atlantis* to the otherworldly homebase of Atlantis). Not in all cases, but in many, the otherworld adventure is formative and informative.

Stargate does share with *Star Trek* the islandness of planets to some degree. Like islands in the traditional 'island narratives', planets in both series function as condensed versions of one or more aspects of our world, bringing individual social, political, ethical, moral, religious, cultural or linguistic issues to the fore and highlighting them for the dual purposes of the plot (entertainment) and focusing the viewer's thought on the issues (edification). In *Stargate* the planets also function very much in terms of isolated otherworlds, but not all otherworlds are planetary, unlike in *Star Trek*. In particular, in *Stargate* the concept of 'ascension' to a higher, non-corporeal state of existence, that is not necessarily different in terms of location but rather in terms of dimension (much like the travel mode through wormholes) adds another layer to possibilities of depicting the otherworld that echo *echtrai* narrative traditions.

One of the clearest instances where characteristics of the *echtra* genre are demonstrated by *Stargate* is in the figure of Daniel Jackson and his interaction with the world beyond the gate. The archaeologist attached to the expedition, as a civilian, Daniel Jackson can be argued to represent the everyman viewer. He is (initially) awkward in battle situations and openly expresses a sense of wonder at the alien cultures encountered. His function is similar to that of Eustace in the *Voyage* and Niketas in *Baudolino* – a way for the average intended member of the audience to engage with the material.[16]

---

16 See above, pp. 92 and 105.

In the original *Stargate* movie (1994), Jackson can also be analysed as a protagonist of an *echtra* narrative who remains in the otherworld for the love of an otherworldly woman.[17] He finds love and remains behind on the alien planet, Abydos, when the rest of the team return to Earth. He remains behind in the understanding that he will never be able to return, as the Abydos gate will be buried to isolate it from Earth without destroying the planet and the people. Through this figure the anagogical aspect of the *echtra* is retained in *Stargate*, since he also has a connection to mysticism, as Stan Beeler points out.[18] Jackson believes strongly that he had acquired supernatural powers in the episode 'Maternal Instinct' (*SG-1* Season 3 episode 20), set in a secluded monastery on a planet called Kheb, visually clearly inspired by Buddhist architecture, and finally does so as he ascends to a higher plane of existence at the conclusion of Season 5 ('Meridian', episode 21).[19]

This theme of the traveller staying behind in the otherworld is one of the staples in *echtrai* narratives. It is aptly summarised by Mac Mathúna, and since details of his summary are relevant to our discussion, I quote the relevant passage in full:

> During his stay there [= in the Otherworld], the man sees and enjoys the wonderful pleasures and treasures of the other domain, often defeats an enemy and/or monster, and usually has a liaison with an Otherworld woman, who may have invited him there in the first place. He often returns to this world, bringing back gifts, treasures and insignia; he sometimes goes back again to the Otherworld or remains there and is never heard of again.[20]

---

17 The subject of the otherworldly woman in the medieval Irish literary tradition has recently received renewed attention, particularly in Joanne Findon, *Bound and Free: Voices of Mortal and Otherworld Women in Medieval Irish Literature* (Toronto: Pontifical Institute of Mediaeval Studies, 2024). Due to the timing of publication I have not had the opportunity to incorporate this work in my discussion.

18 Beeler, '*Stargate SG-1*', p. 270.

19 Beeler, '*Stargate SG-1*', p. 270. Beeler also points out that the Ancients' doctrine of ascension in the *Stargate* franchise generally seems to share elements of (in other words be inspired by) Zen Buddhism (p. 276).

20 Séamus Mac Mathúna, 'The Question of Irish Analogues in Old Norse-Icelandic Voyage Tales in the *fornaldarsögur* and the *Gesta Danorum* of Saxo Grammaticus', in *Between Worlds: Contexts, Sources, and Analogues of Scandinavian Otherowlrd Journeys*, ed. by Matthias Egeler and Wilhelm Heizmann (Berlin: De Gruyter, 2020), pp. 283–345. The comment in brackets is mine.

This echoes Elizabeth A. Bohls's observation about medieval historical traditions of travel and travel narratives in general: 'Travel fulfills obligations and enhances status, but it also feeds dangerous desires. A traveller might come back transformed – for better or worse – or might not come back at all'.[21] Daniel Jackson is part of the team that defeats an alien 'monster' who occupies the alien planet Abydos, a member of the species termed Goa'uld who are the main antagonists in the first seasons of the subsequent spin-off TV series, *Stargate SG-1*. The monster poses as the Egyptian god Ra.[22] The second topos – the liaison with the otherworld woman is represented by Daniel's marriage to Sha're, one of the human inhabitants of the planet. His decision to stay behind on Abydos is the movie's equivalent of the hero staying behind in the otherworld, to be 'never heard of again'. In the storyworld of the initial movie, this narrative arc is complete.[23]

The fascination with the idea of the traveller staying behind in the otherworld finds an echo also in modern interpretations of medieval 'discovery' of the Americas. Kervran, for instance, constructs a narrative of early medieval Irish monks seeking out islands in search of solitude, swept away by winds as far as the Americas, and staying there: 'Certains ne tentèrent rien pour revenir en Europe; ce sont d'autres qui les découvrirent là par hazard. Mais il en est qui sont revenus' ('Some did not make any attempt to return to Europe; it was others who had found them there by accident. But there are some who returned').[24] While the romantic notion of staying behind in the otherworld is shared by this arguably fanciful and fictional reconstruction and the *echtra*, the notion of the monks staying behind on an island where they are brought accidentally and against their will, and found there by others, some of whom do return, has closer parallels elsewhere. It is inspired by *immrama* and is echoed also in the *immram*-inspired *Star Trek*. One thinks in particular of the *Voyager* episode 'The 37's' (*Voyager* 2.1), where the ship's crew on their way home encounter a colony established by people abducted by aliens from Earth in the first half of the twentieth century and brought to this distant planet. While the *Voyager* crew, given the choice, unanimously choses to continue their journey home, the colonists choose to stay.

Returning to *Stargate*, the first spin-off, the television series *Stargate SG-1* provides an opportunity for the character to return from the 'otherworld'

21 Bohls, 'Introduction', p. xiv.

22 Gil, 'Remember the Nox', p. 179.

23 The television series picks up where the movie had left off; see discussion in Gil, 'Remember the Nox', p. 191.

24 Kervran, *Brandan*, pp. 50–51; my translation.

to engage on the subsequent series of expeditions, but as I propose to show in the following discussion, *echtra* elements are present in multiple individual episodes, and are often associated specifically with Daniel. Indeed, his return to Earth through the stargate ultimately occurs because his wife, Sha're, is abducted by a new set of 'otherworldly' (= Goa'uld) opponents.[25] This echoes the plot of *Echtra Láegaire*, where the trip to the otherworld is set in motion after 'an Otherworld king, Fiachna mac Rétach, comes to the land of mortals seeking assistance against his enemies' who had abducted his wife.[26] The opening of *Stargate SG-1* as a series also echoes *Echtra Nerai*, as, like Nera, the earth team follow (though after a pause) an otherworldly raiding party back to the otherworld.[27]

I do not propose to suggest that either case constitutes a deliberate echo of these specific medieval Irish tales on the part of the scriptwriters, nor would I suggest reading the earthly archaeologist-cum-linguist-turned-galactic-explorer Daniel Jackson as an equivalent of a fairy king, but I do suggest that both *Stargate SG-1* and *Echtra Láegaire* demonstrate iterations of the same *topos* (and the same applies to the parallel with *Echtra Nerai*). *Stargate* thus is not merely to be classified as an *echtra* narrative for the sake of argument, but actually demonstrates some of the crucial *topoi* of that narrative genre.[28] A potential, but I would suggest fallacious, counter-argument to my point is that one might extend the argument *ad absurdum* by postulating that the topos of the stolen wife is a common narrative device starting any number of stories, including, of course, that of the Trojan war, mentioned above in connection to Lucy's temptation in the *Voyage*.[29] However, in *Stargate* the specific topos, I would argue, is that the stolen wife is from the otherworld and it is her husband who comes from the otherworld to this world to seek the help of warriors of this world.[30] This specific form of the topos matches both the Old Irish narrative and the storyline of *Stargate SG-1*, seasons 1–3. Jackson fails to recover his wife, and her final appearance is in 'Forever in a Day' (Season 3 Episode 10). True to

25 Gil, 'Remember the Nox', p. 180.

26 Mac Mathúna, 'The Question', p. 290; Mac Mathúna, *Iceland and the Immrama*, p. 23.

27 *Stargate SG-1* pilot episode 1.1 'Children of the Gods'; Meyer, ed. and trans, 'The Adventures of Nera', pp. 216–17; Duignan, *The Echtrae*, p. 43.

28 The search for a vanished wife is motif number H1385.3; related to the rescue of wife from fairyland (motif F322.2) in the folktale motif catalogue compiled for Old Irish material in Tom Pete Cross, *Motif-Index of Early Irish Literature*, Indiana University Folklore Series 7 (Bloomington: Indiana University Press, 1952), pp. 260, 354.

29 Chapter 2, p. 68–69.

30 Mac Mathúna uses the turn of phrase 'assistance of the men of this world', but I think in both cases we can specifically refer to fighting men, 'The Question', p. 290.

form for the otherworldly bride motif, this final appearance includes time-bending as Sha're uses alien technology to communicate with Jackson, making him think he had experienced an entire period of mourning for her in the space of a split second.

It seems deeply appropriate that personal story of the in-story walking encyclopedia of legends (essentially 'Bulfinch's mythology' incarnate), Daniel Jackson, is one of a combination of *echtrai*-related *topoi*.[31] He is the 'hero' who stays in the otherworld for the love of an otherworldly woman (in the original film); he is the husband who seeks his wife abducted by the otherworldly inhabitants (in *SG-1* seasons 1–3); he is the hero who sails off into the unknown of the deathless otherworld never to be heard of again (season 5, absent through season 6, though he returns in season 7).[32]

Jackson is also the focal character because – as the walking talking encyclopedia – he is the series' anchorage in mythologies and legends used for the individual episode plots and larger story-arcs. He, like Niketas in *Baudolino*, digests the material for the reader, anchoring it in the familiar. The writers of *Stargate* use the reverse defamiliarisation technique in much the same way Eco does.[33] The narrative and the mythologies, act as backdrops for exploring different ideas and concepts. As Beeler points out, the ease with which interstellar travel occurs in *Stargate* (by use of the gates and their wormholes, which permit instantaneous transportation between worlds) is key in 'allowing the writers to foreground character studies and plotlines of the SG-1 team against a rich backdrop of cultures that are readily available for research'.[34] It also, along with the reliance on mythological and historical models for the cultures in question, allows the writers to present the audience with a variety of problems posed by utopian, ustopian

---

31 For more on Thomas Bullfinch, see Marie Sally Cleary, *Myths for the Millions: Thomas Bulfinch, His America, and His Mythology Book*, Kulturtransfer und Geschlechterforschung (Frankfurt am Main: Peter Lang, 2007).

32 See also discussion in Van Bever Donker and Stephanie Yorke, 'Re-Imagining the Colonial Encounter', pp. 737–38.

33 See above, pp. 89–90.

34 Beeler, '*Stargate SG-1*', p. 273. In this section of Chapter 6 I explore the implications of reading planets as otherworlds in the science fiction series *Stargate* and, to some extent, *Star Trek*. Johnson-Smith, *American Science Fiction TV* (pp. 157–58) mentions a television series from 1985 entitled *Otherworld* consisting of eight episodes where the main characters have adventures in alternate realities. The title—and summary, as provided by Johnson-Smith—imply at least some degree of inspiration from earlier literatures. Potential connections with the reception history of Old Irish *echtrai* in the context of modern science fiction television may be worth exploring.

and dystopian societies without spending too much time with the travel process itself. This distinguishes *Stargate* from the *immram* mode of *Star Trek* (where the planets *are* the travel, like the islands of the Old Irish voyage narratives). Nevertheless, the planetary narrative paradigm in *Stargate*, as in *Gulliver's Travels* and in *Star Trek*, permits exploration of the implications, possibilities and even problems of utopias, or perhaps better, given the problems, ustopias.[35] There are individual societies encountered by both the *SG-1* and the *Atlantis* teams that thus invite analysis from the perspective of the utopian narrative tradition. Whilst not the only aspect that connects these new media to the intertextual matrix of *echtrai* and *immrama*, it is with this subject that the following section of this discussion is concerned.

6.2 *Stargate* Ustopias

While the Irish otherworlds provide a helpful template against which to read these space-travel narratives, it is possible that they do so less because the series build on the medieval tradition – although it is demonstrably part of their cultural background – but rather because they create, like the medieval Irish narratives, what John Carey describes as 'verbal worlds', where 'all things are possible'.[36] For *Stargate*'s in particular, Carey's formula for the opposition '*this world: Otherworld*' as '*real world: world-as-described*' is particularly useful.[37]

The ustopias of *Stargate*'s island planets are in many cases otherworldly, sharing features with the Old Irish otherworld of *echtra* narratives, though sometimes in subversive form. They are particularly interesting because often juxtaposed with utopias. A case in point are *SG-1* season 1 episodes 8 and 9. In the *SG-1* episode 'The Nox' (season 1 episode 8), a seemingly primitive, though peaceful and apparently happy, civilization turns out to be extremely advanced, to the degree that their technology has the appearance of magic, for both the explorers and the audience. Whenever the peaceful and advanced Nox re-appear later on (and the Nox who does

35 Cf. Morgan, 'Celts in Spaaaaace!', pp. 122–23.

36 Carey, 'Otherworlds', p. 32.

37 It can also be applied, but perhaps necessitating more layers, to the virtuoso treatment of 'reality' in Eco's *Baudolino*; see discussion above, pp. 98–109. One thinks in particular of Carey's identification of 'the story's setting and the story itself' as 'the same thing' ('Otherworlds', p. 36).

re-appear is female) in other episodes, they have all the appearance of having come *a tírib beo* ('from lands of [the] living'), as the otherworldly woman of *Echtrae Chonnlai* does.[38] Old Irish literature has a number of otherworlds with a variety of associated names. Moylan lists *tir tairngiri* ('land of promise'), *mag mell* ('pleasant plain'), *tir na nOg* ('land of youth'), for instance, all of which he characterises as 'sacred *elsewheres*', not all of them necessarily island-shaped.[39]

A similarly blissful society is represented in the following episode, 'Brief Candle' (*SG-1* season 1 episode 9), without strife, with endless feasting and everyone showing contentment, seems to echo the words of the otherworldly woman of *Echtrae Chonnlai*: *Domelom fledo buanae cen frithgnam* ('We enjoy lasting feasts without toil').[40] Yet this appearance hides a terrifying truth that is discovered only when it affects a member of the exploration team: the lifespan of the planet's inhabitants, through technological intervention by an advanced and malign alien, lasts only a fraction of the average human lifespan. The irony in reading 'Brief Candle' as an *echtra* is that here, too the male protagonist is invited to stay with the otherworldly inhabitants by an otherworldly woman who falls in love with him.[41] Here, however, the lands are not of everlasting life. The inhabitants never do grow old, but in a fashion contrasting with the inhabitants of the Old Irish otherworld. The technology left by the malign alien affects the protagonist differently, however, since he had already lived far longer than any of the planet's brief-lived inhabitants, and he undergoes a process of speed-aging.

---

38 Hans Pieter Atze Oskamp, '*Echtra Condla*', *Études celtiques*, 14 (1974), 207–28 (p. 212). For a brief introduction to the tale, see Carey, 'Voyage Literature', p. 1743. See also discussion in Mac Cana, 'The Sinless Otherworld', pp. 96–7. Mac Cana argues that the two tales, *Echtrae Chonnlai* and *Immram Brain*, present, though somewhat differently, the same otherworld (p. 97). See also the discussion in Egeler, *Islands*, pp. 41–61.

39 Moylan, 'Irish Voyages', p. 301.

40 Oskamp, '*Echtra Condla*', pp. 221, 225; discussed p. 212. It is worth pointing out here that both utopian/ustopian societies depicted in these episodes of *Stargate* are devoid of the martial aspect present in the *echtra* narrative; their inhabitants are not military-minded or heroic (though their Terran visitors are both); Oskamp, '*Echtra Condla*', p. 214 and Egeler, *Islands*, pp. 51, 62, for that aspect of the otherworld and otherworld journeys. For discussion of descriptions of the otherworld through lack of negative qualities, see above, pp. 124–25.

41 Compare the discussion of the sexual aspects of the otherworld and its dwellers in the Irish tradition, in Mac Cana, 'The Sinless Otherworld', pp. 100–08. The inhabitants of Argos (also called P3X-8596 by the Earth expedition), the 'Otherworld' (=planet) in 'Brief Candle' appear to enjoy life and love in an innocent, though physical manner.

Thus within the short span of time covered by the episode, the aging contrast between the traditional immortal otherworldly woman and her mortal lover is shown, despite the subversion of the topos in the ustopian representation.[42] In some of the Old Irish otherworld narratives, as in *Echtrae Chonnlai*, the hero is offered immortality if he goes to live in the otherworld. Here, O'Neill instead tastes of the accelerated mortality of the inhabitants.

By contrast, in the two similar episodes in *Stargate Atlantis* where the otherworldly woman falls in love with the mortal man, both women are ascended beings (Season 1 Episode 14 'Sanctuary'; Season 2 Episode 12 'Epiphany'). While the first, Chaya, does not invite him to join the ascended (primarily because of her own marginal status as an exile). Chaya is particularly striking as an example of an otherworldly woman in the Irish tradition, as she is not only endowed with supernatural abilities (as an ascended – energy-based – being, who only appears human) but in her corporeal form is described by the doctor who gives her a medical check as 'as lovely on the inside' as on the outside ('Sanctuary'). Indeed, her perfect health, too perfect, according to the doctor, is humanly impossible and thus causes alarm among her hosts.

The second otherworldly woman, Teer, offers Sheppard, the military leader of the main exploration team of the Atlantis expedition, to join her and her people in ascending to the higher plane of existence at the end of the episode, an offer he declines. The contrast here with the *echtrai* is that in the Old Irish narrative such an invitation can mark the start of an adventure. Within the framework of the *Stargate* series, the on-screen adventure could not continue – at least not in the established form – if the protagonist accepts the offer of joining the otherworld through ascension. Indeed, that is the way for a character to be written out of the series, particularly when an actor leaves, as in the case of Daniel Jackson's acceptance of the offer of ascension in *Stargate SG-1*, discussed above.[43] In this case, this was to enable the actor portraying the character, Michael Shanks, to leave the show.[44] Thus, to return to the series, the character had to come back to the physical world to regain human form. Something similar happens in *Star Trek* with Wesley Crusher, as we have seen, who also accepts adventures beyond

42 Oskamp, '*Echtra Condla*', p. 213. For a medieval instance of the subversion of the same topos, see Egeler, *Islands*, pp. 63–64.

43 See above, p. 161.

44 Gil, 'Remember the Nox', pp. 196–97.

human comprehension and also leaves the series.[45] Thus, the Old Irish otherworld voyage motifs are adapted to the constraints of a new set of storytelling conventions.

The two examples from *SG-1* present specific cases in *Stargate* where otherworldly planets show features associated with the supernatural properties of the otherworld, while the *Atlantis* examples show similarity between motifs found in the way the Ascended beings are conceived in the *Stargate* imaginarium and the Old Irish otherworld. More generally, the motivation of the exploration in the *Stargate* world is linked to the acquisition of knowledge and technology. It is thus more pecuniary than that of *Star Trek*'s utopian variety of exploration for the sake of understanding the galaxy and its inhabitants better.

The focus on acquisition of alien technologies thus echoes the wealth aspect of the otherworld, particularly as it is depicted in *echtra* narratives. One thinks in particular of the misleadingly named *Immram Brain*. Following the references to eternal life and general happiness, quoted above in connection to the discussion of utopias in the chapter on Swift and *Gulliver's Travels*, the otherworldly woman in her invitation to Bran also refers to wealth:[46]

> Móini, dússi cach datho
> hi Ciúin, cáine étatho,
> étsecht fri céul co m-bindi,
> óol fíno óingrindi.
>
> Carpait órdi hi Maig Réin
> taircet la tule don gréin,
> carpait arggait i Maig Mon
> ocus crédumi cen on.
>
> (Wealth, treasures of every hue,
> Are in Ciuin, a beauty of freshness
> Listening to sweet music,
> Drinking the best of wine

45 See above, p. 148.

46 The quoted text and translation are stanzas 13 and 14 from Meyer, ed. and trans., *The Voyage of Bran*, pp. 8 and 9.

Golden chariots in Maig Réin,
Rising with the tide to the sun,
Chariots of silver in Mag Mon,
And of bronze without blemish.)

The presence of wine and musical entertainment is a staple in the *Stargate* *SG-1* otherworlds. Chariots represent material goods, and – in the guise of technology – it is these that the adventurers on the SG team seek on behalf of their Earth-based commanding organisation.

While I do not wish here to push this beyond a parallel, it is telling that the term 'chariot' itself occurs in the *SG-1* episode 'Thor's Chariot' (Season 1 Episode 10), where it stands for an advanced alien spaceship belonging to a member of the benevolent Asgard race known as Thor. The key mythology and legendarium on which this episode is built, like all Asgard episodes, is the Old Norse material, best known today through the prism of the retelling by the twelfth-century writer and politician Snorri Sturlusson (1179–1241).[47] Connections and parallels exist between the medieval literatures and cultures of Ireland and Scandinavia, not least in the travel narrative genres.[48] Other connections appear to also be present in the *SG-1* Norse-inspired episodes 'Thor's Hammer', and 'Thor's Chariot' (season 1 episodes 6 and 10), although perhaps also accidentally, as the local human woman who helps the heroes is called Gairwyn, a distinctly non-Scandinavian name. This name appears to be a compound of the Welsh words *gair* (n.m. 'word') and *gwyn*, the masculine form of the adjective meaning 'white', 'shining',

47 For Snorri's biography, see Kevin J. Wanner, *Snorri Sturluson and the* Edda. *The Conversion of Cultural Capital in Medieval Scandinavia* (Toronto, Buffalo and London: University of Toronto Press, 2008), pp. 18–25; for Old Norse myth in contemporary culture, see Carolyne Larrington, *Old Norse Myths That Shape the Way We Think* (London: Thames and Hudson, 2023), esp. chapter 4 for discussion of Thor (Þórr) and his modern afterlives (focusing in particular on Marvel comic book and movie adaptations). Thor's hammer, the visual representation of which also echoes Norse artefacts, features in the earlier *SG-1* episode 'Thor's Hammer' (Season 1 Episode 10); cf. Larrington, *Old Norse Myths*, fig. 39.

48 Mac Mathúna, 'The Question'; Mac Mathúna, *Iceland and the Immrama*. See also, for example, Rosemary Power, 'Norse-Gaelic Contacts: Genres and Transmission', *Journal of the North Atlantic*, 4 (2013), 19–25; Egeler, *Islands*; and comments in Helen Fulton and Sif Rikhardsdottir, 'Introduction. Transmission of Charlemagne in Scandinavia, Wales, and Ireland', in *Charlemagne in the Norse and Celtic Worlds*, ed. Helen Fulton and Sif Rikhardsdottir (Cambridge: D. S. Brewer, 2022), pp. 1–14 (pp. 1–2).

that can also mean 'blond'.[49] She is the one who essentially functions as the voice of her people in speaking with the protagonists, and becomes an ally, so in this respect also 'fair word' is an appropriate name. In terms of utopian readings it may be significant that word *gwyn* can also mean 'blessed' or 'happy' (also 'holy') and this echoes Gairwyn's position as one of the humans who are protected from the evil Goa'uld by the benign race of Thor's people (the Asgard). Her planet is thus definable as an utopia.

The most striking visualization of the utopian in *Stargate* is arguably the floating technologically advanced, but uninhabited, city of Atlantis itself. As Sarah R. MacKinnon observes, '[t]he angular shapes of the buildings, Ancient script on inner walls and the sharpness of the boundary between the city and the sea creates an otherworldly sense of estrangement that convinces the audience that such a city does not, and could not, exist on Earth'.[50] While MacKinnon does not explicitly refer to Shklovsky or Brecht, the 'estrangement' she invokes is the equivalent of 'defamiliarisation'.[51] The use of the Atlantis legend at the core of the narrative in this series centralizes the notion of islandness. It is the island of Atlantis, according to Patke, is the exemplary case for 'when the idea of an island answers to an abiding human interest that has proved both mysterious and compelling for more than two thousand years of human history, at least in the Western world, but with counterparts in other seas'.[52] Atlantis is also a prime candidate for the re-location of the Irish otherworld within a sci-fi environment, as the mythology of *Stargate* establishes the world of the Ancients – the race who had built the wonderous starship-city, and had sunk it to the bottom of the ocean in another galaxy – as the casebook example of what Patke describes as a 'recognition that something exceptionally significant and splendid existed once but is no longer accessible'.[53] The conflation of the Irish tradition of the 'Fortunate Islands' in the West (also identifiable as the geographically localizable physical goal of Saint Brendan's westward journey) with the legend of Atlantis has in fact happened much earlier.[54]

49 *Geiriadur Prifysgol Cymru* s.v. *gair*; *gwyn*[1], <https://geiriadur.ac.uk/gpc/gpc.html> [accessed 29 March 2024].

50 MacKinnon, '*Stargate Atlantis*', pp. 39–40.

51 See discussion above, p. 62.

52 Patke, *Poetry and Islands*, p. 48, in the context of a broader discussion of the legend of Atlantis and its afterlife (pp. 48–54).

53 Patke, *Poetry and Islands*, p. 53.

54 Patke, *Poetry and Islands*, p. 53; Egeler, *Islands*, pp. 133–34 and further references therein.

6.3 Postcolonial *Echtrai*

Though some societies encountered by the travellers and the viewers in *Stargate* are idyllic or at least sufficiently evolved and enlightened to not suffer from internal self-inflicted conflict, as shown in the section above, an utopian reading is not on the surface obvious for the series as a whole. In *Stargate: SG-1* most humans in the Milky Way galaxy are first colonial/postcolonial subjects of alien (Goa'uld) rule and then pre-colonial subjects of attempts of religious colonization (by the Ori).[55] As Beeler convincingly argues, the main antagonists of the initial seasons of *Stargate SG-1*, the Goa'uld, serpent-like creatures that burrow into human bodies and take over all higher functions, are 'a postcolonial theorist's ideal enemy, since they not only transport and enslave natives but also physically possess their bodies'.[56] Similarly, in his reading, the Goa'uld slaves and 'human incubators', the Jaffa, 'become symbolic representatives of the problem of colonialism'.[57] In this, *Stargate* approaches the ideological interests of *Star Trek* with its 'anticolonialist' Prime Directive – the general order not to interfere with internal affairs of other civilizations (and avoid contact with less technologically advanced civilisations who had not yet ventured out into space).[58] As Booker notes, the main antagonists of *Star Trek Original Series* are both labelled 'Empire'.[59]

While none of the major antagonist species in *Stargate: SG-1* or *Stargate: Atlantis* carry this label, they nevertheless share some of the features of colonizing and dominating powers.[60] The emphasis in *Stargate*, however, is less on domination through brute force of cunning (as with Klingon, or Romulan and Cardassian empires in *Star Trek*) but rather through domination through religion. The major antagonists in the early seasons of *SG-1*, the

---

55 MacKinnon, '*Stargate Atlantis*', p. 37; referring generally to domination but not in specifically colonial/postcolonial terms.

56 Beeler, '*Stargate SG-1*', p. 275. See also discussion in Van Bever Donker and Stephanie Yorke, 'Re-Imagining the Colonial Encounter', pp. 739–41.

57 Beeler, '*Stargate SG-1*', p. 275.

58 Booker, 'The Politics', pp. 196, 204. *Pace* Booker, who suggests that in *Star Trek*'s utopia 'there are no real working-class characters' p. 196 (reiterated on p. 198), the various series' representation of miners seems to stand for the working classes generally. One thinks in particular of the *Original Series* Season 1 Episode 6 'Mudd's Women' and in terms of later developments also the *Voyager* Season 7 Episode 20 'Author, Author' (where the miners are holographic).

59 Booker, 'The Politics', p. 201.

60 Van Bever Donker and Yorke, 'Re-Imagining the Colonial Encounter', p. 735.

Goa'uld, as has already been mentioned, not only take over their human hosts, but also pretend to be the gods of ancient human mythologies, initially Egyptian only, but later also others.[61] The major antagonists of the last two seasons (9 and 10) are the Ori, who as 'ascended' beings existing only in the form of energy and possessed of much greater powers and knowledge than physical beings are in a prime position to highjack religious beliefs. The Wraith of *Stargate: Atlantis*, a vampiric species subsisting on sucking the life-force from humans, rather than taking over bodies like the Goa'uld, are not initially represented posing as gods, but in Season 2 of the series are also revealed to have 'worshipers' ('The Hive', Season 2 Episode 11).

The pretence of deity identity has its parallels (and possible roots) in the Old Norse tradition, in Snorri Sturluson's *Prose Edda*, specifically the *Gylfaginning* 'deception of Gylfi', at the conclusion of which the Æsir speaking to Gylfi are revealed to be human, and not the deity Æsir that they were pretending to be.[62] In medieval Irish material, however, a similar trend can be observed, as what were probably initially deities are euhemerized and anthropomorphized.[63] The treatment of the gods of ancient legends as mortal beings (albeit in the case of *Stargate* not human, and in the case of the Ori of seasons 9–10 not technically mortal in the human sense) thus has a venerable history. It is used in medieval Irish material sometimes to highlight contrasts between a protagonist saint (usually Saint Patrick) and his pagan interlocutors, with the Christian audience of the texts presumably on the side of the saint.[64] The medieval narratives thus contrast different interpretations of old legends, and different worldviews.

The human and the alien in *Stargate* as in *Star Trek* also can be used to represent alternative worldviews and modes of living. As we have seen, in Lewis's *Voyage*, the opposition between Eustace and Reepicheep represents a contrast of modes of thought between technology-obsessed 'modernity'

---

61 Bever Donker and Stephanie Yorke, 'Re-Imagining the Colonial Encounter', pp. 739–41. Note, however, that Donker and York (incorrectly) identify 'Celtic' as 'not European', pp. 741–42 in their list of religions co-opted by the Goa'uld.

62 For the text, see Anthony Faulkes, ed., *Snorri Sturluson. Edda. Prologue and* Gylfaginning, 2nd edn (London: Viking Society for Northern Research/University College London, 2005). For discussions see, for example, Rory W. McTurk, 'Fooling Gylfi: Who Tricks Who?', *Alvíssmál*, 3 (1994), 3–18 and Christopher Abram, '*Gylfaginning* and Early Medieval Conversion Theory', *Saga-Book*, 33 (2009), 5–24.

63 See Mark Williams, *Ireland's Immortals*, pp. 39–68, particularly discussion of *Echtrae Chonnlai* and *Immram Brain*.

64 See, for instance, Harry Roe and Ann Dooley, trans., *Tales of the Elders of Ireland. A New Translation of Acallam na Senórach*) (Oxford: Oxford University Press, 1999).

that had lost its moral rudder (Eustace), and a medieval chivalric mode of thinking (the Narnian mouse). Similarly, there is a contrast in approaches (and military ethics) between the human members of the SG-1 team and Stargate Command on the one hand, and aliens such as their alien ally Teal'c on the other. Indeed, as Beeler observes, 'although a warrior by trade, unlike the members of the Earth military he has a strong ethical conception of battle that is highly reminiscent of the courtly behaviour of medieval knights'.[65] The predominantly pre-technological and pre-modern nature of otherworldly civilisations is explained in *Stargate: SG-1* and *Stargate: Atlantis* as the result of the intervention of advanced and malign alien races intent on not permitting humanity on these worlds to develop sufficiently to challenge them or pose a threat. In *Stargate: Atlantis* most humans of the Pegasus Galaxy, where the Atlantis base is located, are preyed upon by the vampire-like 'Wraith' for whom humans are no more than herd of cattle, to be periodically 'culled' (term used in the series) and consumed.[66] This post-colonial situation positions the protagonists, and Earth, which had developed in relative isolation, both outside this colonialist system and as active protectors of the subjugated subalterns.

As Christoph Singer observes of shorelines as boundary lines in general, the 'setting offers itself as a literary testing ground on which the dreams and nightmares are synchronically realized by the respective societies', and by the narrative for the reader.[67] While the Old Irish material engaged with the open sea and the islands in it in the form of *immram* narratives, and with other lands – utopian or otherwise – as 'otherworld' in *echtra* narratives, the twentieth- and twenty-first-century science fiction stories of *Stargate: SG-1* and *Stargate: Atlantis* query human cultural assumptions and civilization, including issues of colonialism and domination against a fictional narrative where all humanity, represented by the protagonists, is pitched against, and contrasted with, an external and alien universe where the real-world power balances are queried and inverted.[68]

65 Beeler, '*Stargate SG-1*', p. 270.

66 An ecocritical, animal studies, reading of *Stargate Atlantis* is invited by this summary, but is beyond the scope of this chapter.

67 Singer, *Sea Change*, p. 16.

68 As Van Bever Donker and Stephanie Yorke, observe, 'the series also inverts the power dynamics of the historical colonial encounter by making the explorers vulnerable rather than the discovered peoples'; 'Re-Imagining the Colonial Encounter', p. 743.

CHAPTER 7

Conclusion

The discussion in this book has focused on texts, broadly defined, which in a traditional sense might be classified as fantastic.[1] They do not pretend to mirror the world in a way conventionally termed as 'realistic'. As such, one of the most important questions to be asked in the conclusion to this discussion is therefore 'so what?'. Why would it matter that some non-realistic discussions of the world can be categorised in one way and not another, allowing them to be seen as a group? Why does it matter that these texts constitute echoes and continuations of an Old Irish narrative tradition? How does understanding these texts, and understanding them in the very specific new way suggested here, as a complex matrix defined by the criteria of the Old Irish genre system categories *immram* and *echtra*, from which they have inherited some of their characteristics, help us in the grand scheme of things?

To answer these – admittedly somewhat rhetorical questions – I take my cue once again from Umberto Eco's theory of narrative universes:

> The world is not a parameter according to which we should judge narrative universes, as desired by a banally realistic aesthetics; narrative universes are the parameter that enables us to judge our interpretations of the world. This does not mean, as some would have it, that the world is a text or a story; it means that we have to interpret it *as if* it were.[2]

Eco's suggestion that an ability to interpret and read narrative universes might help us come to terms with interpreting and 'reading' the world we live in, is a constructive inversion of the systematic undermining of the sense of reality which we have observed in his treatment of truth, lies, and reality (narrative and otherwise) in *Baudolino*.[3] It may also help throw some

1 See Tzvetan Todorov's classic definition of the fantastic, *Introduction*, p. 29, quoted in the introduction above, p. 40.

2 'A Response by Eco', p. 194. Emphasis Eco's.

3 See Chapter 3, pp. 98–109.

 | DOI:10.1163/9789004734548_008

light on the pervasive presence of the 'otherworld', whether as island ustopias, utopias, eutopias, or other planets, in the texts here discussed.

This book thus serves two broad purposes.[4] In the first place, it proposes a new way of writing literary history, and the history of literary reception: not just as a look at the past, but as a look also through the prism of the past, where reception is used also as a frame to understand the narratives as part of a continuum, not necessarily chronological (here one thinks of Eco's idea of simultaneity of influence) but sometimes mutual.[5] The specific coupling of Old Irish narrative genres chosen here to illuminate the selected texts is in that regard a representative example. I have aimed to show that Old Irish literature and its taxonomies can be used in new ways to help understand post-medieval and modern cultures. The choice of Old Irish also highlights the importance, and benefits, of centring literary corpora that are often relegated to academic margins.[6] The second purpose is of a more subversive nature: to query whether what the narratives in question tell us about our world, and how they affect our understanding of our world, might itself be transformed in light of this different view of their interrelation.

Each text examined here has a unique relationship with the 'real' world of the reader. In the case of the Old Irish *immrama* and the *Navigato sancti Brendani* in particular, the fascination for the modern audience has been largely in seeing in these texts the fictionalised accounts of real voyages: following the argument that these may reflect European contact with the Americas pre-dating not only Columbus but also the Vikings.[7] Regardless of whether this particular *immram* reflects a real-world journey, Brendan's Island in turn made its way onto medieval and early modern maps and spurred a flurry of expeditions in search for it in the sixteenth and seventeenth centuries.[8] At first blush this might be seen as a cross-contamination of the literary and geographic genres, but we must remember that Brendan was a saint and the earliest maps on which his journey featured were medieval *mappae mundi*, and of a religious nature – their intention was to produce an image of the world of the Christian faith, not an aid to practical

4 This discussion is linked both to the objectives set out on p. 2 and p. 6 and to the three purposes of choosing this particular group of texts, discussed in the Introduction, p. 15.

5 Eco, 'Borges'; see also discussion above, p. 42. This corresponds to the third point in my description of this book's goals on p. 15.

6 This corresponds to the first two points in my description of this book's goals on p. 15.

7 Mackley, *The Legend*, p. 9, with reference to Severin, *The Brendan Voyage*, and Ashe, *Land to the West*; see also Kervran, *Brandan*.

8 Kervran, *Brandan*, p. 21.

navigation inspired though it might be by legend.[9] The otherworlds of Eco, Swift and Lewis are parables, curved mirrors of the world we live in, and indeed Eco and Swift locate their marvellous lands within the geography of the real world. Meanwhile, *Star Trek* offers not only parables but inspiration for real-world scientific advances.[10] In each of the later texts, however, crucial aspects of the *immram* and *echtra* traditions are continued and reflected in new ways and in response to the changing needs of new audiences. One of these features is the paradoxical combination of wonder and familiarity that, as Mulligan observes of the *Navigatio*, characterises many of the protagonists' island experiences.[11] Further, if the *Navigatio*, according to Mulligan, 'maps the features and practices rooted in the Bible's Jerusalem onto the North Atlantic', the later texts also re-direct the travel trajectories both within the spatial coordinate system of the original and within the new coordinate systems, expanded (by addition of further dimensions), mapping similar journey features onto new spatial frameworks.[12]

In terms of the first purpose, the new history of literary reception, this book proposes a thematic approach – the examination as a single intertextual matrix of several texts produced at different times and by means of different media, classified according to those taxonomies currently common in the Western world as belonging to different genres. As R. M. Liuzza observes, 'if we allow ourselves to look past the strict definitions and dismantle' some pre-conceptions of genre, 'resonances, parallels and echoes between medieval and modern works' are allowed to emerge, which 'may help illuminate not only some aspects of contemporary literature but also some of the enduring power of the older stories'.[13] The Old Irish narratives are particularly suited to reception studies ironically not because of the stability and uniformity of the preserved tradition, but rather because

9 Kervran, *Brandan*, p. 21, refers to the presence of Brendan's Island on the Hereford Mappa Mundi. Reference to it, and to Brendan's visit to the island, named *Perdita* (lit. 'Lost') is also made in the geographical section of the twelfth-century encyclopedia *Imago mundi*, referred to earlier in this book; Honorius Augustodunensis, *Imago mundi*, I.35, ed. by Flint, p. 66. See above, p. 39–41.

10 See e.g. discussion in Ethan Siegel, *Star Trek Technology. The Science of Star Trek from Tricorders to Warp Drive* (Minneapolis, MN: Voyageur Press, 2017), pp. 6, 22.

11 Mulligan, *A Landscape of Words*, p. 47.

12 Mulligan, *A Landscape of Words*, p. 47; for a discussion of the increase in dimensions employed in the journey narratives discussed in this book, see the 'Introduction' above, pp. 44–46.

13 Liuzza, 'The Future', p. 61.

of its multifaceted fluidity. Oskamp, writing of *Echtrae Chonnlai*, highlights this (useful) difficulty:

> Looking at the texts through twentieth-century eyes the analyser wants to determine: "What is this tale about?", "What does it really say?", "What was it meant for?" But which tale is he talking about? [...] Could the function of the tale, could its significance in seventh-century society really be the same as that in fourteenth-, or even sixteenth-century Ireland? Was it copied with the same intention? Was it understood the same way? The answer is obvious: of course not.[14]

When examining a tradition drawing on the Old Irish narratives of fantastic journeys, therefore, we are dealing not only with a complicated and uncertain corpus in terms of the reception works, but also with an unstable cloud where the stable 'original' is supposed to be, against which these could be read.

This book thus belongs doubly to the spatial school of thought: not only is my focus on voyages – whether to the 'otherworld', to fantastic reimagined versions of the distant East or West, or to fantastic islands or planets – and therefore on the movement in space, but my grouping of the texts, dictated by typological considerations rather than chronological ones, is synchronous rather than diachronous. Following Eco's idea, cited above, I have aimed to allow the texts to speak to each other rather than merely transmitting patterns from the past into the future. In that respect, therefore, the book belongs, perhaps in its turn somewhat anachronistically, to a cultural setting outlined by Michel Foucault in his discussion of 'Other spaces' in the 1960s: 'We are in the epoch simultaneity: we are in the epoch of juxtaposition, the epoch of the near far, of the side-by-side, of the dispersed'.[15] Like structuralism, the approach discussed by Foucault in that particular paragraph of his essay, this book's focus on simultaneity 'does not entail a denial of time; it does involve a certain manner of dealing with what we call time and what we call history'.[16] This book also focuses on space without losing the engagement with the historical aspect. To consider

14 Oskamp, '*Echtra Condla*', p. 211.

15 I quote the English translation of the essay, published in Foucault, 'Of Other Spaces'; the original French text, published in 1984 as 'Des Espaces Autres', is based on a lecture given in 1967 (p. 22, n. 1).

16 Foucault, 'Of Other Spaces', p. 22.

the implications of this combination it is useful to look at the way in which earlier in the passage from which I quote, Foucault represents the historical focus of the nineteenth-century: he states that it is dominated by the second law of thermodynamics.

In essence, the second law of thermodynamics is one that dictates the unidirectionality of the progression of time.[17] The most common expression of this law usually involves the concept of entropy. This makes it useful for thinking about the gradual proliferation with time of genre characteristics and the kinds of features taken into account in typological analyses, which, as multiple accounts of the historical development of particular genres, appear to increase in number and complexity with time. The relevant expression of the second law of thermodynamics, as formulated in accessible terms by R. Stephen Berry is as follows:

> All systems in nature evolve by going from states of lower entropy to states of higher entropy [...] unless some work is done in the process of changing the state. Another way to say this is that systems evolve naturally from states of lower probability to states of higher probability.[18]

Essentially, the idea is that in the physical world the progression is from order to chaos. In terms of the medieval *immram* and *echtra* tradition we can think of this as the progressive expansion and addition of characteristics that leads to a wider gap between the increasingly numerous later texts, which belong to one or the other 'genre', when more genre-specific characteristics emerge and are implemented. One way of coping with the increased entropy of the corpus is to employ force by introducing a different taxonomic system (energy is required to reverse entropy, according to the second law of thermodynamics).[19] Another way, taken in this book, is to accept the genre entropy and employ fuzzy sets to account for the variation of possible states. Throughout the discussion in this book, therefore, the synchronic approach has not been, as Foucault rightly points out, a denial of history, but rather has constituted superimposed snapshots of a

17 R. Stephen Berry, *Three Laws of Nature. A Little Book on Thermodynamics* (New Haven and London: Yale University Press, 2019), p. 30.

18 Berry, *Three Laws of Nature*, p. 42.

19 I would suggest that this is in essence what Rieder is proposing in relation to what he describes as two conflicting, and naturally emerging genre systems—the traditional academic and what he terms the 'mass cultural'; Rieder, *Science Fiction.*

succession of particular states of literary production. Like the measurements of the state of the air in the room, however, they seem static but in fact represent averages across successive permutations of the components through time.[20]

To illustrate this point with the corpus at hand: I have put *Gulliver's Travels*, *The Voyage of the Dawn Treader* and *Star Trek* alongside each other as members to varying degrees of the same fuzzy set as *Navigatio sancti Brendani* and *Immram Curaig Maíle Dúin*, for the sake of discussion, because they thematically fit within the definition of the *immram*, taken as a genre. The intertextual connections that have emerged across representations of otherworldly female figures, idealised places, and othered places (ustopias), tropological messages encoded in individual travellers, or island spaces, show that these texts are also, along the axes outlined by the genre characteristics, related to each other in a more direct, genealogical sense.

Swift was influenced by the island journey tradition and the use of islands for making a moral or tropological point. Lewis was influenced – as a medievalist and Christian thinker – by the same medieval tradition, the same tropological inspiration, but also, in his turn, by Swift. Roddenberry's *Star Trek* is also tropological, using the planets to raise moral issues for the society to which it is addressed in exactly the way that Swift does, and it is not inconceivable that Swift's Gulliver was as large an influence on *Star Trek* conceptually as the Hornblower novels of C. S. Forester in terms of form and in prompting the creation of a British Navy-inspired Starfleet.[21] Eco's *Baudolino* has a less overt tropological message (except in the striking discussion of otherness in the land of Deacon John), but queries assumptions systematically, and undermines certainties, while at the same time using a reverse of the technique of defamiliarization to acquaint the reader with the familiar medieval world. The same approach is taken in *Stargate*, which, like Eco's *Baudolino*, has more in common with *echtrai* than *immrama*, since without the journey description, and keeping only the destination(s), the story would still exist.

I have treated all these as 'texts' explicitly in this book, eliding not only contemporary genre distinctions but also the lines dividing the media. This has also been partly to counter notions of literary hierarchy. 'One reason

---

20 Compare Berry's description of thermodynamic states: 'Virtually every macrostate we encounter is some kind of time average over many, many microstates through which out observed system passes during our observation', Berry, *Three Laws of Nature*, p. 41.

21 Lane and Bowles, *Star Trek. The Adventure*, p. 18.

that TV series are often seen as an "inferior" form of popular art may be the difficulty of ascribing their "authorship"', writes Chris Gregory.[22] Yet this is precisely the reason, as I have argued before, that we can read such works with the same eyes (the same methods and the same approaches) that have traditionally been used by medievalists for anonymous medieval texts.[23] Interestingly, Gregory compares television to ancient and medieval 'story-tellers or "bards"'.[24] Putting aside assumptions of difference thus allows us to focus on the ways in which these texts, which inherit and build on the same tradition, share features inherited from that older material, and ways in which they intervene in the process of its reception.

The texts examined in this book are all to some extent marginal.[25] Old Irish travel narratives are much less frequently invoked in discussions of medieval (European) literature than their Continental counterparts. The fictional work of the great medievalists C. S. Lewis and Umberto Eco, because fantastic, perhaps, is not the stuff of major mainstream literary studies courses. Swift's text is less frequently discussed from perspectives other than the perspective of political satire. The phenomenally popular sci-fi *Star Trek* and *Stargate* belong to the medium of television, which as Johnson-Smith observes, 'hovered in the wings for so long whilst its big screen relation took both commendation and criticism'.[26] Yet taking these franchises alongside the works of Swift, Lewis and Eco allows the tropological and utopian aspects of the otherworlds depicted in each text to emerge more sharply. The continuities which emerge despite – or perhaps even because – of this synchronic approach invoke the sense of continuity in cultural tradition more generally expressed by Lewis:

> Humanity does not pass through phases as a train passes through stations: being alive, it has the privilege of always moving yet never leaving anything behind. Whatever we have been, in some sort we are still.

---

22 Gregory, *Star Trek*, p. 4, see also his comments on p. 5.

23 Petrovskaia, 'The Fool and the Wise Man'.

24 Gregory, *Star Trek*, pp. 7–8.

25 Amis observes that although it may seem that initially 'what attracts people to science fiction is not in the first place literary quality in the accustomed sense of that term', readers who do engage with the genre 'may well come to find such quality there, perhaps in an unaccustomed form, if they ever take trouble to look for it' (*New Maps*, p. 9); interestingly Amis excludes Ireland from his list of producers of twentieth-century science fiction (p. 17).

26 Johnson-Smith, *American Science Fiction TV*, p. 4.

> Neither the form nor the sentiment of this old poetry has passed away without leaving indelible traces on our minds.[27]

Lewis was writing specifically of the courtly love tradition, but the same can be expanded to apply to travel narratives. This sense of continuity has been a major theme in this book. In our case, however, the writers discussed might in some ways be interpreted as the equivalent of the stations in Lewis's metaphorical description. I would take issue with him, however, on the notion that these interrupt the natural flow. I would argue that the train journey also is a continuum, punctuated by stations as it might be, so long as one does not get off or change trains.

Continuity, indeed, has been a major feature in the discussion not only diachronically but also synchronically, in the form of the theory of fuzzy sets. This can be extended from the concept of genre to which I initially applied the notion of fuzzy set in this discussion, to include the opus of the individual writers treated in the first three chapters. Thus, another connection between Lewis, Eco, and Swift lies in the influence the 'day job' of each had on their work. The words written by Lewis about Jonathan Swift in a letter to his brother (commenting on a biography of Swift he had recently read) might be applied to himself: 'the v. obvious point that *most* of his life was spent doing his job'.[28] My argument here is not that Lewis was not first and foremost a Christian author, but rather that he is also a medievalist, and that it may be worth revisiting the extent of the influence of his day-job on his creative output.[29] The different 'areas' of activity of each man are thus also overlapping fuzzy sets.

This overlap can also account for a further connection between Lewis's and Swift's texts in particular (and the overlap with the monastic-influenced genre of *immram*) – the heavy tropological aspect of Lewis's fantasy tale. While some moralizing can be seen in Eco's discussion of the fantastic creatures' ignorance of their physical differences, the rest of the narrative is less of a social or ethical critique or satire and more, as we have seen, an exercise in questioning the fabric of reality. Lewis, by contrast, is much more straightforwardly moralizing throughout the novel, much like the monastic

27 Lewis, *The Allegory of Love*, p. 1.

28 Lewis, letter to his brother, April 28th, 1940, p. 405 and n. 244 for the identification of the biography in question as Robert Wyse Jackson, *Jonathan Swift, Dean and Pastor* (1939).

29 See also comments to that effect in Baxter, *The Medieval Mind*, pp. 10–14.

narrative of the *Navigatio*.[30] His educational day-job and his identity as Christian apologist overlap heavily with his creative output and identity as medievalist, prompting him to choose the *Navigatio* as model.

Eco's engagement with the Irish travel tradition is to draw it into a new kaleidoscopic image, disorienting the reader, and challenging us to question our notions of truth, reality, and fiction. Lewis's engagement with the *immrama* is dialogical. In the conversation between Lewis and his context, the *Navigatio* is the interlocutor. Lewis's reader is a witness to Lewis's response (to questions which none except medievalists would have been witness to).

Whereas Eco's interests in the nature of interpretation and postmodern sensibilities yield a re-interpretation of the fantastic voyage in a fluid type of fictional 'reality' which may even lead the reader to question their own, Lewis's version of the *immram* genre is grounded in a more stable world of classical truth-values and absolutes.[31] The two authors thus deal differently with similar problems posed by the pervasive fantastic of their medieval sources. Eco's novel is at least putatively a historical one, but with a postmodernist bent, while Lewis's *Voyage* is written as a fairy-tale for children. The difference between Lewis's 'classical taste' and Eco's postmodernist sensibilities has been observed amongst others by Frits van Oostrom, in his discussion of the two authors' attitudes to the multi-voiced composition of the *Roman de la Rose* (particularly the section added by Jean de Meun).[32] Lewis himself considers modernism (and would certainly consider postmodernism) a break greater than that between the medieval and Renaissance periods, describing himself as a 'dinosaur' belonging to the older type of literary and cultural world.[33] Thus, my reading of the *Voyage* within the framework of reception and transmission of the medieval Irish voyage narratives takes Lewis at his word, and follows Ward in seeing him 'as a medievally-minded writer himself'.[34]

---

30 This aspect of the *Navigatio* is particularly apparent when it is compared with the Anglo-Norman version of Benedeit; see Sobecki, 'From the *désert liquide* to the Sea of Romance'.

31 See Lewis's inaugural lecture as Professor of Medieval and Renaissance English Literature at Cambridge University, delivered in 1954, 'De descriptione'. See also further discussion below.

32 Frits van Oostrom, *Wereld in Woorden. Geschiedenis van de Nederlandse Literatuur 1300–1400* (Amsterdam: Bert Bakker, 2013), p. 349; Van Oostrom ascribes to Jean de Meun the characteristic *meerstemmigheid aan thema's en opinies* 'multi-voicedness of themes and opinions' (my translation).

33 Lewis, 'De descriptione', pp. 448–52.

34 Ward, *Planet Narnia*, p. 11.

The difference between *Baudolino* and *Voyage* is the difference between a (secular) *echtra* and the (religion-influenced) *immram*: 'In the *echtrae* [...], the journey (which is by no means necessarily over sea) is an unimportant aspect of the story; the sea-voyage from island to island is, on the other hand, the *sine qua non* of the *immram*'.[35] The process of the journey to the East is important to the narrative of *Baudolino* but neither is it the whole story, nor is the detail of the journey as important as the goal of the journey, the preceding and the following narrative and character development.

The intertextual matrix in this book extends also beyond the primary sources and into the secondary literature. A connection between Lewis's *The Discarded Image* and Foucault's article on heterotopias which I have been quoting, is a case in point. Foucault mentions the medieval world and the medieval conceptions of space, and indeed does so in ways that form a distinct echo of Lewis's ideas:

> For the real scandal of Galileo's work lay not so much in his discovery, or rediscovery, that the earth revolved around the sun, but in his constitution of an infinite, and infinitely open space. In such a space the place of the Middle Ages turned out to be dissolved, as it were; a thing's place was no longer anything but a point in its movement, just as the stability of a thing was only its movement indefinitely slowed down.[36]

This is distinctly reminiscent of Lewis's statement that the 'really important difference [between our universe and the medieval one] is that the medieval universe, while unimaginably large, was also unambiguously finite'.[37] Lewis also conveys a sense of stability of the medieval model, and its certainty, compared to ours:

> Again, because the medieval universe is finite, it has a shape, the perfect spherical shape, containing within itself an ordered variety. Hence to look out on the night sky with modern eyes is like looking about one in a trackless forest – trees forever and no horizon. To look up at the towering medieval universe is much more like looking at a great building. The 'space' of modern astronomy may arouse terror, or

35 Dumville, '*Echtrae and Immram*', p. 79.

36 Foucault, 'Of Other Spaces', p. 23.

37 Lewis, *The Discarded Image*, p. 99. The comment in square brackets is mine.

> bewilderment or vague reverie; the spheres of the old present us with an object in which the mind can rest, overwhelming in its greatness but satisfying in its harmony.

Although Foucault does not quote Lewis or cite *The Discarded Image* (there is no bibliography at all in his essay) the echo in his 1967 lecture of Lewis's 1964 book is either direct influence or a symptom of a wider trend in thought at the time. We are back here to Eco's 'anxieties of influence'.[38]

In this contrast of old and new, classical/traditional and subversive and revolutionary (one thinks again of Eco's poignant subversion of stability), it seems appropriate to introduce the use of a concept developed in twentieth-century mathematics to the analysis of the reception of medieval Irish texts. In a discussion of mathematical reasoning, Henri Poincaré observes that 'Mathematics can, therefore, like the other sciences, proceed from the particular to the general'.[39] In this respect, the analysis presented in this book might be seen as a marginal member of the fuzzy set which the humanities constitute, as it edges towards the 'other sciences'. The study employs, and demonstrates the potentials of, the principle of recategorisation of texts, using fuzzy genre sets as an analytical tool. Applied to the corpus of travel narratives discussed here, it has yielded a new intertextual matrix and brought into sharper relief some of the hitherto obscured connections – thematic, functional, symbolic, and contextual – between these texts. My thesis is that the same analytical principles can be applied to other, more mainstream and general corpora to yield similarly interesting and informative results, going, like Poincaré's mathematics, 'from the particular to the general'. If a side-effect of such analyses is to gradually supersede the current – unhelpful to my mind – division of texts by media and the divisions of high and low 'literary' status, and by the bye also of the periodization and its inherent boundaries, so much the better.

As Elizabeth McMahon and Bénédicte André point out, 'Oral and written literatures can bridge time, reach back through and beyond colonial modernity so that we can hear voices of the past in the living present. They can trace continuums into the present and, conversely, lead us to wonder at the

38 See above, p. 15.

39 Henri Poincaré, 'On the Nature of Mathematical Reasoning', chapter 1 in *The Foundations of Science Science and Hypothesis, The Value of Science, Science and Method*, trans. by George Bruce Halsted (Cambridge: Cambridge University Press, 2014), p. 40.

ruptures and estrangements of community or individuals over time'.[40] They cite the theses of spatial theorists Henri Lefebvre and Edward Soja, who postulate a direct relationship between the imagined spaces of literary imagination and the real spaces inhabited by real people – the former not only mediates our perception of the latter, but downright forms the space itself.[41] The phenomenon, thus, of fiction forming reality is not only a feature Baudolino's world but also of ours. Perhaps that in itself is a product of Eco's mediation between us and our reality. The texts examined in this book all share this feature – they mediate between us and the spaces we do, might, or would like to inhabit.

This book has thus aimed to start a new conversation by showing that the 'strange new worlds' that it is the 'continuing mission' of the starship Enterprise to explore, and other similar cultural imaginings, are in fact 'strange new *other*worlds'; that the Old Irish genres of *echtrai* and *immrama* are not fossilized remains of extinct traditions eliciting excitement only of the professional literary archaeologist, but rather that like the ascended ancients of the *Stargate* story-world they are still very much alive, and continue their existence in new and evolved states. It is my hope that this conversation will continue and, as Montaigne so eloquently puts it: *On répond toujours trop bien pour moi, si on répond à ce que je dis.*[42]

40 Elizabeth McMahon and Bénédicte André, 'Literature and the Literary Gaze', in *The Routledge International Handbook of Island Studies*, ed. by Godfrey Baldacchino (London and New York: Routledge, 2018), pp. 296–311.

41 McMahon and André, 'Literature and the Literary Gaze', p. 296. The reference is to Lefebvre's *La production de l'espace* and Edward Soja's *Thirdspace. Journeys to Los Angeles and Other Real-and-Imagined Places* (Oxford: Blackwell, 1996).

42 'One can never do better as far as I'm concerned, then respond to what I say' (my translation); Montaigne, 'L'art de conferer', in Montaigne, *Les essais*, ed. by Denis Bjaï et al., (Paris: Librairie Générale Française, 2001), III.viii, p. 1448.

Bibliography

Abram, Christopher, '*Gylfaginning* and Early Medieval Conversion Theory', *Saga-Book*, 33 (2009), 5–24

Acheraïou, Amar, and Nursel Içöz, ed., *Joseph Conrad and the Orient* (Lublin: Maria Curie-Skłodowska University Press, 2012)

Adams, Gillian, 'A Fuzzy Genre: Two Views of Fantasy', *Children's Literature*, 28 (2000), 202–14

Ahlquist, Anders, ed., *The Early Irish Linguist: An Edition of the Canonical Part of the* Auraicept na n'Eces (Helsinki: Societas scientiarum fennica, 1982)

Akbari, Suzanne Conklin, 'Introduction', in *Marco Polo and the Encounter of East and West*, ed. by Akbari et al., pp. 3–20

Akbari, Suzanne Conklin, and Amilcare Ianucci, with John Tulk, ed., *Marco Polo and the Encounter of East and West* (Toronto, Buffalo and London: University of Toronto Press, 2008)

Alexander, Lisa Doris, 'Star Trek: Deep Space Nine', in *The Routledge Handbook of Star Trek*, ed. by Leimar Garcia-Siino, Sabrina Mittermeier, and Stefan Rabitsch (New York and London: Routledge, 2022), pp. 37–45

Alff, David, 'Swift's World of *Gulliver's Travels*', in *Routledge Companion to Imaginary Worlds*, ed. by Mark Wolf (London: Routledge, 2017), pp. 332–38

Amis, Kingsley, *New Maps of Hell. A Survey of Science Fiction* (London: Victor Gollancz, 1961)

Anderson, John D., 'The Navigatio Brendani: A Medieval Best Seller', *The Classical Journal*, 83 (1988), 315–22

Angenendt, Arnold, 'Die irische *Peregrinatio* und ihre Auswirkungen auf dem Kontinent vor dem Jahre 800', in *Die Iren und Europa im früheren Mittelalter*, ed. by Heinz Löwe, 2 vols (Stuttgart: Klett-Cotta, 1982), vol. 1, pp. 52–79

Ashe, Geoffrey, *Land to the West: St Brendan's Voyage to America* (London: Collins, 1962)

Astell, Ann W., *Political Allegory in Late Medieval England* (Ithaca and London: Cornell University Press, 1999)

Atalay, Bülent, *Math and the Mona Lisa. The Art and Science of Leonardo da Vinci* (New York: Collins and Smithsonian Books, 2006)

Attebery, Brian, *Strategies of Fantasy* (Bloomington: Indiana University Press, 1992)

Atwood, Margaret, 'The Road to Ustopia', *The Guardian*, October 14, 2011 <www.theguardian.com/books/2011/oct/14/margaret-atwood-road-to-ustopia> [accessed 18 February 2024]

Bacon, Francis, *The Essays*, ed. by John Pritcher (London: Penguin, 1985)

Bakhtin, Mikhail M., *The Dialogic Imagination. Four Essays*, ed. by Michael Holquist, trans. by Caryl Emerson and Michael Holquist (Austin: University of Texas Press, 1981)

Bakhtin, Mikhail, *Problems of Dostoyevsky's Poetics*, ed. and trans. by Caryl Emerson (Minneapolis and London: University of Minnesota Press, 1984)

Ball, Warwick, *East of the Wardrobe. The Unexpected Worlds of C. S. Lewis* (Oxford: Oxford University Press, 2022)

Bampi, Massimiliano, 'Genre', in *A Critical Companion to Old Norse Literary Genre*, ed. by Massimiliano Bampi, Carolyne Larrington, and Sif Rikhardsdottir (Cambridge: D. S. Brewer, 2020), pp. 15–30

Barber, Richard, *The Holy Grail. Imagination and Belief* (London: Allen Lane, 2004)

Barrett, Michèle, and Duncan Barrett, *Star Trek: The Human Frontier* (New York: Routledge, 2017)

Barron, W. R. J., and Glyn S. Burgess, ed., *The Voyage of Saint Brendan. Representative Versions of the Legend in English Translation* (Exeter: University of Exeter Press, 2002)

Bartoli, Renata Anna, *La Navigatio sancti Brendani e la sua fortuna nella cultura romanza dell'età di mezzo* (Fasano, Brindisi: Schena, 1993)

Baxter, Jason M., *The Medieval Mind of C. S. Lewis: How Great Books Shaped a Great Mind* (Downers Grove: IVP Academic, 2022)

Bayoumi, Moustafa, and Andrew Rubin, ed., *The Selected Works of Edward Said. 1966–2006* (London and Dublin: Bloomsbury Publishing, 2021)

Beckingham, C. F., and B. Hamilton, ed., *Prester John, the Mongols, and the Ten Lost Tribes* (Aldershot: Ashgate Variorum, 1996)

Beeler, Stan, '*Stargate SG-1* and the Quest for the Perfect Science-Fiction Premise', in *The Essential Science Fiction Television Reader*, ed. by J. P. Telotte (Lexington: University Press of Kentucky, 2008), pp. 267–82

Bennett, Tony, *Outside Literature* (London: Routledge, 1990)

Bernoussi, Mohamed, 'Baudolino, une fascination sémiotique pour le mensonge', *Cahiers de Narratologie*, 22 (2018) <https://doi.org/10.4000/narratologie.8216>

Berry, R. Stephen, *Three Laws of Nature. A Little Book on Thermodynamics* (New Haven and London: Yale University Press, 2019)

Best, Richard Irvine, ed. and tr., 'The Adventures of Art son of Conn, and the Courtship of Delbchaem', *Ériu* 3 (1907), 149–173

Bieler, Ludwig, '*Casconius*, the monster of the *Navigatio Brendani*', *Éigse* 5 (1945–47), 139–40

Bodart-Bailey, Beatrice M., '*Gulliver's Travels*, Japan and Engelbert Kaempfer', *Otsuma Journal of Comparative Culture*, 22 (2021), 75–100

Blondell, Ruby, *Helen of Troy. Beauty, Myth, Devastation* (Oxford: Oxford University Press, 2013)

Bohls, Elizabeth A., 'Introduction', in *Travel Writing, 1700–1830. An Anthology*, ed. by Elizabeth A. Bohls and Ian Duncan (Oxford: Oxford University Press, 2005), pp. xiii–xxvii

Booker, M. Keith, 'The Politics of Star Trek', in *The Essential Science Fiction Television Reader*, ed. by P. Telotte (Lexington: University Press of Kentucky, 2008), pp. 195–208.

Booker, M. Keith, *Star Trek: A Cultural History* (Lanham: Rowan and Littlefield, 2018)

Booker M. Keith, and A. M. Thomas, *The Science Fiction Handbook* (Chichester: Wiley Blackwell, 2009)

Bondanella, Peter, 'Italo Calvino and Umberto Eco: Postmodern Masters', in *The Cambridge Companion to the Italian Novel*, ed. by Peter Bondanella and Andrea Ciccarelli (Cambridge: Cambridge University Press, 2003), pp. 168–81

Bondanella, Peter, ed., *New Essays on Umberto Eco* (Cambridge: Cambridge University Press, 2009)

Bondanella, Peter, *Umberto Eco and the Open Text: Semiotics, Fiction, Popular Culture* (Cambridge: Cambridge University Press, 1997)

Bondanella, Peter, and Andrea Ciccarelli, ed., *The Cambridge Companion to the Italian Novel* (Cambridge: Cambridge University Press, 2003)

Bony, Alain, *Discours et vérité dans* Les Voyages de Gulliver *de Jonathan Swift* (Lyon: Presses Universitaires de Lyon, 2002)

Borges, Jorge Luis, *Biblioteca personal* (Madrid: Alianza Editorial, 2000)

Borges, Jorge Luis, *Ficciones* (Madrid: Alianza Editorial, 1999)

Borges, Jorge Luis, 'La Biblioteca de Babel', in *Ficciones* (Madrid: Alianza Editorial, 1999), pp. 86–99

Borges, Jorge Luis, 'La forma de la espada', in *Ficciones* (Madrid: Alianza Editorial, 1999), pp. 137–45

Borges, Jorge Luis, 'Jonathan Swift: Viajes de Gulliver', in Borges, *Biblioteca personal* (Madrid: Alianza Editorial, 2000)

Borges, Jorge Luis, 'Pierre Menard, autor del Quijote', in Borges, *Ficciones* (Madrid: Alianza Editorial, 1999), pp. 41–55

Bracher, Frederick, 'The Maps in "Gulliver's Travels"', *Huntington Library Quarterly*, 8 (1944), 59–74

Braine, F. S., 'Technological Utopias: The Future of the Next Generation', *Film & History: An Interdisciplinary Journal of Film and Television*, 24 (1994), 1–18

Breatnach, Caoimhín, 'The Transmission and Structure of *Immram curaig Ua Corra*', *Ériu*, 53 (2003), 91–107

Brewer Derek, 'C. S. Lewis, (1898–1963)', in *Medieval Scholarship. Biographical Studies on the Formation of a Discipline*, 2, *Literature and Philology*, ed. by Helen

Damico, with Donald Fennema and Karmen Lenz (New York and London: Garland Publishing, 1998), pp. 405–13

Brewer, Keagan, *Prester John: The Legend and its Sources* (London: Routledge, 2019)

Bross, Kristina, *Future History: Global Fantasies in Seventeenth-Century American and British Writings* (Oxford: Oxford University Press, 2017)

Brown, Devin, *Inside the Voyage of the Dawn Treader: A Guide to Exploring the Journey Beyond Narnia* (Nashville: Abingdon Press, 2013)

Brown, Terence 'Cultural Nationalism, Celticism and the Occult', in *Celticism*, ed. by Terence Brown (Amsterdam and Atlanta: Rodopi, 1996), pp. 221–30

Bruce, Susan, ed., *Three Early Modern Utopias. Thomas More: Utopia / Francis Bacon: New Atlantis / Henry Neville: The Isle of Pines*, Oxford World's Classics (Oxford: Oxford University Press, 1999)

Buchanan, Ian, *A Dictionary of Critical Theory*, 1st edn (Oxford: Oxford University Press, 2010) <https://www.oxfordreference.com/view/10.1093/acref/9780199532919.001.0001/acref-9780199532919-e-669> [accessed 6 November 2024]

Buchanan, Ron, '"Side by Side": The Role of the Sidekick', *Studies in Popular Culture*, 26 (2003), 15–26

Bucknell, Clare, 'Satire', in *Jonathan Swift in Context*, ed. by Joseph Hone and Pat Rogers (Cambridge: Cambridge University Press, 2024), pp. 125–31

Burgess, Glyn S., and Clara Strijbosch, ed., *The Brendan Legend. A Critical Bibliography* (Dublin: Royal Irish Academy, 2000)

Burgess, Glynn S., and Clara Strijbosch, ed., *The Brendan Legend: Texts and Versions* (Leiden and Boston: Brill, 2006)

Byrne, Aisling, *Otherworlds: Fantasy and History in Medieval Literature* (Oxford: Oxford University Press, 2015)

Calvino, Italo, *Le città invisibili*, 3rd edn (Turin: Einaudi, 1972)

Calvino, Italo *Invisible Cities*, trans. by William Weaver (New York: Harcourt Brace Jovanovich, 1974)

Calvino, Italo, *Se una notte d'inverno un viaggiatore* (Turin: Einaudi, 1979)

Campbell, Mary B., *The Witness and the Other World. Exotic European Travel Writing, 400–1600* (Ithaca and London: Cornell University Press, 1988)

Capozzi, Rocco, 'Knowledge and Cognitive Practices in Eco's Labyrinths of Intertextuality', in *Literary Philosophers. Borges, Calvino, Eco*, ed. by Jorge J. E. Garcia, Carolyn Korsmeyer and Rudolphe Gasché (New York and London: Routledge, 2002), pp. 165–84

Carey, John, 'Aerial Ships and Underwater Monasteries: The Evolution of a Monastic Marvel', *Proceedings of the Harvard Celtic Colloquium*, 12 (1992), 16–28

Carey, John, *Ireland and the Grail* (Aberystwyth: Celtic Studies Publications, 2007)

Carey, John, 'The Location of the Otherworld in Irish Tradition', in *The Otherworld Voyage in Early Irish Literature. An Anthology of Criticism*, ed. by Jonathan

Wooding (Dublin: Four Courts Press, 2000), pp. 113–9; originally published in *Éigse*, 19 (1982), 36–43

Carey, John, 'Otherworlds and Verbal Worlds in Middle Irish Narrative', *Proceedings of the Harvard Celtic Colloquium* 9 (1989), 31–42

Carey, John, 'Time, Space and the Otherworld', *Proceedings of the Harvard Celtic Colloquium*, 7 (1987), 1–27

Carey, John, 'Voyage Literature' in *Celtic Culture: A Historical Encyclopedia*, ed. by John T. Koch (Santa Barbara: ABC-CLIO, 2006), pp. 1743–46

Carpenter, Andrew, 'Literary Scene. Ireland', in *Jonathan Swift in Context*, ed. by Joseph Hone and Pat Rogers (Cambridge: Cambridge University Press, 2024), pp. 255–62

Carruthers, Gerard, and Alan Rawes, 'Introduction: Romancing the Celt', in *English Romanticism and the Celtic World*, ed. by Gerard Carruthers and Alan Rawes (Cambridge: Cambridge University Press, 2003), pp. 1–19

Cavagna, Mattia, and Silvère Menegaldo, 'Entre la terre et la mer, entre le Paradis et l'Enfer : l'île dans la *Navigatio sancti Brendani* et ses versions en langues romanes', *Les lettres romanes*, 66 (2012), 7–35

Chadwick, Owen, *John Cassian*, 2nd edn (Cambridge: Cambridge University Press, 1968)

Chance, Jane, ed., *Tolkien the Medievalist* (London and New York: Routledge, 2003)

Charles-Edwards, Thomas M., 'The Social Background to Irish *Peregrinatio*', *Celtica*, 11 (1976), 43–59

Christopher, Joe R., 'Modern Literature', in *Reading the Classics with C. S. Lewis*, ed. by Thomas L. Martin (Grand Rapids, MI: Baker Academic, and Carlisle: Paternoster Press, 2000), pp. 145–264

Classen, Albrecht, 'The *Carmina Burana*: A Mirror of Latin and Vernacular Literary Traditions from a Cultural-Historical Perspective: Transgression is the Name of the Game', *Neophilologus*, 94 (2010), 477–97

Cleary, Marie Sally, *Myths for the Millions: Thomas Bulfinch, His America, and His Mythology Book*, Kulturtransfer und Geschlechterforschung (Frankfurt am Main: Peter Lang, 2007)

Clements, Niki Kasumi, *Sites of the Ascetic Self: John Cassian and Christian Ethical Formation* (Notre Dame, Indiana: Notre Dame University Press, 2020)

Coletti, Theresa, 'Eco's Middle Ages and the Historical Novel', in *New Essays on Umberto Eco*, ed. by Peter Bondanella (Cambridge: Cambridge University Press, 2009), pp. 71–89

Coletti, Teresa, *Naming the Rose: Eco, Medieval Signs, and Modern Theory* (Ithaca: Cornell University Press, 1988)

Compean, Richard Edward, 'Swift and the Lucianic Tradition', Unpublished PhD Dissertation, University of California Davis, 1976

Conan Doyle, Sir Arthur, *The Lost World: Being an Account of the Recent Amazing Adventures of Professor E. Challenger, Lord John Roxton, Professor Summerlee and Mr. Ed Malone of the 'Daily Gazette'* (London: J. Murray, 1966 [1912])

Connell, Charles, 'Reading the Middle Ages: The "Post-Modern" Medievalism of C. S. Lewis', *Sehnsucht: The C.S. Lewis Journal*, 1 (2007), 19–28

Conrad, Joseph, *Youth. Heart of Darkness. The End of the Tether*, ed. by Owen Knowles (Cambridge: Cambridge University Press, 2010)

Cooper, Helen, *The English Romance in Time: Transforming Motifs from Geoffrey of Monmouth to the Death of Shakespeare* (Oxford: Oxford University Press, 2004)

Coulter, Cornelia Catlin, 'The "Great Fish" in Ancient and Medieval Story', *Transactions and Proceedings of the American Philological Association*, 57 (1926), 32–50

Crawford, Jason, *Allegory and Enchantment. An Early Modern Poetics* (Oxford: Oxford University Press, 2017)

Cronin, Michael, *Translation in the Digital Age* (London and New York: Routledge, 2013)

Cronin, Michael, 'Utopia for Modern Languages and How We Can Get There', *The MHRA Centenary Lectures*, MHRA, 2018, <https://www.mhra.org.uk/centenary/cronin100> [accessed 12 December 2023]

Cross, Tom Pete, *Motif-Index of Early Irish Literature*, Indiana University Folklore Series, 7 (Bloomington: Indiana University Press, 1952)

Davies, Sioned, trans., *The Mabinogion* (Oxford: Oxford University Press, 2009)

Davies, Sioned, 'Mythology and the Oral Tradition: Wales', in *The Celtic World*, ed. by Miranda Green (New York: Routledge, 1996), pp. 785–94

Davies, Surekha, 'The Wondrous East in the Renaissance Geographical Imagination: Marco Polo, Fra Mauro and Giovanni Battista Ramusio', *History and Anthropology*, 23 (2012), 215–34

Dendle, Peter, 'Cryptozoology in the Medieval and Modern Worlds', *Folklore*, 117 (2006), 190–206

Dickens, Charles, *Great Expectations and Hard Times* (Bloomsbury: Nonesuch Press, 1937, republished in 2005)

Dickson, David, 'Dublin', in *Jonathan Swift in Context*, ed. by Joseph Hone and Pat Rogers (Cambridge: Cambridge University Press, 2024), pp. 270–76

Dillard, J. M., *Where No One Has Gone Before: A History in Pictures* (New York: Pocket Books, 1994)

Dillon, Miles, *Early Irish Literature. An Introduction to the Sagas and Legends of Ancient Ireland* (Chicago: Chicago University Press, 1948)

Dionne, Craig, 'The Shatnerification of Shakespeare', in *Shakespeare after Mass Media*, ed. by Richard Burt (New York: Palgrave Macmillan 2002), pp. 173–91

Dodds, Klaus, and Veronica della Dora, 'Artificial Islands and Islophilia', in *The Routledge International Handbook of Island Studies*, ed. by Godfrey Baldacchino (London and New York: Routledge, 2018), pp. 392–415

Donoghue, Denis, 'Hibernus Ludens', *The Hudson Review*, 16 (1963), 450–54

Downing, David C., *Into the Wardrobe: C. S. Lewis and the Narnia Chronicles*, (San Francisco: Wiley, 2005)

Duffy, Seán, *Brian Boru and the Battle of Clontarf* (Dublin: Gill & Macmillan, 2014)

Duignan, Leonie, *The* Echtrae *as an Early Irish Literary Genre* (Rahden: Verlag Marie Leidorf, 2011)

Dumville, David N., '*Echtrae* and *Immram*: Some Problems of Definition', *Ériu*, 27 (1976), 73–94

Dutta, Mary Buhl, '"Very Bad Poetry, Captain": Shakespeare in Star Trek', *Extrapolation*, 36 (1995), 38–45

Eco, Umberto, *Baudolino* (Milan: Bompiani, 2000)

Eco, Umberto, *Baudolino*, trans. by William Weaver (London: Vintage, 2003)

Eco, Umberto, 'Borges and My Anxiety of Influence', in Eco, *On Literature*, trans. by Martin McLaughlin (London: Random hours Vintage, 2006), pp. 118–35

Eco, Umberto, *The Limits of Interpretation* (Bloomington and Indianapolis: Indiana University Press, 1994)

Eco, Umberto, *Mouse or Rat? Translation as Negotiation* (London: Phoenix, 2004)

Eco, Umberto, 'On Some Functions of Literature', in Eco, *On Literature*, trans. by Martin McLaughlin (London: Random hours Vintage, 2006), pp. 1–15

Eco, Umberto, *Serendipities. Language and Lunacy*, translated by William Weaver (London: Phoenix, 1999 [1998])

Eco, Umberto, *Storia delle terre e dei luoghi leggendari* (Milan: Bompiani, 2013)

Eco, Umberto, 'To See Things and Texts', in Eco, *Mouse or Rat? Translation as Negotiation* (London: Phoenix, 2004), pp. 104–122

Eco, Umberto, 'Why the Island is Never Found' in Eco, *Inventing the Enemy and Other Occasional Writings*, trans. by Richard Dixon (Boston and New York: Houghton Mifflin Harcourt, 2012), pp. 192–216

Eco, Umberto, in conversation with Charlotte Ross, 'A Response by Eco', in *Illuminating Eco: On the Boundaries of Interpretation*, ed. by Charlotte Ross and Rochelle Sibley (London and New York: Routledge, 2016; first published London: Ashgate, 2004), pp. 193–99

Electronic Dictionary of the Irish Language <https://dil.ie/> [accessed 5 November 2024]

Edmond, Rod, and Vanessa Smith, ed., *Islands in History and Representation* (London: Routledge, 2003)

Eddy, William A., *Gulliver's Travels: A Critical Study* (Princeton: Princeton University Press, London: Humphrey Milford, 1923)

Eddy, William A., 'A Source for *Gulliver's Travels*' *Modern Language Notes*, 36 (1921), 419–22

Egeler, Matthias, *Islands in the West. Classical Myth and the Medieval Norse and Irish Geographical Imagination* (Turnhout: Brepols, 2017)

Einstein, Albert, and Nathan Rosen, 'The Particle Problem in the General Theory of Relativity', *Physical Review*, 48 (1935), 73–77

Estrada, Ernesto, and Philip Knight, *A First Course in Network Theory* (Oxford: Oxford University Press, 2015)

Even-Zohar, Itamar, 'Polysystem Theory', *Poetics Today*, 11 (1990), 9–94

Fallon, Richard, 'Arthur Conan Doyle's *The Lost World*: Illustrating the Romance of Science', *English Literature in Translation, 1880–1920*, 63 (2020), 162–92

Farronato, Christina, *Eco's Chaosmos: From the Middle Ages to Postmodernity* (Toronto, Buffalo and London: University of Toronto Press, 2003)

Farronato, Cristina, 'Umberto Eco's *Baudolino* and the Language of Monsters', *Semiotica*, 144 (2003), 319–342

Faulkes, Anthony, ed., *Snorri Sturluson. Edda. Prologue and* Gylfaginning, 2nd edn (London: Viking Society for Northern Research/University College London, 2005)

Fazekas, Andrew S., *Star Trek. The Official Guide to Our Universe. The True Science Behind the Starship Voyages* (Washington, DC: National Geographic, 2016)

Fimi, Dmitra, 'Introduction', in *Imagining the Celtic Past in Modern Fantasy*, ed. by Dmitra Fimi and Alistair J. P. Sims (London: Bloomsbury Academic, 2023), pp. 1–8

Fimi, Dmitra, and Alistair J. P. Sims, *Imagining the Celtic Past in Modern Fantasy* (London: Bloomsbury Academic, 2023)

Findon, Joanne, *Bound and Free: Voices of Mortal and Otherworld Women in Medieval Irish Literature* (Toronto: Pontifical Institute of Mediaeval Studies, 2024)

Fischer, Benjamin, and Philip C. Derbesy, 'Literary Catholicity. An Alternate Reading of Influence in the Work of C. S. Lewis and G. K. Chesterton', *Religion and the Arts*, 19 (2015), 389–410

Fitzgerald, Robert P., 'The Allegory of Luggnagg and the Struldbruggs in "Gulliver's Travels"', *Studies in Philology*, 65 (1968), 657–76

Fitzpatrick, Kelly Ann, *Neomedievalism, Popular Culture, and the Academy. From Tolkien to Game of Thrones* (Cambridge: D. S. Brewer, 2019)

Flint, Valerie I. J., 'Honorius Augustodunensis', *Authors of the Middle Ages*, II, *Historical and Religious Writers of the Latin West*, 5–6, ed. by Patrick J. Geary (Aldershot, Hants: Variorum Reprints, 1995), pp. 89–183

Fogarty, Hugh, '*Aislinge Óenguso*: a *remscél* Reconsidered', in *Narrative in Celtic Tradition: Essays in Honor of Edgar M. Slotkin*, ed. by Joseph F. Eska (New York: Colgate University Press, 2011), pp. 56–67

Follett, Westley, 'An Allegorical Interpretation of the Monastic Voyage Narratives in Adomnán's *Vita Columbae*', *Eolas. The Journal of the American Society of Irish Medieval Studies*, 2 (2007), 4–27

Ford, A. J., *Marvel and Artefact. The 'Wonders of the East' in its Manuscript Contexts* (Leiden and Boston: Brill, 2016)

Ford, Patrick K., 'Branwen: A Study of the Celtic Affinities' *Studia Celtica*, 22–23 (1987–88), 29–41

Ford, Paul, *A Companion to Narnia* (New York: Harper Collins, 1994)

Foucault, Michel, '*Of Other Spaces*', trans. by Jay Miskowiec, *Diacritics*, 16 (1986), 22–27

Fowler, Alastair, *Kinds of Literature. An Introduction to the Theory of Genres and Modes* (Oxford: Clarendon Press, 2002)

Friede, Susanne, 'Baudolino' in *Umberto Eco Handbuch. Leben – Werk – Wirkung*, ed. by Erik Schilling (Stuttgart / Berlin: J. B. Metzler / Springer, 2021), pp. 189–95

Friedman, Michael, 'Introduction', in Immanuel Kant, *Metaphysical Foundations of Science*, trans. by Michael Friedman, Cambridge Texts in the History of Philosophy (Cambridge: Cambridge University Press, 2004)

Fulton, Helen, and Sif Rikhardsdottir, 'Introduction. Transmission of Charlemagne in Scandinavia, Wales, and Ireland', in *Charlemagne in the Norse and Celtic Worlds*, ed. by Helen Fulton and Sif Rikhardsdottir (Cambridge: D. S. Brewer, 2022), pp. 1–14

Fulton, Roger, *The Encyclopaedia of TV Science Fiction*, 2nd edn (London: Boxtree, 2000)

Gantz, Jeffrey, trans., *Early Irish Myths and Sagas* (Harmondsworth: Penguin, 1981)

Garcia, Jorge J. E., Carolyn Korsmeyer and Rudolphe Gasché, ed., *Literary Philosophers. Borges, Calvino, Eco* (New York and London: Routledge, 2002)

Garcia-Siino, Leimar, 'Star Trek: Voyager', in *The Routledge Handbook of Star Trek*, ed. by Leimar Garcia-Siino, Sabrina Mittermeier, and Stefan Rabitsch (New York and London: Routledge, 2022), pp. 46–55

Garcia-Siino, Leimar, Sabrina Mittermeier and Stefan Rabitsch, 'Introduction: Open Hailing Frequencies', in *The Routledge Handbook of Star Trek*, ed. by Leimar Garcia-Siino, Sabrina Mittermeier, and Stefan Rabitsch (New York and London: Routledge, 2022), pp. 1–5

Garcia-Siino, Leimar, Sabrina Mittermeier, and Stefan Rabitsch, ed., *The Routledge Handbook of Star Trek* (New York and London: Routledge, 2022)

Geiriadur Prifysgol Cymru, University of Wales, 2023 <https://geiriadur.ac.uk/gpc/gpc.html> [accessed 29 March 2024]

Giardini, Marco, *Figure del regno nascosto. Le leggende del Prete Gianni e delle dieci tribù perdute d'Israele fra Medioevo e prima età moderna* (Florence: Olschki, 2016)

Gil, Steven John, '"Remember the Nox": *Stargate: SG-1*'s Narrative Structure and the Changing Form of Television Fiction', *New Review of Film and Television Studies*, 12 (2014) 178–202

Gill, R. B., 'The Uses of Genre and the Classification of Speculative Fiction', *Mosaic: An Interdisciplinary Critical Journal*, 46 (2013), 71–85

Gomel, Elena and Danielle Gurevitch, 'Introduction', in *The Palgrave Handbook of Global Fantasy*, ed. by Elena Gomel and Danielle Gurevitch (Cham: Springer / Palgrave Macmillan, 2023), pp. xv–xx

Gomel, Elena, and Danielle Gurevitch, ed., *The Palgrave Handbook of Global Fantasy* (Cham: Springer / Palgrave Macmillan, 2023)

Gomel, Elena and Danielle Gurevitch, 'What is Fantasy and Who Decides?', in *The Palgrave Handbook of Global Fantasy*, ed. by Elena Gomel and Danielle Gurevitch (Cham: Springer / Palgrave Macmillan, 2023), pp. 3–13

Greenwood, Emily, *Afro-Greeks: Dialogues between Anglophone Caribbean Literature and Classics in the Twentieth Century* (Oxford: Oxford University Press, 2010)

Gregory, Chris, *Star Trek: Parallel Narratives* (Basingstoke and London: Macmillan, 2000)

Gulya, Jason J., *Allegory in Enlightenment Britain. Literary Abominations* (Cham: Palgrave Macmillan, 2022)

Guynes, Sean, and Dan Hassler-Forest, ed., *Star Wars and the History of Transmedia Storytelling* (Amstedam: Amsterdam University Press, 2017)

Hagan, Justice, 'Star Trek: Picard', in *The Routledge Handbook of Star Trek*, ed. by Leimar Garcia-Siino, Sabrina Mittermeier, and Stefan Rabitsch (New York and London: Routledge, 2022), pp. 74–79.

Halmos, Paul R., *Naïve Set Theory* (Princeton: Princeton University Press, 1960)

Harder, Jisca, '"For As Often As He Slept": A Comparative Analysis of Medieval Insular Vernacular Dream-Narratives', unpublished RMA thesis, Utrecht University, 2022 <https://studenttheses.uu.nl/handle/20.500.12932/42282> [accessed 24 March 2024]

Hardwick, Lorna, 'Aspirations and Mantras in Classical Reception Research: Can There Really Be Dialogue between Ancient and Modern' in *Framing Classical Reception Studies. Different Perspectives on a Developing Field*, ed. by Maarten De Pourcq (Leiden and Boston: Brill, 2020), pp. 15–32

Hardy, Elizabeth Baird, '"Where Many Books Have Gone Before": Using Star Trek to Teach Literature', *Set Phasers to Teach! Star Trek in Research and Teaching*, ed. by in Stefan Rabitsch, Martin Gabriel, Wilfried Elmenreich, and John N. A. Brown (Cham: Springer, 2018), pp. 1–11

Hark, Ina Rae, 'Star Trek: The Original Series', in *The Routledge Handbook of Star Trek*, ed. by Leimar Garcia-Siino, Sabrina Mittermeier, and Stefan Rabitsch (New York and London: Routledge, 2022), pp. 9–17

Harrison, Alan, *Ag Cruinniú Meala: Anthony Raymond (1675–1726). Ministéir Protastúnach, agus Léann na Gaeilge i mBaile Átha Cliath*, Leabhair thaighde, 60 (Dublin: An Clóchomhar, 1988)

Harrison, Alan, *The Dean's Friend: Anthony Raymond 1675–1726: Jonathan Swift and the Irish Language* (Dublin: de Burca, 1999)

Hart, Dabney Adams, *Through the Open Door. A New Look at C. S. Lewis* (Tuscaloosa: University of Alabama Press, 1984)

Harth, Phillip, 'The Problem of Political Allegory in *Gulliver's Travels*', *Modern Philology*, 73 (1976), 40–47

Hasan, Zaki, 'Star Trek: Enterprise', in *The Routledge Handbook of Star Trek*, ed. by Leimar Garcia-Siino, Sabrina Mittermeier, and Stefan Rabitsch (New York and London: Routledge, 2022), pp. 56–64

Hayani El Mechkouri, Kamal, 'La construction de l'espace chez Umberto Eco', *Cahiers de narratologie*, 33, *L'art du roman chez Umberto Eco* (2018) <https://doi.org/10.4000/narratologie.8071>

Heaney, Seamus, and Richard Kerney, 'Borges and the World of Fiction: An Interview with Jorge Luis Borges', *The Crane Bag*, 6 (1982), 71–8

Hillers, Barbara, 'Voyages Between Heaven and Hell: Navigating the Early Irish *Immram* Tales', *Proceedings of the Harvard Celtic Colloquium*, 13 (1993), 66–81

Hillers, Barbara, 'Medieval Irish *Wandering of Ulysses* Between Literary and Orality', in *Classical Literature and Learning in Medieval Irish Narrative*, ed. by Ralph O'Connor (Cambridge: D. S. Brewer, 2014), pp. 83–97

Hone, Joseph, and Pat Rogers, ed., *Jonathan Swift in Context* (Cambridge: Cambridge University Press, 2024)

Honorius Augustodunensis, *Imago mundi*, ed. by Valerie I. J. Flint, Archives d'histoire doctrinale et littéraire du Moyen Âge, 49 (1982)

Hooks, Bell, 'Choosing the Margin as a Space of Radical Openness', *Framework: The Journal of Cinema and Media*, 36 (1989), 15–23

Houston, Chlöe, 'Utopia, Dystopia or Anti-utopia? Gulliver's Travels and the Utopian Mode of Discourse', *Utopian Studies*, 18 (2007), 425–42

Hughes, Kathleen, 'The Changing Theory and Practice of Irish Pilgrimage', *Journal of Ecclesiastical History*, 11 (1960), 143–151

Hutchinson, Steven, 'Mapping Utopias', *Modern Philology*, 85 (1987), 170–85

Interactieve Kaarten. Gemeente Amsterdam <maps.amsterdam.nl> (City of Amsterdam, 2023) [accessed 7 december 2024]

Irwin, William Robert, *The Game of the Impossible* (Urbana: University of Illinois Press, 1974)

Isaacs, Bruce, 'A Vision of Time and Place: Spiritual Humanism and the Utopian Impulse', in *Star Trek and Myth. Essays on Symbol and Archetype at the Final Frontier*, ed. by Mathew Wilhelm Kapell (Jefferson: McFarland, 2010), pp. 182–196

Jackson, Kenneth, 'The Adventure of Laeghaire mac Crimhthainn', *Speculum* 17 (1942), 377–389

James, Edward, 'Tolkien, Lewis and the Explosion of Genre Fantasy', in *The Cambridge Companion to Fantasy Literature*, ed. by Edward James and Farah Mendehlson (Cambridge: Cambridge University Press, 2012), pp. 62–78

Jauss, Hans Robert, *Toward an Aesthetic of Reception* (Brighton: Harvester Press, 1982)

Johnson-Smith, Jan, *American Science Fiction TV: Star Trek, Stargate and Beyond* (London: I.B. Tauris, 2012)

Jones, Aled Llion, 'Good Time(s), Bad Time(s): Myth and Metaphysics in Some Medieval Literature?', *Proceedings of the Harvard Celtic Colloquium*, 38 (2018), 47–74

le Juez, Brigitte, and Olga Springer, ed., *Shipwreck and Island Motifs in Literature and the Arts* (Leiden and Boston: Brill/Rodopi, 2015)

Kazimierczak, Karolina, 'Adapting Shakespeare for *Star Trek* and *Star Trek* for Shakespeare: *The Klingon Hamlet* and the Spaces of Translation', *Studies in Popular Culture*, 32 (2010), 35–55

Kelling, H. D., 'Some Significant Names in Gulliver's Travels', *Studies in Philology*, 48 (1951), 761–78

Kerney, Richard, 'Poetry, Language and Identity: A Note on Seamus Heaney', *Studies: An Irish Quarterly Review*, 75 (1986), 552–63

Kervran, Louis, *Brandan. Le grand navigateur celte du VIe siècle* (Paris: Éditions Robert Lafont, 1977)

Kline, Naomi Reed, *Maps of Medieval Thought. The Hereford Paradigm* (Woodbridge: Boydell Press, 2001)

Koch, John T., ed., *Celtic Culture: A Historical Encyclopedia* (Santa Barbara: ABC-CLIO, 2006)

Koch, John. T., *'Echtrai'*, in *Celtic Culture: A Historical Encyclopedia*, ed. by John T. Koch, (Santa Barbara: ABC-CLIO, 2006), p. 646

Koch, John T., *'Immrama'*, in *Celtic Culture: A Historical Encyclopedia*, ed. by John T. Koch, (Santa Barbara: ABC-CLIO, 2006), p. 959

Konstantakos, Ioannis M., 'The Island that was a Fish: an Ancient Folktale in the *Alexander Romance* and in Other Texts of Late Antiquity', in *Aspects of Orality and Greek Literature in the Roman Empire*, ed. by Consuelo Ruiz-Montero (Newcastle-upon-Tyne: Cambridge Scholars Publishing, 2019), pp. 281–300

Kruger, Haidee, *Postcolonial Polysystems: The Production and Reception of Translated Children's Literature in South Africa* (Amsterdam: John Benjamins, 2012)

Krysinski, Wladimir,'Borges, Calvino, Eco: The Philosophies of Metafiction', in *Literary Philosophers. Borges, Calvino, Eco*, ed. by Jorge J. E. Garcia, Carolyn Korsmeyer and Rudolphe Gasché (New York and London: Routledge, 2002), pp. 185–204

Lane, Andy, and Anna Bowles, *Star Trek. The Adventure. Stardate 18.12.02. Hyde Park, London* (London: Titan Publishing Group, 2002)
Larrington, Carolyne, *Old Norse Myths That Shape the Way We Think* (London: Thames and Hudson, 2023)
Lawyer, John E., 'Three Celtic Voyages: Brendan, Lewis and Buechner', *Anglican Theological Review*, 84 (2002), 319–43
Lazo, Andrew, 'A Kind of Midwife. J. R. R. Tolkien and C. S. Lewis – Sharing Influence', in *Tolkien the Medievalist*, ed. by Jane Chance (London and New York: Routledge, 2003), pp. 36–49
Le Saux, Françoise, 'Laȝamon's *Brut*' in *Arthur of the English. The Arthurian Legend in Medieval English Life and Literature*, ed. by W. R. J. Barron (Cardiff: University of Wales Press, 2001), pp. 22–32
Le Saux, Françoise, 'Wace's *Roman de Brut*' in *Arthur of the English. The Arthurian Legend in Medieval English Life and Literature*, ed. by W. R. J. Barron (Cardiff: University of Wales Press, 2001), pp. 18–22
Leary-Owhin, Michael E., and John P. McCarthy, ed., *The Routledge Handbook of Henri Lefebvre, The City and Urban Society* (London and New York: Routledge, 2020)
Lefebvre, Henri, *La production de l'espace* (Paris: Anthropos, 1974)
Lefebvre, Henri, *The Production of Space*, trans. by Donald Nicholson-Smith (Oxford: Blackwell, 1991)
Leitch, Megan G., *Sleep and its Spaces in Middle English Literature: Emotions, Ethics, Dreams* (Manchester: Manchester University Press, 2021)
Leitch, Megan G., and K. S. Whetter, ed., *Arthurian Literature xxxvi: Sacred Space in Arthurian Romance* (Woodbridge: Boydell and Brewer, 2021)
Lewis, C. S., *The Allegory of Love. A Study in Medieval Tradition* (Oxford: Oxford University Press, 1958 [1936])
Lewis, C. S., *The Collected Letters of C. S. Lewis. Volume ii. Books, Broadcasts, and the War, 1931–1949*, ed. by Walter Hooper (New York, Harper Collins, 2004)
Lewis, C. S., *The Collected Letters of C. S. Lewis. Volume iii. Narnia, Cambridge, and Joy, 1950–1963* ed. by Walter Hooper (New York, Harper Collins, 2007)
Lewis, C. S., '*De descriptione temporum*', in *20th Century Literary Criticism. A Reader*, ed. by David Lodge (Harlow: Addison Wesley Longman, 1972), pp. 443–53; originally published in *They Asked for a Paper. Papers and Addresses* (London: Bles, 1962)
Lewis, C. S., *The Discarded Image. An Introduction to Medieval and Renaissance Literature* (Cambridge: Cambridge University Press, 1994 [1964])
Lewis, C. S., *English Literature in the Sixteenth Century, Excluding Drama* (Oxford: Clarendon Press, 1954)

Lewis, C. S., 'On Science Fiction' in Lewis, *Of Other Worlds: Essays and Stories*, ed. by W. Hooper (New York and London: Harcourt, 1966), pp. 55–86

Lewis, C. S., *They Asked for a Paper. Papers and Addresses* (London: Bles, 1962)

Lewis, C. S., *The Voyage of the* Dawn Treader (Dublin and London: HarperCollins, 2014); first edition Geoffrey Bles, 1952

Lewis, Henry, and P. Diverres, ed., *Delw y Byd* (*Imago Mundi*) (Cardiff: Cardiff University Press, 1928)

Lindley, David, 'The Birth of Wormholes' *Physical Review Focus* 15, 11 (2005) <https://link.aps.org/doi/10.1103/PhysRevFocus.15.11> [accessed 19 May 2023]

Liuzza, R. M., 'The Future is a Foreign Country: The Legend of the Seven Sleepers and the Anglo-Saxon Sense of the Past', in *Medieval Science Fiction*, ed. by Carl Kears and James Paz (London: King's College London Centre for Late Antique & Medieval Studies, 2016), pp. 61–78

Lodge, David, ed., *20th Century Literary Criticism. A Reader* (Harlow: Addison Wesley Longman, 1972)

Logan, G. M., and R. M. Adams, ed., *Thomas More. Utopia* Cambridge Texts in the History of Political Thought, 2 (Cambridge: Cambridge University Press, 1989)

Lotman, Yuri M., 'Autocommunication: "I" and "Other" as Addressees (On the Two Models of Communication in the System of Culture)', in *Culture and Communication. Signs in Flux. An Anthology of Major and Lesser-Known Works by Yuri Lotman*, ed. by Andreas Schönle, trans. by Benjamin Paloff (Boston: Academic Studies Press, 2020), pp. 4–33

Lotman, Yuri M., *La sémiosphère*, trans. by Anka Lodenko (Limoges, Presses Universitaires de Limoges, 1999)

Lotman, Yuri M., 'On the Semiosphere', trans. by Wilma Clark, *Sign System Studies*, 33.1 (2005), 205–229

Lotman, Yuri M., *Universe of The Mind. A Semiotic Theory of Culture*, trans. by Ann Shukman (London: Tauris, 1990)

Loughlin, Chris, 'When was Celtic Futurism? The Irish *Immrama* as Proto-Science-Fiction', *SFRA Review* 52.1 *Selected LSFRC 2021 Papers* (2022), 214–22 <https://sfrareview.files.wordpress.com/2022/02/5201-ls-immarama.pdf> [accessed 7 April 2024]

Lawlor, John, *C. S. Lewis. Memories and Reflections* (Dallas: Spence, 1998)

Lu, Wei, 'Sci-Fi Realism and the Allegory of Dystopia: With Kazuo Ishiguro's *Never Let Me Go* as an Example', *Comparative Literature Studies*, 57 (2020), 702–14

Lucian, *True History. Introduction, Text, Translation, and Commentary*, ed. and trans. by Diskin Clay, and ed. by James H. Brusuelas (Oxford: Oxford University Press, 2021)

Magennis, Hugh, 'The Anonymous Old English Legend of the Seven Sleepers and its Latin Source', *Leeds Studies in English*, 22 (1991), 43–56

Mac Cana, Proinsias, *Branwen Daughter of Llŷr: A Study of the Irish Affinities and of the Composition of the Second Branch of the Mabinogi* (Cardiff: University of Wales Press, 1958)

Mac Cana, Proinsias, *The Learned Tales of Medieval Ireland* (Dublin: DIAS, 1980)

Mac Cana, Proinsias, '*Mongán Mac Fiachna* and *Immram Brain*', *Ériu*, 23 (1972), 102–42

Mac Cana, Proinsias, 'The Sinless Otherworld of *Immram Brain*', *Ériu*, 27 (1976), 95–115

Mac Mathúna, Séamus, *Iceland and the Immrama: An Enquiry into Irish Influence on Old Norse-Icelandic Voyage Literature*, Münchner Nordistische Studien, 48 (München : utzverlag, 2021)

Mac Mathúna, Séamus, ed., *Immram Brain – Bran's Journey to the Land of the Women*, Buchreihe der Zeitschrift für celtische Philologie, 2 (Tübingen: Max Niemeyer Verlag, 1985)

Mac Mathúna, Séamus, 'The Question of Irish Analogues in Old Norse-Icelandic Voyage Tales in the *fornaldarsögur* and the *Gesta Danorum* of Saxo Grammaticus', in *Between Worlds: Contexts, Sources, and Analogues of Scandinavian Otherowlrd Journeys*, ed. by Matthias Egeler and Wilhelm Heizmann (Berlin: De Gruyter, 2020), pp. 283–345

MacKinnon, Sarah R., '*Stargate Atlantis*: Islandness of the Pegasus Galaxy', *Shima*, 10 (2016), 36–49 https://doi.org/10.21463/shima.10.2.06

Mackley, J. S., *The Legend of St Brendan. A Comparative Study of the Latin and Anglo-Norman Versions* (Leiden and Boston: Brill, 2008)

Mackley, J. S., 'Some Celtic Otherworld Motifs in Brendan's Voyage to Paradise', Paper presented to the International Medieval Congress, Leeds (2010), online archived version <http://nectar.northampton.ac.uk/4949/> [accessed 24 March 2023]

MacLeod, Robbie Andrew, 'Love and Gender in Medieval Gaelic Saga', unpublished PhD thesis, University of Glasgow, 2024 <https://theses.gla.ac.uk/84302/> (accessed 25 November 2024)

Manning, David, 'The Church of England', in *Jonathan Swift in Context*, ed. by Joseph Hone and Pat Rogers (Cambridge: Cambridge University Press, 2024), pp. 232–39

The Mariners Magazine; or, Sturmy's Mathematical and Practical Arts... By Capt. Samuel Sturmy (London, 1669)

Martin, Erik, 'Alienation/Defamiliarisation/Estrangement (*ostranenie*)', in *Central and Eastern European Literary Theory and the West*, ed. by Michał Mrugalski, Schamma Schahadat and Irina Wutsdorff (Berlin: De Gruyter, 2022), pp. 881–86

Martin, Marie, *Learning by Wandering. An Ancient Irish Perspective for a Digital World* (Oxford and Bern: Peter Lang, 2010)

Massey, Jeff, '"On Second Thought, Let's Not Go To Camelot... 'Tis a Silly Space": Star Trek and the Inconsequence of SF Medievalism', in *Medieval Science Fiction*, ed. by Carl Kears and James Paz (London: King's College London Centre for Late Antique & Medieval Studies, 2016), pp. 95–114

Matthews, David, *Medievalism: A Critical History* (Cambridge: D. S. Brewer, 2015) <https://doi.org/10.1515/9781782043973>

Meyer, Kuno, ed. and trans, 'The Adventures of Nera', *Revue Celtique*, 10 (1889) 212–228

McCone, Kim, ed. and tr., *Echtrae Chonnlai and the Beginnings of Vernacular Narrative Writing in Ireland*, Maynooth Medieval Irish Texts, 1 (Maynooth: Department of Old and Middle Irish, National University of Ireland, 2000)

McDonald, Peter, ed., *The Poems of W. B. Yeats: Volume Two: 1890–1898* (London: Routledge, 2021)

McLaughlin, Martin, 'Calvino, Eco and the Transmission of World Literature', in *Transmissions of Memory. Echoes, Traumas, and Nostalgia in Post–World War II Italian Culture*, ed. by Patrizia Sambuco (Vancouver, Madison, Teaneck and Wroxton: Fairleigh Dickinson University Press, 2018), pp. 3–19

McLaughlin, Martin, 'Calvino's Rewriting of Marco Polo: From the 1960s Screenplay to *Invisible Cities*', in *Marco Polo and the Encounter or East and West*, ed. by Akbari, et al., pp. 182–200

McLaughlin, Roisin, 'Fénius Farsaid and the Alphabets', *Ériu*, 59 (2009), 1–24

McMahon, Elizabeth, and Bénédicte André, 'Literature and the Literary Gaze', in *The Routledge International Handbook of Island Studies*, ed. by Godfrey Baldacchino (London and New York: Routledge, 2018), pp. 296–311

McTurk, Rory W., 'Fooling Gylfi: Who Tricks Who?', *Alvíssmál*, 3 (1994), 3–18

Menzies, Ruth, 'Re-writing *Gulliver's Travels*: the Demise of a Genre?' *e-Rea. Revue électronique d'études sur le monde anglophone*, 3 (2005) <https://doi.org/10.4000/erea.613>

Mercer, Sabine, 'Truth and Lies in Umberto Eco's *Baudolino*', *Philosophy and Literature*, 35 (2011), 16–31

Mercier, Vivian, *The Irish Comic Tradition* (Oxford: Oxford University Press, 1962)

Merrifield, Andy, 'Henri Lefebvre. A Socialist in Space', in *Thinking Space*, ed. by Mike Crang and Nigel Thrift, Critical Geographies, 9 (London and New York: Routledge, 2000), pp. 167–82

Metz, Christian, *Language and Cinema* (The Hague: Mouton, 1974)

Meyer, Kuno, ed. and trans., *The Voyage of Bran Son of Febal to the Land of the Living* (London: David Nutt, 1895; facsimile reprint Felinfach: Llanerch Publishers, 1994)

Meyer, Paul, '*L'Image du monde*, rédaction du MS. Harley 4333', *Romania*, 21 (1892), 481–505 <https://doi.org/10.3406/roma.1892.5743>

Michie, Sarah, 'The Lover's Malady in Early Irish Romance' *Speculum*, 12 (1937), 285–419

Miller, William H., *Picture History of British Ocean Liners. 1900 to the Present* (Mineola, New York: Dover Publications, 2001)

Mittermeier, Sabrina, 'Star Trek: Discovery' in *The Routledge Handbook of Star Trek*, ed. by Leimar Garcia-Siino, Sabrina Mittermeier, and Stefan Rabitsch (New York and London: Routledge, 2022), pp. 65–73

Mittermeier, Sabrina, and Marieke Spychala, ed., *Fighting For the Future. Essays on* Star Trek: Discovery (Liverpool: Liverpool University Press, 2020)

Mittman, Asa Simon, *Maps and Monsters in Medieval England* (London and New York: Routledge, 2006)

Mochel-Caballero, Anne-Frédérique, '"Where the Waves Grow Sweet": From Sea Adventure to Transcendence in The Voyage of the Dawn Treader by C.S. Lewis', *Fantasy Art and Studies*, 11 (2021) <https://u-picardie.hal.science/hal-03784545> [accessed 14 March 2024]

Montaigne, *Les essais*, ed. by Denis Bjaï et al., (Paris: Librairie Générale Française, 2001)

Montgomery, P. Andrew, 'Classical Literature', in *Reading the Classics with C. S. Lewis*, ed. by Thomas L. Martin (Grand Rapids, MI: Baker Academic, and Carlisle: Paternoster Press, 2000), pp. 52–71

Morgan, Cheryl, 'Celts in Spaaaaace!', in *Imagining the Celtic Past in Modern Fantasy*, ed. by Dimitra Fimi and Alistair J. P. Sims (London: Bloomsbury Academic, 2023), pp. 117–34

Moseley, C. W. R. D., trans., *The Travels of Sir John Mandeville* (Harmondsworth: Penguin, 1983)

Moylan, Tom, 'Irish Voyages and Visions: Pre-figuring, Re-configuring Utopia', *Utopian Studies*, 18, Special issue 'Irish Utopian' (2007), 299–323

Mullan, John, 'Catching the Prester John Bug', *London Review of Books*, 25 (2003) < https://www.lrb.co.uk/the-paper/v25/n09/john-mullan/catching-the-prester-john-bug> [accessed 6 March 2024]

Müller, Eduard, ed. and trans., 'Two Irish Tales', *Revue Celtique*, 3 (1876–78), 342–60

Mulligan, Amy C., *A Landscape of Words: Ireland, Britain and the Poetics of Space, 700–1250* (Manchester: Manchester University Press, 2019)

Murasaki Shikibu, *The Tale of Genji*. Abridged, trans. by Royall Tyler (London: Penguin, 2006)

Murray, Kevin, 'Genre Construction: the Creation of the *Dinnshenchas*', *Journal of Literary Onomastics*, 6 (2017), 11–21

Nabokov, Vladimir, 'James Joyce (1882–1941). *Ulysses* (1922)' in Vladimir Nabokov, *Lectures on Literature*, ed. by Fredson Bowers, with introduction by John Updike (San Diego, New York, and London: Harcourt Brace & Co, 1980), pp. 285–370

Nabokov, Vladimir, *Lectures on Russian Literature*, ed. by Fredson Bowers (New York: Harcourt Inc., 1981), pp 97–136

Ní Mhaonaigh, Máire, 'The Peripheral Centre: Writing History on the Western "Fringe"', *Interfaces: A Journal of Medieval European Literatures*, 4 (2017), 59–84 <https://doi.org/10.13130/INTERFACES-04-05>

Ní Mhaonaigh, Máire, 'The Literature of Medieval Ireland, 800–1200: from the Vikings to the Normans', in *The Cambridge History of Irish Literature*, ed. by Margaret Kelleher and Philip O'Leary (Cambridge: Cambridge University Press, 2006), pp. 32–73

Ó Broin, Brian, '*Aisling*', in *Celtic Culture: A Historical Encyclopedia*, ed. by John T. Koch (Santa Barbara: ABC-CLIO, 2006), p. 33

O'Connor, Ralph, 'Irish Narrative Literature and the Classical Tradition, 900–1300', in *Classical Literature and Learning in Medieval Irish Narrative*, ed. by Ralph O'Connor (Cambridge: D. S. Brewer, 2014), pp. 1–22

O'Corráin, Donnchadh, 'Irish and Nordic Exchange. What They Gave and What They Took', in *Heritage and Identity. Shaping the Nations of the North*, ed. by J. M. Fladmark (London: Routledge, 2002), pp. 61–72

Ó Dochartaigh, Caitríona, 'Language and Identity in Early Medieval Ireland', *Études Irlandaises*, 27 (2002), 119–31

O'Donnell, Thomas C., *Fosterage in Medieval Ireland. An Emotional History* (Amsterdam: Amsterdam University Press, 2020)

O'Donoghue, Denis, *Brendaniana. St. Brendan the Voyager in Story and Legend* (Dublin: Browne and Nolan, 1893)

O'Loughlin, Thomas, 'Brendan, St', in *Celtic Culture: A Historical Encyclopedia*, ed. by John T. Koch (Santa Barbara: ABC-CLIO, 2006), pp. 244–45

O'Meara, John, and Jonathan Wooding, 'The Latin Version', in *The Voyage of Saint Brendan. Representative Versions of the Legend in English Translation*, ed. by W. R. J. Barron and Glyn S. Burgess (Exeter: University of Exeter Press, 2002), pp. 13–64

Ogline, Jill, 'Edmund Pevensie and the Character of the Redeemed', *Inklings Forever*, 2 (1999), 48–53

Ording, Philip, *99 Variations on a Proof* (Princeton: Princeton University Press, 2019)

Orff, Carl, *Carmina Burana. Cantiones Profanae* (Wauconda: Bolchazy-Carducci, 1996)

Orlandi, Giovanni, and Rossana E. Guglielmetti, ed. and trans., *Navigatio sancti Brendani: alla scoperta dei segreti meravigliosi del mondo*, Per Verba, 30 (Florence: Galluzzo and Fondazione Ezio Franceschini, 2014)

Oskamp, Hans Pieter Atze, '*Echtra Condla*', *Études celtiques*, 14 (1974), 207–28.

Oskamp, Hans Pieter Atze, ed., *The Voyage of Máel Dúin: A Study in Early Irish Voyage Literature followed by an Edition of Immram curaig Máele Dúin from the*

Yellow Book of Lecan in Trinity College, Dublin (Groningen: Wolters-Noordhoff, 1970)

Padel, Oliver, *Arthur in Medieval Welsh Literature* (Cardiff: University of Wales Press, 2013)

Parsons, Geraldine, '*Aisling* (Vision)', in *The Encyclopedia of Medieval Literature in Britain*, ed. by Siân Echard and Robert Rouse (Wiley Online Library, 2017), n.p. <https://doi.org/10.1002/9781118396957.wbemlb067>

Patch, Howard Rollin, 'Some Elements in Mediæval Descriptions of the Otherworld', PMLA, 33 (1918), 601–43

Patey, Douglas Lane, 'Swift's Satire on "Science" and the Structure of *Gulliver's Travels*', ELH, 58 (1991), 809–39

Patke, Rajeev S., *Poetry and Islands. Materiality and the Creative Imagination* (London: Rowan and Littlefield, 2018)

Pedrycz, Witold, and Fernando Gomide, *An Introduction to Fuzzy Sets: Analysis and Design* (Cambridge, MA: MIT Press, 1998)

Penrose, Sir Roger, *The Emperor's New Mind. Concerning Computers, Minds and The Laws of Physics*, Oxford Landmark Science, revised impression (Oxford: Oxford University Press, 2016 [1989])

Perosa, Sergio, *From Islands to Portraits. Four Literary Variations* (Amsterdam: IOS Press and Tokyo: Ohmsha, 2000)

Petrovskaia, Natalia I., ed., *Delw y Byd. A Medieval Welsh Encyclopedia* (Cambridge: MHRA, 2020)

Petrovskaia, Natalia I., 'The Fool and the Wise Man: The Legacy of the Two Merlins in Modern Culture', in *The Legacy of Courtly Literature. From Medieval to Contemporary Culture*, ed. by Deborah Nelson-Campbell and Ruben Cholakian (Cham: Palgrave Macmillan, 2017), pp. 175–205

Petrovskaia, Natalia I., *This is Not a Grail Romance. Understanding Historia Peredur vab Efrawc* (Cardiff: University of Wales Press, 2023)

Petrovskaia, Natalia I., 'Poisson et pêche dans la littérature irlandaise et galloise : le bétail de la mer', *Anthropozoologica*, 53 (2018), 139–46 <https://doi.org/10.5252/anthropozoologica2018v53a12>

Petrovskaia, Natalia I., *Transforming Europe in the* Images of the World, *1110–1500. Fuzzy Geographies* (Amsterdam: Amsterdam University Press, 2025)

Pickering, David, 'Chesterton, Lewis, and the Shadow of Newman. A Study in Method', *New Blackfriars*, 104 (2023), 142–60

Poe, Harry Lee, *The Completion of C. S. Lewis (1945–1963): From War to Joy* (Wheaton: Crossway, 2022)

Poe, Harry Lee, *The Inklings of Oxford: C. S. Lewis, J. R. R. Tolkien, and Their Friends* (Grand Rapids: Zondervan, 2009)

Poincaré, Henri, *The Foundations of Science. Science and Hypothesis, The Value of Science, Science and Method*, trans. by George Bruce Halsted (Cambridge: Cambridge University Press, 2014)

Polo, Marco, *The Travels*, trans. by Ronald Latham (Harmondsworth: Penguin, 1958)

Poppe, Erich, '*Imtheachta Aeniasa* and its Place in Medieval Irish Textual History', in *Classical Literature and Learning in Medieval Irish Narrative*, ed. by Ralph O'Connor (Cambridge: D. S. Brewer, 2014), pp. 25–39

Porter, Lynette, *Charming Villains and Modern Monsters: Science Fiction in Shades of Gray on 21st Century Television* (Jefferson: McFarland, 2010)

Power, Rosemary, 'Norse-Gaelic Contacts: Genres and Transmission', *Journal of the North Atlantic*, 4 (2013), 19–25

Priest, Hannah, '"Oh, the funnies, the funnies": The Medieval Monstrous Races in *The Voyage of the Dawn Treader* and *Baudolino*', in *Our Monstrous (S)kin: Blurring the Boundaries Between Monsters and Humanity*, ed. by Sorcha Ní Fhlainn (Oxford: Interdisciplinary Press, 2009)

Prior, Oliver Herbert, ed., *L'Image du monde de maitre Gossuin. Rédaction en prose* (Lausanne and Paris: Payot, 1913)

Probyn, Clive, *Jonathan Swift and the Anglo-Irish Road* (Leiden: Brill and William Fink, 2020)

Пропп, Владимир Яковлевич [Propp, Vladimir Yakovlevich], *Морфология сказки* [*Morfologia Skazki*], 2nd edn (Moscow: Наука, 1969); first published in 1928

Rabitsch, Stefan, '"And Yet, Everything We Do Is Usually Based On The English": Sailing The *mare incognitum* of Star Trek's Transatlantic Double Consciousness with Horatio Hornblower', *Science Fiction Film and Television*, 9 (2016), 439–72

Rabitsch, Stefan, *Star Trek and the British Age of Sail: The Maritime Influence Throughout the Series and Films* (Jefferson: McFarland, 2019)

Rees, Christine, *Utopian Imagination and Eighteenth-Century Fiction* (London and New York: Longman, 1996)

Reid, Conor, 'The Lost Worlds of Arthur Conan Doyle's Professor Challenger Series', *Journal of the Fantastic in the Arts*, 28 (2017), 271–89

Rieder, John, *Science Fiction and the Mass Cultural Genre System* (Middletown, Connecticut: Wesleyan University Pess, 2017)

Rigney, Ann, 'The Many Dimensions of Literature' in *The Life of Texts. An Introduction to Literary Studies*, ed. by Kiene Brillenburg Wurth and Ann Rigney (Amsterdam: Amsterdam University Press, 2019), pp. 43–76

Ritter, Kathleen, *Stargate SG-1. The Ultimate Visual Guide* (London, New York, Munich, Melbourne and Delhi: DK, 2006)

Robinson, Douglas, *Estrangement and the Somatics of Literature: Tolstoy, Shklovsky, Brecht* (Baltimore: John Hopkins University Press, 2008)

Roche, Norma, 'Sailing West: Tolkien, the Saint Brendan Story, and the Idea of Paradise in the West', *Mythlore*, 17 (1991), 16–20

Roe, Harry, and Ann Dooley, trans., *Tales of the Elders of Ireland. A New Translation of Acallam na Senórach*) (Oxford: Oxford University Press, 1999)

Rogers, Shef, 'Travel and Exploration', in *Jonathan Swift in Context* ed. by Joseph Hone and Pat Rogers (Cambridge: Cambridge University Press, 2024), pp. 93–99

Romanets, Maryna, 'Travellers, Cartographers, Lovers: Ideologies of Exploratory Desire in Contemporary Irish Poetry', *Nordic Irish Studies*, 3 (2004), 35–49

Rundles, W. G. L., 'Le Nouveau Monde, l'autre monde et la pluralité des mondes' in *Actas do Congresso Internacional de História dos Descobrimentos*, IV (Lisbon: Oficinas Gráficas da Papelaria Fernandes, 1961), pp. 347–382

Rundles, W. G. L., *Geography, Cartography and Nautical Science in the Renaissance* (Aldershot and Burlington: Ashgate Variorum, 2000)

Russell, Jeffrey Burton, 'The Flat Error: The Modern Distortion of Medieval Geography', *Mediaevalia*, 15 (1989), 337–53

Russell, Paul, '"What Was Best of Every Language": the Early History of the Irish Language", in *A New History of Ireland*, 1, *Prehistoric and early Ireland*, ed. by Dáibhí Ó Cróinín (Oxford: Oxford University Press, 2005), pp. 405–450

Said, Edward, 'Traveling Theory', in *The Selected Works of Edward Said. 1966–2006*, ed. by Moustafa Bayoumi and Andrew Rubin (London and Dublin: Bloomsbury Publishing, 2021), pp. 197–219

Scafi, Alessandro, *Il paradiso in terra. Mappe del giardino dell'Eden* (Milan: Bruno Mondadori, 2007)

Scafi, Alessandro, *Mapping Paradise. A History of Heaven on Earth* (Chicago: Chicago University Press, 2006)

Schakel, Peter J., *Imagination and the Arts in C. S. Lewis: Journeying to Narnia and Other Worlds* (Columbia and London: University of Missouri Press, 2002)

Schakel, Peter J., 'Restoration and Eighteenth Century', in *Reading the Classics with C. S. Lewis*, ed. by Thomas L. Martin (Grand Rapids, MI: Baker Academic, and Carlisle: Paternoster Press, 2000), pp. 187–202

Schechter, Eric, *Classical and Nonclassical Logics. An Introduction to the Mathematics of Propositions* (Princeton: Princeton University Press, 2005)

Schilling, Erik, ed., *Umberto Eco Handbuch. Leben – Werk – Wirkung* (Stuttgart: J. B. Metzler and Berlin: Springer, 2021)

Schmeller, J. A., ed., *Carmina Burana. Lateinische und deutsche Lieder und Gedichte einer Handschrift des XIII. Jahrhunderts aus Benedistbeuern auf der K. Bibliothek zu Munchen* (Breslau: Wilhelm Koebner, 1894)

Schneider, Peter, *Extragalactic Astronomy and Cosmology* (Berlin and Heidelberg: Springer, 2015)

Selmer, Carl, ed., *Navigatio sancti Brendani abbatis: From Early Latin Manuscripts* (Notre Dame: University of Notre Dame Press, 1959)

Severin, Timothy *The Brendan Voyage* (London: Hutchinson, 1978)

Seymour, M. C., ed., *Mandeville's Travels* (Oxford: Clarendon Press, 1967)

Sherry, Norman, *Conrad's Eastern World* (Cambridge: Cambridge University Press, 1966)

Shklovsky, Viktor, 'Art as Technique' in *Russian Formalist Criticism: Four Essays*, ed. by Lee T. Lemon, Marion J. Reis, and Gary Saul Morson (Lincoln and London: University of Nebraska Press, 1965), pp. 5–24

Шкловский, Виктор Борисович, [Shklovsky, Viktor Borisovich], *О теории прозы* [*O Teorii Prozi*] (Moscow: Krug, 1925)

Siegel, Ethan, *Star Trek Technology. The Science of Star Trek from Tricorders to Warp Drive* (Minneapolis, MN: Voyageur Press, 2017)

Sinding, Michael, 'Metaphor, Allegory, Irony, Satire and Supposition in Factual and Fictional Narrative', in *Narrative Factuality: A Handbook*, ed. by Monika Fludenik and Marie-Laure Ryan (Berlin: De Gruyter, 2020), pp. 165–84

Singer, Christoph, *Sea Change: The Shore from Shakespeare to Banville*, Spatial Practices. An Interdisciplinary Series in Cultural History, Geography and Literature, 20 (Amsterdam and New York: Rodopi, 2014)

Singleton, Charles S., 'Dante's Allegory', *Speculum*, 25 (1950), 78–86

Slessarev, Vsevolod, ed., *Prester John. The Letter and the Legend* (Minneapolis: University of Minnesota Press and London: Oxford University Press, 1959)

Sobecki, Sebastian I., 'From the *désert liquide* to the Sea of Romance: Benedeit's *Le voyage de Saint Brendan* and the Irish *immrama*', *Neophilologus*, 87 (2003), 193–207

Soja, Edward, *Thirdspace. Journeys to Los Angeles and Other Real-and-Imagined Places* (Oxford: Blackwell, 1996)

Sparke, Linda S., and John S. Gallagher III, *Galaxies in the Universe. An Introduction* (Cambridge: Cambridge University Press, 2000)

Spiegel, Simon, 'Utopia', in *The Routledge Handbook of Star Trek*, ed. by Leimar Garcia-Siino, Sabrina Mittermeier, and Stefan Rabitsch (New York and London: Routledge, 2022), pp. 467–75

Stanek, Łukasz, *Henri Lefebvre on Space: Architecture, Urban Research, and the Production of Theory* (Minneapolis and London: University of Minnesota Press, 2001)

Stargate, dir. by Roland Emmerich (Centropolis/MGM, 1994)

Stargate: Atlantis (Acme Shark/MGM, 2004–2009)

Stargate SG-1 (MGM, 1997–2007)

Stargate: Universe (Acme Shark/MGM, 2009–2011)

Star Trek: Deep Space Nine (Paramount Television, 1993–1999)

Star Trek Discovery (CBS, 2017–2024)

Star Trek: Enterprise (Paramount Network Television, 2001–2005)

Star Trek Picard (CBS, 2020–2023)

Star Trek: The Next Generation (Paramount Television, 1987–1994)

Star Trek: The Original Series (Desilu Productions, 1966–1969)

Star Trek: Voyager (Paramount Network Television, 1995–2001)

Stauder, Thomas, and Umberto Eco, 'Un colloquio con Umberto Eco intorno a *Baudolino*', *Il lettore di provincia*, 110 (2001), 3–14;

Stauder, Thomas, and Umberto Eco, *Colloqui con Umberto Eco. Come nascono i romanzi* (Milano: La nave di Teseo, 2024)

Stilgoe, John R., *What Is Landscape?* (Cambridge, MA, and London: MIT Press, 2015)

Stokes, Whitley, ed. and tr., 'The Death of Crimthann son of Fidach, and the Adventures of the Sons of Eochaid Muigmedón', *Revue Celtique* 24 (1903), 172–207

Stokes, Whitley, ed. and tr., 'The Irish Ordeals, Cormac's adventure in the Land of Promise, and the Decision as to Cormac's sword', in Whitley Stokes and Ernst Windisch, ed., *Irische Texte mit Wörterbuch*, 3.1 (Leipzig: Hirzel, 1891), pp. 183–221

Stokes, Whitley, ed. and trans., 'The Voyage of the Húi Corra', in *Revue Celtique*, 9 (1988), 22–69

Stokes, Whitley, ed. and trans., 'The Voyage of Mael Duin (Part I)', *Revue Celtique*, 9 (1988), 447–95

Stokes, Whitley, ed. and trans., 'The Voyage of Mael Duin (Part II)', *Revue Celtique*, 10 (1989), 50–95

Stokes, Whitley, ed., 'The Voyage of Snedgus and Mac Riagla', *Revue Celtique*, 9 (1988), 14–25

Stoppe, Sebastian, *Is* Star Trek *Utopia? Investigating a Perfect Future* (Jefferson: McFarland, 2022)

Stoppe, Sebastian, *Unterwegs zu neuen Welten: Star Trek als politische Utopie* (Darmstadt: Büchner-Verlag, 2014)

Storey, Ian, 'Classical Allusion in C. S. Lewis' *Till We Have Faces*', *The Chronicle of the Oxford University C. S. Lewis Society*, 4 (2007), 5–20

Strijbosch, Clara, *The Seafaring Saint: Sources and Analogues of the Twelfth-Century Voyage of Saint Brendan* (Dublin: Four Courts Press, 2000)

Sturges, Robert S., *Medieval Interpretation: Models of Reading in Literary Narrative, 1100–1500* (Carbondale and Edwardsville: Southern Illinois University Press, 1991)

Swank, Kris, 'The Child's Voyage and the *Immram* Tradition in Lewis, Tolkien, and Pullman', *Mythlore*, 38 (2019), 73–96

Swank, Kris, 'The Irish Otherworld Voyage of *Roverandom*', *Tolkien Studies*, 12 (2015), 31–57

Swift, Jonathan, *The Essential Writings of Jonathan Swift*, ed. by Claude Rawson and Ian Higgins (New York and London: W. W. Norton and Company, 2010)

Szabo, Vicki E., *Monstrous Fishes and the Mead-Dark Sea* (Leiden and Boston: Brill 2008)

Tambling, Jeremy, *Allegory* (London and New York: Routledge, 2010)

Thomson, Clive, 'Bakhtin's "Theory" of Genre', *Studies in Twentieth-Century Literature*, 9 (1984), 29–40, <https://doi.org/10.4148/2334-4415.1150>

Thomson, Derick S., ed., *Branwen Uerch Llyr*, Medieval and Modern Welsh Series 2 (Dublin: DIAS, 2003[1961])

Todorov, Tzvetan, *Introduction à la littérature fantastique* (Paris: Seuil, 1970)

Tracy, Robert, '"All Them Rocks in the Sea": *Ulysses* as *Immram*', *Irish University Review*, 32 (2002), 225–41

Triantafyllos, Sotirios, *Topos in Utopia. A Peregrination to Early Modern Utopianism's Space* (Wilmington: Vernon Press, 2021)

Tuan, Yi-Fu, 'Realism and Fantasy in Art, History, and Geography', *Annals of the Association of American Geographers*, 80 (1990), 435–46

Van Bever Donker, Vincent, and Stephanie Yorke, 'Re-Imagining the Colonial Encounter in *Stargate: SG-1*: Discourses of Linear Progress and Separate Development', *Interventions*, 20. *Violence in a Global Frame* (2018), 734–749

Van Duzer, Chet, '*Hic sunt dracones*: The Geography and Cartography of Monsters', in *The Ashgate Research Companion to Monsters and the Monstrous*, ed. by Asa Simon Mittman and Peter J. Dendle (London and New York: Routledge, 2016), pp. 387–435

van Hamel, Anton Gerard, ed., *Immrama*, Mediaeval and Modern Irish Series, 10 (Dublin: Dublin Institute for Advanced Studies, 1941)

van Hamel, Anton Gerard, ed., 'The text of *Immram curaig Maíldúin*', *Études Celtiques*, 3 (1938), 1–20

van Oostrom, Frits, *Wereld in Woorden. Geschiedenis van de Nederlandse Literatuur 1300–1400* (Amsterdam: Bert Bakker, 2013)

Van Riper, A. Bowdoin, 'Star Trek: The Next Generation'; in *The Routledge Handbook of Star Trek*, ed. by Leimar Garcia-Siino, Sabrina Mittermeier, and Stefan Rabitsch (New York and London: Routledge, 2022), pp. 28–36

VanderKolk, Daniel, 'C.S. Lewis, Celtic Mythology, and Transatlantic Travel: the Story of Brendan the Voyager', conference paper *Translatlantic Connections Conference*, 2015 <https://www.academia.edu/download/36327580/TransAtlSpch.pdf> [accessed 24 March 2024]

Varandas, Angélica, 'The Sacred Space of Gods and Saints: Some Considerations About the Sea and Exile in Irish Mythology and Tradition' in *Creating through Mind and Emotions*, ed. by Mário S. Ming Kong and Maria do Rosário Monteiro (Boka Raton and London: CIC Press / Taylor and Francis, 2022), pp. 423–28

Volmering, Nicole Johanna Bernartina, 'Medieval Irish Vision Literature: A Genre Study', unpublished PhD thesis, University College Cork, 2014 von den Brincken, Anne-Dorothee, 'Presbyter Iohannes, Dominus Dominantium: Ein Wunsch-Welt-bild des 12. Jahrhunderts', in *Ornamenta Ecclesiae. Kunst und Künstler der Romanik. Katalog zur Ausstellung des Schnützgen-Museums in der Josef-Haubrich-Kunsthalle*, I, ed. by A. Legner (Cologne: Schnütgen-Museum, 1985) pp. 83–90

Vu, Ryan, 'Science Fiction before Science Fiction: Ancient, Medieval, and Early Modern SF' in *The Cambridge History of Science Fiction*, ed. by Gerry Canavan and Eric Carl Link (Cambridge: Cambridge University Press, 2018), pp. 13–34

Wagner, B., *Die "Epistola Presbiteri Johannis" lateinisch und deutsch. Überlieferung, Textgeschichte, Rezeption und Übertragungen im Mittelalter. Mit bis-her unedierten Texten* (Tübingen: Max Niemeyer, 2000)

Walker, Jeanne Murray, '*The Lion, The Witch and The Wardrobe* as Rite of Passage', *Children's Literature in Education*, 16 (1985), 177–88

Wanner, Kevin J., *Snorri Sturluson and the* Edda. *The Conversion of Cultural Capital in Medieval Scandinavia* (Toronto, Buffalo and London: University of Toronto Press, 2008)

Ward, Michael, *Planet Narnia. The Seven Heavens in the Imagination of C. S. Lewis* (Oxford: Oxford University Press, 2008)

Waters, E. G. R., ed., *The Anglo-Norman Voyage of St. Brendan by Benedeit. A Poem of the Early Twelfth Century* (reprinted Geneva: Slatkine, 1974 [Oxford, Clarendon Press, 1928])

Wegner, Phillip E., *Imaginary Communities: Utopia, the Nation, and the Spatial Histories of Modernity* (Berkeley: University of California Press, 2002)

Weitekamp, Margaret A., '"Ahead, Warp Factor Three, Mr. Sulu": Imagining Interstellar Faster-Than-Light Travel in Space Science Fiction', *Journal of Popular Culture*, 52 (2019), 1036–57

Williams, David, *Deformed Discourse. The Function of the Monster in Medieval Thought and Literature* (Montreal and Kingston: McGill-Queen's University Press, 1999)

Williams, Mark, *Ireland's Immortals. A History of the Gods of Irish Myth* (Princeton: Princeton University Press, 2016)

Willis, Ika, and Ellie Crookes, 'Introduction', in *Medievalism and Reception*, ed. by Ika Willis and Ellie Crookes (Cambridge: D. S. Brewer, 2024), pp. 1–10

Willis, Ika, and Ellie Crookes, ed., *Medievalism and Reception* (Cambridge: D. S. Brewer, 2024)

Wooding, Jonathan M., 'The Date of *Navigatio S. Brendani abbatis*', *Studia Hibernica*, 37 (2011), 9–26

Wooding, Jonathan M., 'Introduction', in *The Otherworld Voyage in Early Irish Literature. An Anthology of Criticism*, ed. by Jonathan Wooding (Dublin: Four Courts Press, 2000), pp. xi–xxviii

Wooding, Jonathan M., 'Navigatio Sancti Brendani' in *Celtic Culture: A Historical Encyclopedia*, ed. by John T. Koch (Santa Barbara: ABC-CLIO, 2006), p. 1348

Wooding, Jonathan M., ed., *The Otherworld Voyage in Early Irish Literature. An Anthology of Criticism* (Dublin: Four Courts Press, 2000)

Woodward, David, 'Medieval *Mappaemundi*', in *History of Cartography I: Cartography in Prehistoric, Ancient, and Medieval Europe and the Mediterranean*, ed. by J. B. Harley and David Woodward (Chicago and London: University of Chicago Press, 1987), pp. 286–370

Woodward, David, 'Reality, Symbolism, Time and Space in Medieval World Maps', *Annals of the Association of American Geographers*, 75 (1985), 510–21

Yarrow, Simon, *Saints. A Short History* (Oxford: Oxford University Press, 2016)

Yeager, Suzanne M., 'The World Translated: Marco Polo's *Le Devisement dou monde*, *The Book of Sir John Mandeville*, and Their Medieval Audiences', in: *Marco Polo and the Encounter of East and West*, ed. by Suzanne Conklin Akbari and Amilcare Iannucci, with the assistance of John Tulk (Toronto, Buffalo and London: University of Toronto Press, 2008), pp. 156–81

Yri, Kirsten, 'Medievalism and Antiromanticism in Carl Orff's *Carmina Burana*', in *The Oxford Handbook of Music and Medievalism*, ed. by Stephen C. Meyer and Kirsten Yri (Oxford: Oxford University Press, 2020), pp. 269–300

Zadeh, Lotfi A., 'Fuzzy Sets', *Information and Control*, 8 (1965), 338–353

Zarncke, Friedrich, ed., 'Der Brief des Priesters Johannes an den byzantischen Kaiser Emanuel', *Abhandlungn der köninglich sächsischen Gesellschaft der Wissenschaften*, 17 (1879), pp. 873–934, reprinted in *Prester John. The Mongols and the Ten Lost Tribes*, ed. by Charles F. Beckingham and Bernard Hamilton (Aldershot: Ashgate Variorum, 1996), pp. 40–102

Zhu, Lifeng, Weiwei Xia, Jia Liu, and Aiguo Song, 'Visualizing Fuzzy Sets Using Opacity-Varying Freeform Diagrams', *Information Visualization*, 17 (2017), 146–160

Zukas, Alex, 'Cartography and Narrative in the Maps of Herman Moll's The World Described', *XVII–XVIII* 78 (2021). Special issue: *Cartes et cartographies dans le monde anglophone aux XVIIe et XVIIIe siècles / Maps and Mapping in the English-Speaking World in the 17th and 18th Centuries* http://journals.openedition.org/1718/8764

Index

Printed in the United States
by Baker & Taylor Publisher Services